D1759636

Embodied Politics
Dance, Protest and Identities

WITHDRAWN FROM
THE LIBRARY

UNIVERSITY OF

KA 0387463 X

EMBODIED POLITICS

Dance, Protest and Identities

Stacey Prickett

DANCE BOOKS

UNIVERSITY OF WINCHESTER
LIBRARY

For my Parents, Jill and Bruce Prickett,
who started me on this journey

Cover photograph: *Awaz/Voice* (2006) choreography by Chitra Sundaram,
left to right: Jasmine Simhalan, Magdeline Gorringe, Divya Kasturi, photo
by Stacey Prickett

First published in 2013 by Dance Books Ltd.,
Southwold House, Isington Road, Binsted, Hampshire, GU34 4PH

© Stacey Prickett
ISBN: 978-1-85273-166-3
A CIP catalogue for this title is available from the British Library

Printed in Great Britain

UNIVERSITY OF WINCHESTER

0367463X 306 684
02

Contents

Acknowledgements

The roots of this book can be traced back to my initial forays into dance scholarship and the trail of discovery that led to the history of a workers dance movement in the USA, and involved me in archival research in diverse sites across many years. Multiple visits to some key archives revealed intriguing gems of information, and many people helped uncover obscure sources. Special thanks are due to to Helen Roberts at the National Resource Centre for Dance, University of Surrey, and Nicholas Bell of the Music Collections of the British Library. Appreciation also goes to staff at the New York Public Library of the Performing Arts, Jerome Robbins Dance Division for their help. I also thank staff at the Victoria and Albert Museum's Archive of Art and Design and Theatre Museum Collection; the National Co-operative Archives; San Francisco Performing Arts Library and Museum; the Tamiment Library, New York University; and the Library of Congress. My gratitude also goes to those who followed up leads for me, often on short notice: Debbie Williams, Joanna Dee Das and Judith Andrews. The histories that follow are enriched by the stories of those involved in the dance activities, as performers, creators, critics and/or viewers. I was fortunate to draw on the memories and experience of the following at various times (listed in alphabetical order): Sujata Banerjee, Jess Curtis, Jane Dudley, Rita Felciano, Joe Goode, Joanna Haigood, Joanna Harris, Keith Hennessy, Divya Kasturi, Krissy Keefer, Jessica Robinson Love, Sara Shelton Mann, Sushma Mehta, Edna Ocko, Prarthana Purkayastha, Sonia Sabri, Edith Segal, and Gauri Sharma Tripathi. John White was particularly generous in sharing his stories of the Woodcraft Folk, memories and rare programmes from the 1930s left-wing pageants in England. Shari Segel provided missing historical detail and provided generous permission to use her aunt Edith's archives.

My journey has been accompanied by an amazing group of scholars, practitioners and writers who offered support, insight into the dance fields and critical scrutiny in equal measure: Theresa Buckland, Ann David, Lynn Garafola, Andrée Grau, Sanjeevini Dutta, Helena Hammond, Royona Mitra, Geraldine Morris, and Chitra Sundaram. Victoria Phillips Geduld generously shared rare source material. Larraine Nicholas in particular provided insight into the left-wing dance in Britain and exchanged ideas without which this book would not exist. Discussions with Helen Thomas, Stephanie Jordan and Gay Morris helped me clarify and develop some initially tenuous research paths. My colleagues in the Department of Dance have been gracious in their support; thanks also to students who asked questions that kept the inquiry developing, and the University of Roehampton which provided research leave to enable me to finish the book.

Special thanks go to David Leonard at Dance Books, Liz Morrell for her editing expertise, and Chris Jones for her help in researching archives and preparing the index. An early version of chapter 3 was originally published as 'San Francisco Innovators and Iconoclasts: Dance and Politics in the Left Coast City', in *Dance Chronicle*, 2007, 30, pp. 237-290, and is republished with permission. I have researched the copyright of images with due diligence and acknowledge it where known.

Research and writing was conducted with funding from the Arts and Humanities Research Council (Small Grant in the Creative and Performing Arts) and with support from the University of Roehampton. Special thanks go to Diana Hastings and Briar Chatterjea who provided me with a home away from home and encouragement over the years, as did my late friend Katrina Howard. My friends and family in London, America and India have continued to cheer me on, offering escapes and sustenance at the perfect times. My partner Salim Mehta been a willing companion on research trips and at dance performances, supporting me with humour and warmth along the way.

List of illustrations

Illustrations located between pages 90 and 91.

Chapter 1 images:
Edith Segal in Lenin Memorial Pageant rehearsal (1928).
Edith Segal, Lenin Memorial Pageant (1928), Madison Square Garden.
Edith Segal, undated.
Nature Friends Dance Group, undated, summer camp at Lake Midvale, New Jersey.
Edith Segal, *The Belt Goes Red* (1930) Lenin Memorial Pageant at Memorial Square Garden.

Chapter 2 images:
Helen Elton c. 1934.
Kate Eisenstaedt's Central European dance class (1934).
War Dance, choreography by Kate Eisenstaedt, *Towards To-morrow Pageant of Co-operation*, 1938.
Ballet of Mourning Women, choreography by Margaret Barr, *Towards To-morrow Pageant of Co-operation*, 1938.

Chapter 3 images:
Robert Henry Johnson and Amara Tabor Smith in *Sailing Away* (2010), Zaccho Dance Theatre.
Norman Rutherford, Keith Hennessy, Jess Curtis and Kim Epifano in Contraband's *Mira II* (1994).
Jules Beckman, Jess Curtis and Keith Hennessy in *Ice, Car, Cage* (1997/98)
Debby Kajiyama and Lena Gatchalian in the Dance Brigade's *Cave Women... The Next Incarnation!* (2003).

Chapter 4 images:
Anusha Subramanyam in classical bharatanatyam choreography, *Murugan* (2001).
Anusha Subramanyam in her own choreography, *From the Heart* (2010).
Mavin Khoo in *Sufi:Zen* (2010), choreography by Gauri Sharma Tripathi with Khoo and Jonathan Lunn, Akademi production at the South Bank Centre.
Sapnay/Dreams (2005) choreography by Mavin Khoo and Gauri Sharma Tripathi, dancer facing camera, Rachel Waterman, Akademi production, Trafalgar Square.
Awaz/Voices (2006), choreography by Chitra Sundaram, dancers (left to right) Divya Kasturi, Amina Khayyam and Prarthana Purkayastha, Trafalgar Square.

Abbreviations for notes

Archival sources are abbreviated in the notes as follows:

BL ABC: British Library, Music Division, Alan Bush Collection
LOC: Library of Congress, Washington DC, Performing Arts, Federal Theatre Project
NRCD: National Resource Centre for Dance, University of Surrey, Fernau Hall (F. Hall) Archives
NYPL: New York Public Library for the Performing Arts, Jerome Robbins Dance Division
NYU: Tamiment Library, Robert F. Wagner Labor Archives, New York University
SF PALM: San Francisco Performing Arts Library and Museum
V&A: Victoria and Albert Museum, Archive of Art and Design and Theatre Museum Collection (THM)

Introduction

There are no reds in modern dance today. Once there were left-wingers who, with bare feet thrust up from the ankles and fists doubled out from the wrists, outdid dancing with polemics. 'Dance is a weapon' was their battle cry'. Margaret Lloyd, 1949[1]

As I was searching for a dance history essay topic, I came across Margaret Lloyd's statement about the existence of 'reds' or communists in American modern dance, which led me to extensive research to uncover details of the leftist dance movement in New York in the 1930s. Its beginning was traced back to 1924 when Edith Segal, a young New York dancer, took the bold step of performing a solo to commemorate the death of the Communist leader Vladimir Lenin at a highly political event, a Lenin Memorial Meeting in Chicago. As one of the outspoken 'reds', Segal developed a dance practice based on ideas about art as a political tool to awaken consciousness and affect change in society. Labelled as agit-prop (agitation-propaganda) this overt example prompted further reflection on relationships between art and politics, with central questions shaping later investigations into the socio-political contexts of dance practices. As I moved between London and the San Francisco Bay Area, I came into contact with a rich range of performances with a political edge, and I needed to situate research in the specifics of its context. I began to question how connections between arts and politics have shifted between the 1920s and 1930s and now, as we enter into the teens of the 21st century. What distinctions and similarities exist between dance practices that are decades and continents apart? In various ways, some of the themes that inspired a revolutionary dance in the USA have remained and were evident in London performances I viewed as a student and later as a lecturer: notions of class; institutional power and resistance; the relationship of artistic practice, training and expressivity to the representation of gender, nation and ethnicity.

The initial focus of the book is on recreational dances of American workers in the 1920s and 1930s, where archival material opened new avenues of inquiry around dance activities linked to Marxist ideologies. In the process of research, a single article on workers dance groups in England in the 1930s inspired the search for their history, a partial account of which establishes a second historical chronicle. Although their timeframes overlap, distinctive trajectories emerge in the wider arts contexts in New York and London. Dances by contemporary artists in the late 20th and early 21st centuries offer different political discourses for exploration, seen in alternative dance

---

1 Margaret Lloyd (1949) *The Borzoi Book of Modern Dance*, p. 173.

practices and performance in San Francisco, where a strong countercultural zeitgeist is shaped by innovative approaches to artistic expression. In contrast, the postcolonial classical forms of South Asian dance in Britain have developed through an engagement with mainstream institutions, where notions of politics are embedded in relations of power at deeper levels which are not always obvious until one delves beneath the surface.

An increasing number of publications on the politics of performance encompass everything from popular dance to burlesque to historical and national dance practices. Alexandra Kolb's 'Introduction' in *Dance and Politics* (2011), for example, chronicles multiple strategies across the historical and stylistic spectrum for bringing social issues to the fore. As Kolb details, however, the term 'political' has become so commonplace that it seems all-encompassing and is in danger of shifting into nothingness, while some might argue that this has already occurred.[2] Explicit political images abounded during my research trips to the British Library in the summer of 2013, where the site was enlivened by posters for a 'Propaganda: Power and Persuasion' exhibition. One could purchase a notebook, underground ticket holder or tea towel featuring a range of images: a poster from a Chinese film, *The White Haired* Girl (1950, a Chinese ballerina in *arabesque en pointe* holding a gun), Rosie the Riveter flexing her bicep (World War II American female labourer showing off her arm muscle) or the Suffragette slogan calling for 'Votes for Women' (simple black print on white background). All of these themes have been scrutinised by dance scholars, and are now turned into everyday commodities removed from politics. The examples of the political power of the body on display supported dominant ideologies (China and USA, respectively) or a motivating call to action to challenge policies (the battle for women's right to vote).[3] The central ideas – embodiment, politics and protest – found in the exhibition also emerge in the dance practices presented here, linked to key concepts of class, hegemony, social justice and politics of representation.

Politics and the Everyday

I was originally drawn to the passion of left-wing modern dancers in 1930s New York City. My talks with the leaders of a revolutionary dance movement such as Segal; Jane Dudley, the choreographer, teacher and

---

2 Alexandra Kolb (2011) 'Introduction' in Alexandra Kolb, ed. *Dance and Politics*, see also Mark Franko (2007) 'Dance and the Political' in Susanne Franco and Marina Nordera, eds., *Dance Discourses: Keywords in Dance Research*.

3 See Li Cunxin (2009) *Mao's Last Dancer*, Harmondsworth: Penguin, Stacey Prickett (2011) 'Dancing the American Dream during World War II', in Kolb, op.cit.; and Ramsay Burt (2013) 'The Biopolitics of Modernist Dance and Suffragette Protest', in Gerald Siegmund and Stefan Hölscher, eds., *Dance, Politics and Co-immunity*.

former dancer with the Martha Graham Company; and Edna Ocko, dance critic, accompanist and activist, revealed a strength of conviction that must have translated into a dynamic force when channelled into dance all those decades earlier. They demonstrated vividly how the ideological was imbued in the physical, an embodied politics. The notion of embodiment – expressing ideas and beliefs through the body, connections between physical actions and ideology – have been taken up by multiple disciplines, and increasingly interrogated by dance scholars via sociological, anthropological and cultural studies methodologies. The *Oxford English Dictionary* sets out two definitions for 'embody': 'To give a concrete form to (what is abstract or ideal); to express (principles, thoughts, intentions) *in* an institution, work of art, action, definite form of words, etc.' and 'To cause to become part of a body; to unite into one body; to incorporate (a thing) in a mass of material, (particular elements) in a system or complex unity'.[4] A powerful belief that politics and dance were inseparable was evident in a belief in the social responsibility of the artist, inextricably bound to the radical dancers' sense of self.

That political sense was Marxism, offering a conceptual tool to understand the world, one predicated on the struggle between classes, simplified in many instances to the call 'Workers of the world unite!' Identity was linked fundamentally to class in the late 1920s and 1930s, and perceptions of the function of art in society were based on Marxist ideals rather than the reality of the new world created by the Bolshevik Revolution in 1917. Karl Marx turned to history to explain society, examining the material conditions of a society to understand it as he wrote in 1859: 'The mode of production of material life conditions the social, political and intellectual process in general. It is not the consciousness of men that determine their social existence, but, on the contrary, their social existence that determines their consciousness.'[5] The world view is established by base-superstructure relationships, while a 'scientific' Marxism is predicated on the argument that ideology and culture are a reflection of the material 'base' comprised of power relations that shape society. Binaries proved highly problematic, however, seen in the dominance of ballet in the Soviet Union and its prevalence in Communist China. After an initial period of experimentation and innovation in the USSR between 1917 and 1924, classical ballet was retained in which Proletkult (proletarian culture) suppressed more 'abstract' newer approaches to dance. The innovations were advanced outside the USSR, as New York and London workers mixed political enlightenment with creativity in their search for a socially relevant dance.

---

4 'embody | imbody, v.' OED Online. June 2013. Oxford University Press. 1 September 2013 http://www.oed.com/view/Entry/60907.
5 Karl Marx (1963) *Selected Writings in Sociology and Social Philosophy*, p. 67.

Hegemony and Protest

The concept of hegemony offers strategies to explore power relations in a post-communist world. It emerges out of a critique of Marxism by Italian philosopher Antonio Gramsci, who argued that an emphasis on the material conditions of a society does not allow for subjectivity, and consideration of ideologies and consciousness. As conceptualised today, power is not held only by the forces of the state, but permeates throughout civil society through small and large institutions – everything from the family to the church, trade unions and schools. A normalised world view becomes widely accepted, a 'system of values, attitudes, beliefs, morality etc. that is in one way or the other supportive of the established order and the class interests that dominate it'.[6] For example, Anthony Shay's analysis of state folk dance companies reveals shifting relationships and how hegemonic considerations determine who and what is represented. The Turkish State Folk Dance Ensemble perpetuates a national identity that valorises peasant culture from Anatolia instead of dances linked to the historical Ottoman Empire. The Moiseyev Dance Company repertoire has been comprised of 'Russified' versions of ethnic dances from non-Slavic areas of the USSR.[7] Beyond the decisions of who is represented, the hegemony of ballet is evident in the modification of steps and standardisation of the stylised folk dances.

The historical examples I investigate are explicit in setting out tensions between dominant and subordinate groups, but what relevance does Marxism hold in the 21st century in Europe and the USA? The Berlin wall was dismantled and the Soviet state disbanded in 1989 while I was writing my PhD about Marxism and dance. The dance activism of the late 20th century and early 21st century is devoid of an overt unifying rhetoric. Beyond the historical accounts, how can one write about fundamental social structures that impact upon and are impacted by culture? Power relations between employer/employee, landlord/tenant, state/individual continue to shape ideologies, however, those that emphasise notions of democracy, equality and social justice are increasingly perceived as leftist or socialist. Strategic use of the body as political protest is detailed in Susan Leigh Foster's article, 'Choreographies of Protest' which interrogates multiple models of bodily control.[8] Dancing protest is conceptualised here as practices that critique the status quo, setting out an oppositional stance. In my university BA class on dance, power and politics one student presentation focused on how women in Chile danced alone in the *Cueca solo*. The aim has been to pressure the government to reveal what happened to their loved ones who disappeared

---

6 Carl Boggs (1976) *Gramsci's Marxism*, pp. 36-38. See also Antonio Gramsci (1971) *Selections from The Prison Notebooks*; and Steve Jones (2006) *Antonio Gramsci.*
7 Anthony Shay (2002) *Choreographic Politics*, pp. 61, 203-211.
8 Susan Leigh Foster (2003) 'Choreographies of Protest', *Theatre Journal*. 55, pp. 295-412.

during the dictatorship of General Pinochet that began in 1973 following a USA-sponsored coup on September 11th. The women's danced lament, the poignant absence of a man to partner them, transformed the function of the social dance into a powerful plea for justice. In contrast, the power of many was seen in One Billion Rising for Justice on 14 February 2013. The worldwide action in 207 locations saw one billion people take to the streets, to dance, sing and talk about continued violence against girls and women, in protest against a horrific rape and murder in Delhi, India.[9] The protest explored here arises from strong moral imperatives that challenge institutions of power in a society, be they manifest in the oppression of workers or enduring racial discrimination arising from the legacy of slavery.

Hegemony functions at multiple levels and is in constant shift and negotiation as cultural leaders emerge from the subordinated class. Counter-hegemony occurs with breaking of ideological bonds and confrontation of the ruling class, evident in some subcultural practices which are absorbed into mainstream culture, reinforcing ongoing processes of cultural change. Dance offers a prime site through which to challenge as well as reinforce dominant social values, in some instances linked to concepts of the nation as well as class, while other values are challenged at a more fundamental level – that of the body. An absorption of values held by marginalised groups occurs, evident in how some of the alternative, left-wing or minority dance styles impact upon the dance fields as well as wider cultural landscapes. A clear example is seen in the absorption (or some would argue appropriation) of aspects of hip-hop culture which are now part of a dominant culture industry although underground manifestations of dance still circulate and evolve.[10] This transformation occurred in the visual arts when *Slave Labour,* a mural by the graffiti artist Banksy, was cut out of a wall on the side of a discount store in the Haringey area of London and put up for sale at a Florida auction house, causing huge public outcry. The depiction of a child at a sewing machine, producing the ubiquitous Union Jack bunting that decorated buildings, homes and public spaces during the 2012 British celebrations of the Olympics and the Queen's Jubilee, became an iconic reminder of the exploitation of workers in other countries, enabling the proliferation of cheap goods in the west. Rather than be considered vandalism, this political commentary was treasured as art, protected by a Perspex cover with signs directing viewers to the mural's location.[11] The fluidity of boundaries is evident in some of the

9 I am very grateful to students in my Dance, Power & Politics module, Spring 2013, particularly Kirsty Dawson whose research is mentioned here.

10 See Halifu Osumare (2007) *The Africanist Aesthetic in Global Hip-hop,* for a comprehensive analysis of the globalisation of hip hop culture.

11 The removal has generated more artwork which comments on the 'theft'. See Richard Luscumbe, 'Sale of "stolen" Banksy mural cancelled at 11th hour', *Guardian,* 23 February 2013, accessed 4 March 2013, http://www.guardian.co.uk/artanddesign/2013/feb/23/

case studies that follow, while in other instances the hegemony of dominant dance styles proved formidable, constraining the spread of a leftist dance in Britain which lasted only a few years.

Representation, Identities and Power

Another key issue explored in the dance examples emerges from questions of representation and cultural identity and how race, ethnicity, gender and class are reflected in and shape cultural practices. Cultural studies theorists Paul Gilroy and Stuart Hall provide models for contextualising how identity issues intersect with hegemonic discourses, revealing the impact of demographic and economic shifts since the end of World War II. Hall explored how collective social identities have been fragmented, replacing larger homogeneous and unified ones shaped by rigid class boundaries. Class markers gave us codes through which we read one another and informed collective political action – clearly articulated in the leftist rhetoric of 1930s Marxism. He argues that categories of class, race, gender and nation are structured by historical processes linked to modernity – such as capitalism, urbanisation, the formation of world economy, social and gender divisions of labour. Mass migration in post-war 1950s and 1960s transformed Britain's political, social and economic life and a collective black identity – a political category – emerged to challenge racism, as diasporic minorities sought out their lost histories to construct new identities.[12]

Gilroy interrogates post-colonial transitions and Britain's loss of empire to consider institutional and social hierarchies of power, arguing that race is linked to an 'overarching' class structure which is problematic in today's global economy. Writing predominantly about British society, Gilroy also explores the networks of race, ethnicity and nation that shape experiences of diaspora across the Black Atlantic, so named because of the lasting transnational impact of slavery.[13] Early workers' dance examples explored here prioritise class struggles, while similar relations of power also impact upon themes of social and racial injustice explored in more contemporary dances. Processes of identity formation are always in flux in the USA as well and the specific experiences of assimilation and migration are developed in this book in relation to individual dances.

The exploration of class and social structures reveals how alternative choreographic and recreational dance activities are located in relation to mainstream institutional frameworks, underpinned by the concepts of

---

banksy-missing-mural-auction-stopped?INTCMP=SRCH
12 Stuart Hall (1991) 'Old and new Identities, Old and New Ethnicities', in Anthony King, ed., *Culture, Globalization and the World-System*.
13 Paul Gilroy (2002) *There Ain't No Black in the Union Jack*, (2nd ed.), pp. 18-19; see also Paul Gilroy (1993) *The Black Atlantic*.

sociologist Pierre Bourdieu which help reveal how social meaning is linked to aesthetic choices. For example, Gay Morris articulates these relationships using Bourdieu in the construction of an American dance field in the 20th century and its attainment of cultural capital. Interrelationships exist between a person's habitus – the education and class situations that shape tastes and can be manifest bodily through gesture, posture and lifestyle – their social location and taste.[14] As Helen Thomas summarises, 'the body has come to be inscribed and invested with power, status, and particular symbolic forms that are crucial to the accumulation of certain resources'.[15] Michel Foucault explores institutional relations of power, their disciplinary structures and how they impact upon social bodies.[16] A Foucauldian discourse also underpins the consideration of how the dance activities are situated in relation to dominant social, political and artistic institutions, revealing various degrees of social engagement or a transformative impetus for the individual.

The Personal is Political

In his autobiography, leftist historian Eric Hobsbawm reflected about his time at Cambridge University in the 1930s: 'Of course, everything was political in a sense, though not in the post-1968 sense for which "the personal is political".'[17] He reveals the wider political scene through personal reflections, something resisted by the leftist dancers in the 1930s. The awakening of social consciousness would arise through the collective, a solidarity empowering individual action to change society. In contrast, the construction of community, of a collective sensibility in the late 20th and early 21st centuries can be linked to the emergence of a 'second' wave of feminism in the 1960s. Foucault's theories around the 'technologies of the self' influenced feminist perceptions of embodiment where all aspects of the care and presentation of the body have entered into discourse as political acts, according to Susan Bordo.[18] Diverse productions are situated in relation to the alternative scene in San Francisco while larger social narratives are featured in some of the South Asian dance productions, alongside examples of participatory activities that offer the potential for transformation on an individual level. Both institutional power relations and dance as expression of the personal emerge as significant in the theatrical events and recreational activities explored here.

14 Gay Morris (2006) *A Game for Dancers*; Pierre Bourdieu (1977) *Outline of a Theory of Practice*; Pierre Bourdieu (1984) *Distinction*.
15 Helen Thomas (2003) *The Body, Dance & Cultural Theory*, p. 56.
16 Michel Foucault (1980) in Colin Gordon ed., *Power/Knowledge*; Michel Foucault (1979) *Discipline & Punish*.
17 Eric Hobsbawm (1995) *Age of Extremes*, p. 113.
18 Susan Bordo (1993) *Unbearable Weight: Feminism, Western Culture and the Body in Western Culture*.

Constructing Narratives

Two time frames are examined in the following chapters, requiring different analytical and methodological approaches. Some of the left-wing artists were prolific writers, putting forward their visions of an empowered working class, activated through the power of art which would stir class consciousness. Their documents provide part of the archive through which a history of 'workers' dance in the USA and Britain is read. The historical recovery for dances in the 1920s and 1930s involved detective work to sort through boxes of uncatalogued archives, scrutinising grainy 90-year-old photographs and searching for connecting threads and tidbits of information about what the dances may have looked like. I was also fortunate to interview some of the key artists in the left-wing dance movement, delving beyond familiar accounts of their later careers. Investigation of dance practices in the late 20th and early 21st centuries is informed by attendance at live performances and analysis of recordings, reviews and publicity material, as well as interviews and correspondence with the creators and performers.

In returning to my postgraduate research and investigating new archival sources, Chapter 1 analyses Segal's involvement in the diverse activities in the 1920s and 1930s. The dominant scholarly focus on the 'revolutionary dance' of the time has been on those who went on to become prominent choreographers, teachers and performers (such as Dudley). I return to the roots of the movement, traced back to recreational and participatory activities at workers' summer camps, in political pageants, at strike meetings and less political after-school sessions. The vibrancy of New York's Lower East Side emerges as a catalyst, a converging point for multiple nationalities and generations of Jewish immigrants escaping persecution or searching for economic wealth to fulfil the American dream. Struggles for equal rights, fair pay and improved working conditions for the labourer then led Segal to Detroit where she supported the United Automobile Workers strike actions. Her work with the Federal Theatre Project in the motor city reveals a counter-hegemonic shift where the initially subversive, marginalised activities became an integral part of the first federally funded arts project. Ideological and stylistic links to European socialist theatre and dance performance are also uncovered, arising from travel to Berlin and the Soviet Union in 1931.

In Chapter 2, the socio-political contexts of left-wing dance performances in Britain are investigated alongside institution-building processes that have shaped the dance field today. Connections are established to early modern dance in the USA through Margaret Barr while other dancers (Kate Eisenstaedt and Helen Elton among them) had Central European training during the inter-war years with Rudolf Laban and Gertrude Bodenwieser. Communist composer Alan Bush emerges as an organising force, and he left behind letters which offer rare details of dances and the groups' artistic and ideological beliefs. Rather than feeding into the dance establishment and influencing dominant styles, the left-wing dance groups dispersed once the political environment changed with the outbreak of war in 1939 and Barr's departure from England. During the short time of their existence, however, workers dance activities were seen by large audiences in three large-scale left-wing pageants as well as recreational activities. It is in the left-wing theatre field – particularly Unity Theatre – that their influence was felt among a network of international artists. Archival documents – personal correspondence and diaries – rather than photographs provided descriptive accounts while rare footage of the *Towards To-morrow* pageant of 1938 offered unprecedented views of a mass dance.

The focus of Chapter 3 moves back to the USA, revisiting and developing my 2007 article on dance and politics in San Francisco.[19] A rich alternative dance scene has seen some of its long-standing members enter into the Bay Area cultural mainstream, while increasingly influencing an international community of practitioners. The careers of luminaries such as Margaret Jenkins and Joe Goode have been shaped by the west coast experiences although their creative legacies link back to New York City. Significantly, a collaborative and socially conscious ethos is established in relation to the zeitgeist of radical protest in the 1960s and onwards – a spirit of resistance informs the work of performers who integrate notions of dance as social ritual, be it for healing, pagan or spiritual purposes. Contact improvisation as a creative process is exemplified in the work of the collective Contraband and collaborative creations arising out of post-Contraband activities. Other site and aerial choreographic innovations push physical capabilities of the body while revealing hidden histories of locations and the social significance of space and place. Overt political influences – challenging notions such as the boundaries of the body, the exploration of queer identity, the impact of AIDS, feminist perspectives, are only some of the myriad themes that inspire artistic creation. Strong community bonds shape an international network, the cosmopolitan practices and partnerships help support organisations that keep the field vibrant in the face of diminished public funds.

Politics of representation and policies of multiculturalism have had an impact upon the South Asian dance practices analysed in Chapter 4, which explores how the diasporic forms have become firmly situated within the British dance ecology. There is geographic and aesthetic diversity within the overarching label. The category includes classical styles of bharatanatyam originating in South India; classical kathak from North India; odissi from the state of Orissa; popular styles of *filmi* dances (classified as Bollywood);

---

19 Stacey Prickett (2007) 'San Francisco Innovators and Iconoclasts: Dance and Politics in the Left Coast City', *Dance Chronicle*, 30:2, pp. 237-290.

and bhangra, a modified folk dance form from the Punjab area of northwest India. What sets the South Asian dance community apart, however, is how an institution-building process emerged from within, generating a powerful grassroots advocacy that has influenced professionalisation of the dance forms. The development of training systems and advances in the quality of performance are analysed in relation to socio-political shifts that accompanied different governments in power. While existing scholarship explores discourses surrounding notions of hybridity, the chapter considers where the dance is situated in formal education, represented in public performances and circulated globally in the work of avant-garde South Asian and British Asian choreographers and performers. Danced celebrations of nation and sport in public events in 2012 – the Queen's Jubilee (60th anniversary of the monarch's reign) and the Olympic Games and Paralympic Games – provide the cornerstones to investigate the larger British dance field.

The diverse threads are drawn together in a conclusion that explores connections as well as contrasts, revealing an influential network of artists and practices that span generations of dancers and across continents. This web was reinforced in 2012 when I spoke at *The Body in Crisis* symposium sponsored by the Onassis Foundation in Athens, Greece. Extensive television news coverage had broadcast running battles between protesters and riot police outside Parliament, contrasting with desperate pleas for help as people's lives were devastated by the financial collapse of the nation. Yet my walks through the Plaka tourist centre contrasted greatly with the images of unrest – relaxed crowds populated the streets and cafés while long queues of people sought shade from the hot sun as they awaited entry to ancient sites. Protest marches closed down streets around the Greek Parliament and a day-long metro strike impacted our travel plans, so the signs were certainly there if one looked. The symposium offered encouragement to dancers searching for artistic responses to Greece's economic and social crisis, reinforcing ideas around revolutionary dance and collective strength. My topic was the left-wing dancers in 1930s New York who believed their art was a weapon in the class struggle. In a moment of synchronicity I was joined on the panel by someone whose work I had seen in San Francisco who offered a practical perspective. Stephanie Maher, a dancer, choreographer and teacher, revealed how the personal and political are intertwined, with ideology turned into action as a collaborative spirit imbued her artistic practices, life and work ethics in California in the 1980s and 1990s and more recently in the Ponderosa collective outside Berlin. The evening ended late around communal dinner table, as the passion of the day was channelled by some into a spontaneous folk dance with a bit of improvisation – a display of embodied passion. While the euro crisis remained, a renewed optimism was restored for a brief time. I wondered whether similar evenings were shared by those who believed they could change the world through dance almost a century earlier.

Chapter 1

Edith Segal and Dancing Workers: Pageants, Summer Camps and Picket Lines

'We believe that workers who dance, play and sing together will also fight together for their rights.'[1]

'If I can't dance I don't want to be part of your revolution'.
Mis-attributed to Emma Goldman, feminist anarchist and activist.[2]

By the late 1920s recreational dancers in America were appearing in a range of political and social arenas, laying the foundations for the development of a wider left-wing dance movement. Drawing inspiration from Isadora Duncan and Marxist ideals, they channelled a strong social consciousness into a passion for movement, their history overtaken by concert dance artists who became prominent the following decade.[3] Edith Segal (1902-1997) was the quintessential leader motivating young men, women and children to use dance as a mode of political expression and to awaken the consciousness of their working-class identity. This chapter highlights the practices that occurred in the 1920s, outside the limelight of critical scrutiny. The energy of the recreational dances fed into the creation of the Workers Dance League in 1932, marking a brief period when workers groups shared stages with rising young professional modern dancers. The recreational groups' impassioned portrayals of an idealised world and celebration of people's

---

1 Executive Secretary, Educational Department, International Ladies Garment Workers Union Fannia M. Cohn, (1933) 'A New Era Opens', *Justice*, p. 9.

2 Alix Kates Shulman (1991) 'Dances With Feminists', orig. published in *Women's Review of Books*, IX:3, December, http://sunsite.berkeley.edu/Goldman/Features/dances_shulman.html, Emma Goldman Papers. Quotation attributed to Emma Goldman (1869-1940), anarchist, feminist activist, imprisoned for two years and then deported from the USA because of her politics in 1919.

3 My articles include Stacey Prickett (1994) 'The People: Issues of Identity Within the Revolutionary Dance', in Lynn Garafola, ed., *Of, By and For the People: Dancing on the Left in the 1930s*; (1990) 'Dance and the Workers' Struggle', *Dance Research* and (1989) 'From Workers' Dance to New Dance?', *Dance Research*. See also Ellen Graff (1997) *Stepping Left: Dance and Politics in New York City, 1928-1942*; Mark Franko (1995) *Dancing Modernism/ Performing Politics*; Lynn Garafola (2005) 'Writing on the Left: The Remarkable Career of Edna Ocko', *Legacies of Twentieth-Century Dance*; Elena J. Brown (2002) '"If I can't Dance I Don't Want to Be Part of Your Revolution': Edith Segal and the Revolutionary Dance Movement of the 1930s', *Society of Dance History Scholars Conference* Proceedings; and Susan Manning (2004) *Modern Dance, Negro Dance: Race in Motion*.

power to overcome exploitation exposed new audiences to an early version of modern dance. Starting in New York, groups with labour affiliations also sprang up in San Francisco, Detroit, Boston and other urban centres.

Of those involved in the left-wing movement, Segal had the most extensive connections to those labouring in garment factories, offices, and later in the 1930s, automobile manufacturing. The worker in various guises provided inspiration for her dances, poetry, political action and perpetuation of a Jewish cultural heritage. The range of dances, themes and recreational dance groups that held the imprimatur of Segal's directorial hand reveal the diverse influences that shaped her aesthetic and performance career. Crossing between recreational and professional dance and theatre fields, her group choreography integrated realistic movement with folk dance and modern dance. Fundamental to all was a strong conviction in the fight for equality, justice, and for the perpetuation of Jewish heritage in its secular rather than religious manifestations. Segal's embodied politics demonstrate integral links to workers theatre in Germany, the USSR and the USA; settlement house training and performance; pageantry; and multiple dance styles. Joining the Communist Party in 1927, she retained strong political convictions throughout her life. A continued commitment to communist tenets led to decades of FBI surveillance of activities which today seem innocuous.[4]

Segal was still a vibrant mover when I interviewed her in the late 1980s and early 1990s. Her dance narrative was interspersed with snippets of song and impassioned critiques of capitalism, the high price of clothing and the plight of the homeless. Surrounded by the remnants of a full life – stacks of books, papers, framed letters and tributes – Segal spoke of the scepticism she faced in wanting to convey her political feelings through dance. In archival documents, interviews, reviews and her own reflections, Segal emerges as a dynamic catalyst, at times an outspoken advocate for a political dance, early on labelled as agit-prop (agitation-propaganda). The accounts accessible today reveal a very energetic, compassionate woman who touched many people's lives, but by the criteria of what was to became canonic modern dance aesthetics, she was neither a strong choreographer nor a technically powerful dancer. Rather than perceiving these as negative attributes however, she engaged with recreational dancers in different ways than the major moderns and their proponents. Drawing from a large palette of movement material to devise activities, Segal's blend of recreation and entertainment reinforced ideological beliefs about equality and communal identities. The *Village Voice* dance critic and historian Deborah Jowitt wrote: 'She had a gift, a former colleague says, for whipping nondancers

---

4 I am grateful to Victoria Phillips Geduld for sharing with me Edith Segal's FBI files obtained through the Freedom of Information Act Request No. 1080924-000.

into creditable shape and making them look good'.[5] An exploration of Segal's early career reveals how a number of performative innovations and ideological imperatives shaped her dance practice, at a time when the artistic and political coincided. Across 15 years, between 1924 and 1939, Segal moved from the political margins to a position closer to the theatrical mainstream, from Chicago and New York to Detroit and employment with the Federal Theatre Project.

Interviews with Segal focus predominantly on key dances such as a solo performed by her at a Chicago Lenin Memorial Meeting in 1924, Communist Party pageants and the multi-racial *Black and White* duet originally danced by two women. However, minimal attention is given to her dance activities at summer camps, her Federal Theatre Project work and union-related activities in Detroit. Close reading of archival materials provide insight into performative practices that were on the periphery. The focus here is on this less familiar trajectory, tracing ideological and artistic influences that include Isadora Duncan, the Russian actor Maria Ouspenskaya, the American poet Walt Whitman and the iconic Soviet politician Vladimir Lenin, revealing a rich eclecticism indicative of a vibrant artistic and political world.

Political Environment

The year 1927 provides a historical moment around which to situate the workers dance as a regular practice in the New York City area. Major economic and social changes in the first quarter of the 20th century transformed ideas about progress, technology and the relationship between the body and labour. The assembly line and drive for profit heightened labour tensions, leading to an unprecedented number of strikes, many of which were unsuccessful in altering fundamental economic relationships. Mass consumption and increasing industrialisation went hand-in-hand with the rise of unions. The aftermath of WWI was rife with industrial action, which at times was met with violence or severe repercussions for those involved in labour disputes. Occasional victories fuelled hope for further change, however, as a steel strike resulted in the first eight-hour work day. The ideologies of nation shifted away from America's agrarian economic foundations as is shown by the development of big business, the growth of large corporations and loss of farmers' economic and political capital. The country entered a period of unprecedented growth, demographic change and isolationism.

The later part of the 1920s was marked by protests in response to major trials and repressive government actions perceived as chipping away the civil liberties underpinning American democracy. The closing of the left-

---

5 Deborah Jowitt (1982) 'A Lifetime of Art on the Left', *Village Voice*, July 6, p. 75.

wing journal *The Masses* and the trial of its editors under anti-sedition laws are indicative of fears about the spread of communism after the Russian Bolshevik Revolution in 1917. Passage of the Espionage Act of 1917 restricted the expression of dissent while the Sedition Act of 1918 led to high-profile prosecutions. Among those jailed for voicing opposition to war conscription was Eugene V. Debs, who ran as the Socialist presidential candidate from his jail cell. The years 1919 and 1920 witnessed mass deportations of immigrants because of their leftist politics, with the feminist activist Emma Goldman among those rounded up during what became known as the Red Scare. Contempt for constitutional rights reached its height as 5,000 immigrants were expelled from the land of promise.

The 1920 case of the shoemaker Nicolà Sacco and the unemployed labourer Bartolomeo Vanzetti became an international cause that exposed injustices and prejudice in American society. Accused of a murder and theft in Bridgewater, Massachusetts, they were executed in 1927 despite the flimsy evidence. Prominent writers, artists and intellectuals joined with trade unionists to advocate for their release. An alliance between the American intelligentsia and activist workers emerged around this case and others as 'proletarian' issues drew together religious, race-based and political groups across the ideological spectrum. Many supporters believed Sacco and Vanzetti's anarchist beliefs and Italian heritage contributed to their conviction.[6]

America's population had been transformed by mass immigration in the late 19th and early 20th century, with an influx of arrivals from Russia, Eastern and Southern Europe. There was a perception that the predominant Roman Catholic and Jewish beliefs held by immigrants from these areas threatened the white Protestant mainstream. Christian fundamentalists and a revitalised Ku Klux Klan targeted immigrants, Jews, Catholics and their supporters while continuing attacks against blacks. Citizenship demanded a level of patriotism and assimilation that differed from European identity constructions. Eric Hobsbawm argues that after 1860, immigrants comprised a majority of America's working class. They were deemed the least stable members of the national community, 'an internal enemy against whom the good American could assert his or her Americanism'.[7]

Despite the constraints against free expression, organisations rooted in communist and socialist ideologies were formed as legal entities, but factionalism undermined the power of the left as a political force in government. The Socialist Labor Party was the most mainstream of the leftist

---

6 For comprehensive histories of the USA that focus on civil liberties and worker rights issues, see Eric Foner (1998) *The Story of American Freedom*; Howard Zinn (2003) *The Twentieth Century*.
7 Eric Hobsbawm (1983) 'Mass Producing Traditions, Europe, 1870-1914', in Eric Hobsbawm and Terence Ranger, *The Invention of Tradition*, p. 280.

groups while breakaway organisations such as the International Workers of the World (IWW or 'Wobblies') drew in those marginalised by the left-leaning political parties. Widespread fear of even the symbols of revolution led to passage of state and federal laws such as the Red Flag Act which banned red flags (communist) and black flags (associated with anarchists).[8]

The Great Migration of people from the agricultural South to the industrial centres of the North involved whites as well as blacks, lured by the possibility of employment and a new life. Race riots caused many deaths in cities such as East St Louis (1917) and Chicago (1919) while horrific lynchings continued in the South. Such overt violence was only part of the deep-seated and all-encompassing prejudicial customs and laws that were targeted by the civil rights movement of later decades.

Alongside this long list of repressive laws and exclusionary practices, a counter hegemonic movement emerged that would influence New Deal policies of the 1930s, shape the arts and their relationship to wider society. Inspired by the Soviet Union and a surge of optimism at the end of World War I, a movement grew to enact change in the employment conditions of America's workers. At the same time, the fight against prejudice and government oppression became increasingly organised, as demonstrated by the establishment of the National Association for the Advancement of Colored People (NAACP) in 1909 and the Civil Liberties Bureau (forerunner of the American Civil Liberties Union) in 1917. There were fears of immigrant radicals – of those whose ideologies and customs were deemed alien to North European hegemony.

Discrimination extended to trade unions, with power consolidated in the American Federation of Labor (AFL), whose membership of skilled, white, American-born men excluded many – immigrants, women and unskilled workers.[9] The International Workers Order (IWO) was comprised of fraternal ethnic organisations that banded together when the struggle between Communists and Socialists led the Communists to break from the Socialist-led Jewish Workmen's Circle in 1930. IWO groups valued the traditions and languages of their homelands and joined the newly established Jewish People's Fraternal Order to create a benevolent organisation that drew together existing ethnic societies and established new groups among Italians, Poles, Ukrainians and other immigrant populations. Providing low-cost insurance, the IWO also sponsored cultural events and filled a gap after the 'bolshevisation' of the Communist Party which emphasised an international proletariat and banned foreign language federations.[10] The emergence of a specific working-class identity linked to radical politics, one

---

8 Eric Foner (2010) *Give Me Liberty: An American History*, v. 2, 3d ed. p. 697.

9 Foner (2010) op.cit. pp. 833-834; Zinn, op.cit. pp. 39-40.

10 Paul C. Mishler (1999) *Raising Reds: The Young Pioneers, Radical Summer Camps, and Communist Political Culture in the United States*, pp. 64-66.

embracing a multi-ethnic immigrant population and the emergence of a cultural front have their roots in New York City's Lower East Side, within the intersection of politics, labour and art of the area's Jewish community.

Lower East Side Life

For centuries New York City has been the entrance point for waves of immigrants searching for economic opportunities, escaping religious prosecution or other oppression. After the assassination of Czar Alexander II in 1880, religious pogroms prompted a large exodus of Jews from areas of Eastern Europe and Russia (Poland, Lithuania and Ukraine among them). An open door policy brought approximately two million Jewish refugees to America between 1880 and 1924 when restrictive quotas came into effect. Many of the immigrants began their new lives in the Lower East Side of Manhattan, an area transformed over the years by succeeding groups whose ethnic or national communities dominated the area – black, Irish, Italian, German, with Eastern European and Russian Jews. They settled there, reshaping the neighbourhood in the process. Drawn by the *di goleneh medina* (the golden land dream) Jewish arrivals were faced instead with dark and crowded streets lined by densely populated tenement houses. The scarcity of indoor space meant activities and social interactions spilled outside, which 'created a kind of zone that social and cultural historians have come to view as highly productive of cultural creativity, a zone that blurred the public and private'.[11]

Born to parents who were part of the Jewish exodus from Eastern Europe, Segal grew up on the Lower East Side. Between the ages of six and twenty-one when she eloped, Segal lived at 156 East Broadway. As she explained: 'the Lower East Side WAS the Jewish community... East Broadway... was the street that housed ALL the Yiddish newspapers of the time – the *Forward*, the *Day*, the *Jewish Morning Journal*.'[12] The socialist paper *Jewish Daily Forward* mediated between the Jewish community and American mainstream, publishing articles about etiquette and helping to socialise new arrivals. The *Freiheit* (Freedom) was established by the Communist Party (CPUSA) in 1922; its editor was Moissaye Olgin who also contributed to the *Daily Worker*, another CPUSA periodical.[13]

Classified as Russian, Segal's Polish father worked as a cigarmaker and was a union member who spoke Yiddish. Her English-speaking mother had migrated from Stuchin, Poland, and was a hairdresser and *shaitlmacher* or wigmaker. Orthodox Jewish women wear wigs – although not Segal's

---

11 Hasia R. Diner (2000) *Lower East Side Memories: A Jewish Place in America*, p. 134.
12 NYPL, Edith Segal, Interview with Leslie Farlow, Edith Segal Archives (ES Archives), *MGZMT 3-1153, file number 122-37, p. 6. 14 January 1991.
13 Epstein Mendelsohn (2007) *At the Edge of a Dream*, p. 101.

mother or grandmother – to cover their hair after marriage. The Segal home must have been a scene of vibrant activity, with women coming and going for their hair appointments, adding to the daily buzz of a life with four children. Unlike her only brother, Segal and her two sisters were taught Hebrew at home by a lay rabbi while the family attended synagogue on the high holy days. They lived on the first floor of a five-story red brick apartment building built in 1910. The basement was occupied by the printing shop of the Yiddish songwriter and poet Eliakum Zunser. A restaurant on the ground floor or 'stoop floor' attracted Yiddish writers, including the 'Dante of the Sweatshops', poet Morris Rosenfeld.[14] The Garden Cafeteria was a few doors away at 165 East Broadway, and its description evokes a site of lively economic, political and cultural interactions:

> ...in its heyday, from dawn until late in the evening, the 240-seat dining room was crowded with intellectuals, radicals, socialists, poets, journalists and other neighbourhood residents seated at communal tables. They would drink scalding tea from a glass, eat blintzes, kasha varnishkes, matzo ball soup, herring and various other Jewish culinary delights while discussing life, literature, philosophy, politics and events of the day....[15]

Life-altering opportunities for education lay nearby, and Segal made the most of what was on offer. She studied at the nearby Educational Alliance, a charity organisation established in 1889 to help Jewish immigrants adjust to life in their new country.[16] The Henry Street Settlement where she trained in music, dance and acting was also close by, so her youth was imbued with a rich cultural and political engagement. Historian Hasia Diner analyses the 'sacralisation' of the Lower East Side over the years, its history held as common history among many Jewish-Americans, achieving the status of an imagined community for some without familial connections to the area.[17] Segal's youth, however, fits the myth, is close to the reality that shaped a shared Jewish-American heritage in many ways.

To help out the family financially, Segal undertook a non-academic curriculum at Washington Irving High School. While working as a stenographer, she joined classes in socialism at the Rand School of Social Science, established in 1906 by the American Socialist Society.[18] Despite

---

14 Ibid. pp. 234-235.

15 Joyce Mendelsohn (2009) *The Lower East Side: Remembered and Revisited*, p. 56.

16 Educational Alliance website, 'About Us', http://www.edalliance.org/index.php?submenu=AboutUs&src=gendocs&ref=AboutUs&category=Main, accessed online on 2 January 2013.

17 Diner, op.cit.

18 Description from New York State Archives summary of files seized by the FBI in 1919, when the school was under suspicion of seditious activity, http://www.archives.nysed.gov/a/research/res_topics_bus_lusk_rand.shtml, Accessed online on August 20, 2012.

being a self-declared atheist from the age of 13, Segal's work with secular Jewish groups and the IWO schools helped perpetuate the spread of Yiddish culture and language. While an ethnic identity was a crucial part of Segal's artistry, she did not perceive herself as a Jewish dancer, 'as I have choreographed many dances on other themes'.[19] Rebecca Rossen has interrogated the complexities of Jewishness by analysing perceptions of Jews by each other and non-Jews, and their corporeal manifestations in performances by a number of choreographers of Jewish heritage. Rossen distinguishes between 'Jewish dances' with overt Judaic content and 'dancing Jewish'. She discusses how the dancers had to negotiate the intersection between American-ness and Jewishness from a position of otherness that has dissipated over time, as younger generations moved outside the Lower East Side community.[20]

Piano classes provided a musical foundation and Segal trained in dance and acting at the Henry Street Settlement, although her mother did not approve of her involvement in dance classes. These started with interpretive dance, emphasising individual expression, folk dance, and early modern dance. She honed her performance skills in Neighborhood Playhouse productions over a twelve year period, appearing in her first production at the age of ten. Her career as a poet started early, when she was awarded the first prize for song and music in the Henry Street Settlement Camp Song contest.

Segal's ideals found danced expression in Communist Party pageants and in works created for the various dance groups she directed. The story of how she interrupted a cross-country hitch-hiking trip in 1924 to dance a solo at a Lenin Memorial Meeting in Chicago is often cited as the start of the left-wing dance movement, one established away from the concert dance world. Accompaniment was provided by pianist Rudolph Leibich who played the funeral march at the memorial service for the executed IWW activist and songwriter Joe Hill in 1915. Inspired by Duncan, Segal's solo began with an expression of sorrow as she recalled:

> [In] the first part – to the Workers Funeral March ... I would be a mourner, in short red tunic with black cloth draped over one shoulder. Then I would remove the black, go into the second part done to the *Internationale*, [with] Lenin telling the workers not to mourn but to build. Ripping aside a black scarf of mourning to reveal a red tunic, the tribute ended with an evoca-

19 NYPL, Judith Brin Ingber Edith Segal Questionnaire, 21 December 1987, ES Archives, file 122-51.

20 Rebecca Leigh Rossen (2006) *Dancing Jewish: Jewish Identity in American Modern Dance and Postmodern Dance*. Joshua Perlman (2008) also investigates Jewish identity and modern dance in *Choreographing Identity: Modern Dance and American Jewish Life, 1924-1954*. See also Naomi Jackson (2002) *Converging Movements: Modern Dance and Jewish Culture at the 92nd Street Y*.

tion of joy and optimism for a future under communism, accompanied by the *Internationale*, the anthem of workers around the world.[21]

This early solo bore the impact of her training in the movement system of Emile Jaques-Dalcroze, folk dance and a Duncan-influenced interpretive style while later ballet training and performing experience contributed to the emergence of an aesthetic that amalgamated diverse influences. One photograph in her archive shows Segal in costume for a Russian folk dance which accompanied a San Francisco showing of the film *Five Year Plan*, presumably taken on the same cross-country trip.

Playhouse and Pageants

The settlement house played a significant institutional role in the evolution of the workers' dance, being one aspect of a progressive philanthropic movement offering a range of facilities to immigrant families. Drama, dance and musical training took place alongside classes which helped Americanise the clientele and provide a cultural foundation to enrich their lives. In Manhattan, Lillian Wald established the Henry Street Settlement in 1893, and by 1906 dance and music training was offered. The volunteer teachers included Irene and Alice Lewisohn, the wealthy daughters of a copper magnate. Their exposure to European theatre and dance during extensive travels shaped their outlook. They built and subsidised the 399-seat Neighborhood Playhouse theatre as an alternative to established commercial theatres, enabling young artists to gain performance skills, production experience and establish networks upon which the dance field flourished. The form of *lyric drama* they developed 'displaced the written word as the center of the theatrical production and [they] carried out experiments in scenery, lighting, costuming, sound, music, dance and acting styles'.[22] Inspired by avant-garde practitioners such as Gordon Craig, Alice was drawn to theatre design. Irene's dance classes drew on Genevieve Stebbins' interpretations of the Delsarte's system of expressive movement. Their productions also drew on the talents of Blanche Talmud (1900-1990) who taught at the Neighborhood Playhouse from 1920-1940.[23]

---

21 Edith Segal, interview with author, September 15, 1988. See accounts of interviews by Jowitt, op.cit., while Eleni J. Brown, op.cit. summarises Segal's inspiration and influences, op.cit.; see also Farlow, op.cit.

22 Melanie Blood (2007) 'Cooper Heiresses take the Stage' in *Angels in the American Theater: Patrons, Patronage and Philanthropy*, introduction by Robert A. Schanke, p.39. See also Linda J. Tomko, (1999) *Dancing Class, Gender, Ethnicity and Social Class in American Dance 1890-1920*.

23 Blanche Talmud was an inspirational teacher to many and helped choreograph a number of dance sequences in the lyric dramas. See http://jwa.org/encyclopedia/article/dance-performance-in-united-states, accessed on 5 January 2013.

Linda Tomko's comprehensive study of dance in the Progressive Era highlights the significance of classes offered at settlement houses.[24] While settlement house training shaped a number of prominent actors and dancers over the years (including Helen Tamiris, Sophie Maslow and Anna Sokolow), the underlying ethos behind the Neighborhood Playhouse productions placed the group above the individual: 'the emphasis on ensemble performance and identity of purpose helped to forge in bodily terms a representation, and possibly a sense, of immigrants belonging to a corporate whole larger than their specific historical or ethnic identities.'[25] Tomko links these values to the innovative 'little theatre' movement. They are also evident in the collective sensibilities of the workers' dance and political pageants of the early 1930s.

New York City was a hotbed of performance, with an insatiable appetite for new styles and stars. An inclusive approach to programming saw Russian ballet on the lineup alongside vaudeville acts. In the Henry Street Pageant of 1913, a historical survey of the area featured a range of dances such as 'the Irish Jig, the Highland fling, a German hopping dance, the tarantella, a Russian folk dance, a Yiddish song and a Russian Kasatchek, followed by the Settlement Song and an exit march'.[26] The global performance offerings at the theatre included the Noh-inspired *Tamura* (1918) by Japanese modern dancer Michio Ito. According to theatre scholar John Harrington, rather than universalising art by introducing Asian aesthetics to a Western context, Ito 'brings both immigrant consciousness and Japanese culture to a neighbourhood fully familiar with the first through a distinct and well-defined racial identity of its own'.[27] Drawing from international theatre forms, *The Little Clay Cart* (1924) was inspired by the Lewisohns' Indian travels. Segal appeared in seventeen productions inspired by American history such as *Hiawatha* (possibly the 1911 staging), celebrations of religious rituals (*The Festival of Pentecost, The Feast of Tabernacles*, 1918), and literary adaptations such as Walt Whitman's *Salut au Monde* (1922), which encapsulated a populist and democratic ethos. In addition to the characterisations from around the world, Segal learned to play a range of instruments, enriching her rhythmic awareness, seen in her portrayal of a man in *A Burmese Pwé* (1926). She is credited as a percussionist in a number of the later workers dance group performances. Her experiences at the Neighborhood Playhouse established a theatrical sensibility informed by a holistic aesthetic, giving her the musical tools to function as a composer/accompanist as well as a dance director.

24 Tomko, op.cit p. 113.
25 Ibid. p. 117, The Neighborhood Playhouse also provided space for groups such as the Needle Trades Dance Group, who met twice a week.
26 John Harrington (2007) *The Life of the Neighborhood Playhouse on Grand Street*, p. 41.
27 Ibid. p. 104.

One of Segal's last Playhouse performances was in S. Ansky's *The Dybbuk* (1926), a compilation of Chassidic Jewish folk tales and rituals about a young bride-to-be who becomes possessed by a spirit. *The Dybbuk* has been hailed as a milestone, marking 'the institutional role the Neighborhood Playhouse sought as a link between the Lower East Side and the outside world through the romance of professional theatre and the practical skills it offered to students in the assimilationist framework of the settlement'.[28] Dance featured prominently in the mystical play about spirit possession. Segal played Rachel, the bride's mother, and one of a group of beggars who dance in return for food.

In an interview, Segal related how she developed her character in the Beggar's Dance: 'I was a widowed cripple with two children at home...we had to come back and tell [the director] who "we were". This experience heightened our observation and empathy with those around us – an experience which grew more profound during my entire life.'[29] A *New York Times Magazine* account reinforces the realist impetus: 'The beggars in the *Dybbuk* who are so convincing on the stage were put through a whole course of simulated begging from getting up in the morning to wrapping up in realistic rags in a less exposed corner for a night's rest.'[30] Settlement houses offered space for the intersection of cultural practices where movement was imbued with ideologies of class, ethnicity and politics – a blend which shaped Segal's ethos from the start.

The realist approach to acting was influenced by the Moscow Art Theatre, which arrived in New York in 1923, sparking a transformation in dramatic training and performance. The legacy left by members of the group who established careers in the USA is known as 'the Method', an acting approach based on the work of Konstantin Stanislavsky. The Russian actor Maria Ouspenskaya, whom Segal names as an inspirational teacher who taught improvisational movement at the Playhouse, co-founded the American Laboratory Theatre before making a career as a significant character actor in Hollywood films. Segal had other leftist theatre connections to Artef, a Yiddish theatre group comprised of workers which was established in 1925. The group's founders were theatre activists who developed their ideas at one of the summer camps, thus Artef was linked to the rural escapes known as the 'borscht circuit' or the 'borscht belt'.[31] During the ten years the company produced shows in New York City (starting in 1928), the group became known for its avant-garde approach with an appeal that extended to English-speaking audiences as well as offering productions in a more agit-prop style. Modelling itself on the Moscow Art Theatre, Artef established studios to

28 Ibid. p. 216.
29 Farlow, op.cit.p. 6.
30 Harrington, op.cit. p. 221.
31 David S. Lifson (1965) *The Yiddish Theatre in America*, p. 439.

train its members in theatre crafts such as voice, movement, dance, design and provide them with an understanding of theatre history.[32] A collective sensibility shaped the group's work: cheap tickets were offered through trade unions which ensured audiences at the start when the mainstream newspapers initially refused to publicise its shows. Segal set movement to some of Artef's shows while company members performed in her pageant dances.

As increasingly visible activist dancers organised and took their political protests in movement to the streets, union halls and concert dance stages, they engaged in debates about the relationship between ideology and dance, the social responsibility of artists, aesthetic standards and tensions between the professional and recreational performers. By the time the 1929 stock market crash became a world-wide economic depression, a fledging left-wing dance movement was in full swing, shaping the work of young modern dancer-choreographers, such as fellow Lower East Side dance students Helen Tamiris, Sophie Maslow and Anna Sokolow. The aesthetic and ideological debates surrounding different groups within the left-wing dance movement have been documented extensively so the focus in this chapter is on tracing a confluence of movement, artistic and political practices that fed into the 1930s.

Dance Influences and Beginnings

The 1920s encompassed diverse artistic responses to global upheavals such as war and increasing economic instability. The forays into politically informed performances occurred alongside a vibrant performance field. For example, dance critic Marcia B. Siegel analyses New York's 1928-1929 dance season, which she declared was unprecedented in its number and stylistic range. New York's dance critics John Martin (*New York Times*) and Mary F. Watkins (*The Herald Tribune*) reported on 129 concert dance events. A cosmopolitan season offered an eclectic range of styles, and unusual mixing of genres. Former Ballets Russes choreographer Léonide Massine was dance director at The Roxy, a large cinema which featured live shows while Michel and Vera Fokine presented their 'school-based' Fokine Ballet. The Ziegfield revue included ballerina Tamara Geva, and Agnes de Mille choreographed a revival of the old ballet spectacle *The Black Crook*. While perceptions of dance as high art had yet to be deeply ingrained, stylistic mixing occurred. Although perceived today as 'artists' rather than 'entertainers', the hierarchies of dance art had fluid boundaries. Doris Humphrey and Charles Weidman performed at night spots and Sunday night concert dance stages, as did Tamiris. This shifting of boundaries was quite contentious for those striving to elevate the cultural capital of their work. 'Entertainment', equated with 'popular', held a

---

32 Ibid., also see Irving Howe (1976) *World of our Fathers, The Journey of the Eastern European Jews to American and the Life they Found and Made*, p. 490.

negative connotation. As Siegel notes, 'The Europeans use the term "popular" interchangeably with the term "folk", but in this country [the USA] popular meant not artistic.'[33]

Isadora Duncan inspired a new generation of dancers striving for an expressive vitality responsive to their lives while others codified expressive bodily techniques to convey innovative themes. Martha Graham and Tamiris each gave solo concerts in 1927 which are recognised today as heralding seminal shifts in aesthetics, individuality and expressivity in dance. Impresario Sol Hurok produced a memorial concert in honour of Duncan who died in 1927. Multiple groups carried on her name and legacy, one of which – the New Duncan Dancers – went on to perform under the auspices of the left-wing Workers Dance League in the 1930s. From Europe came the German dancers Harold Kreutzberg and Hans Weiner, who had both trained with Rudolf Laban, while Eugene Von Grona, later to found the First American Negro Ballet, taught German modern dance. The European connection was reinforced by Duncan, the guiding light for young dancers of all ideological persuasions in the 1920s. Making her career in Europe, she returned to the USA twice during World War I. During her 1917-1918 tour Duncan evoked a patriotic nationalism and danced in support of France and the war at a time when anti-war sentiments were prevalent amongst her Bohemian supporters. Ann Daly notes that *La Marseillaise* (1914) and other heroic maternal dances marked a shift away from the diaphanous costumed 'goddess' dances that shaped global aesthetic and interpretive dancing trends.[34] Speeches from the stage announced Duncan's politics, increasingly aligned with bolshevism after the 1917 Russian Revolution. In dance terms her political alignment was evident in the *Marche Slav*, about the rise of the Russian peasantry in opposition to czarist rule.[35]

As Daly notes, Duncan was able to link her support of bolshevism to patriotic sympathies during the war, but the situation changed drastically when she returned to the USA in 1922. The previous year she had moved to Moscow at the invitation of Commissar of the Enlightenment Anatoly Lunacharsky. The dream of a free school was short-lived because of widespread famine and dire economic conditions, and Duncan had to tour the Soviet Union to raise money. However, the schools survived under the guidance of Irma Duncan, one of Isadora's adopted students. Daly highlights how Duncan's life by that point was a contradiction between what she espoused in speeches and interviews and the luxury in which she sought to live. Arriving in New York, she was held overnight on Ellis Island and questioned about her

33 Marcia B. Siegel (1987) 'Modern Dance Before Bennington: Sorting it all out', *Dance Research Journal*, p. 6.
34 Ann Daly (2003) *Done into Dance: Isadora Duncan in America*, pp. 188 and 194.
35 Ibid. p. 195.

politics before being allowed to land. Duncan's marriage to the Soviet poet Sergei Esenin resulted in the revocation of her American citizenship. As Daly explains, after the war 'being a "revolutionary" was no longer a romantic badge of honor associated with the fight for democratic reforms; it now denoted a dangerous communist sympathiser out to destroy the American way of life. Where audiences once had seen freedom in the dancer's body, they now saw sedition.'[36] Scandal followed Duncan, through her polemical speeches, Esenin's alcoholic outbursts, and the display of an ageing body in revealing costumes that defied social and theatre conventions of the time. The Communist Party's *Daily Worker* devoted extensive coverage to the government's treatment of Duncan and conveyed her simplified version of communist tenets: 'I want everyone to dance and sing and be happy. That is my idea of Communism.'[37]

While Duncan was a spiritual influence, Segal's years of eclectic dance included a scholarship to study with Mikhail Mordkin between 1925 and 1927. A star of Moscow's Bolshoi Ballet, Mordkin had partnered Anna Pavlova in her first American tour, performing in classical music venues and paving the way for an influx of Russian dance groups which populated vaudeville theatres. Mordkin returned to lead his own Imperial Russian All-Star Company, appearing alongside jazz singer Al Jolson. To help develop a pick-up corps de ballet for his *Swan Lake* and more contemporary productions in the style of Fokine, Mordkin began offering classical ballet classes.[38] Although she later speaks against the bourgeois foundations of ballet, a 1928 photograph shows Segal in a high passé position, the lines of her leg continued by a well-pointed foot, displaying a physical tension in keeping with ballet training rather than the softly shaped limbs evident in some earlier images.

Segal entered into her first professional contract in 1926, performing in live shows at the Strand and Paramount cinema theatres. In a short space of time, cinema chains offered live performances that held onto vaudeville traditions until the development of sound technology changed the film industry.[39] During a tour on the Publix cinema circuit which took her to Texas and other central states, Segal performed what she described as 'authentic Spanish' dancing, a polka and a version of the 'Dance of the Hours', from the final act of the opera *La Giaconda* by Amilcare Ponchielli (1876). In one photograph, Segal poses on the roof of the Strand Theatre in pointe shoes

---

36 Ibid. p. 197.
37 Anon. (1922) 'Dance Among the Kitchen Pans',*The Daily Worker*, 2 December, p. 6.
38 Susan Carbonneau Levy (1990) *The Russians are coming: Russian dancers in the United States, 1910-1933.*
39 Douglas Gomery (1979) The Movies Become Big Business: Publix Theatres and the Chain Store Strategy, *Cinema Journal*, 18:2, pp. 26-40.

and a mid-length full skirted 'colonial' costume for the Colonial Days show.[40]

Back in New York, Segal organised dance activities for a variety of sponsoring organisations, teaching at the Grand Street Settlement, in union halls and community centres affiliated with the Communist Party USA (CPUSA). Increasingly the arts were utilised as a political tool to attract members. Dance historian Victoria Phillips Geduld discusses the extent to which pronouncements about progress against the capitalist machine were largely propaganda as CPUSA recruitment remained low despite large audiences at political rallies and benefits. Radical organisations offered enticements to compete with a range of corporate welfare activities and those available at other civic institutions, such as the attraction of a swimming pool at the YMCA.[41] Communist Party membership remained small relative to its influence in radical politics and the cultural left. Despite male dominance in leadership positions and a gendered 'masculinism' of the avant-garde while reinforcing traditional roles for women, a left feminist impetus was evident in the CPUSA's grassroots activities. Women comprised approximately one quarter of the CPUSA membership in 1935 and approximately 50% by 1943, and tensions arose between the organisation and the National Women's Party and perceptions of feminism as a white bourgeois movement. Proponents of Communism stressed the universality of their ideology, emphasising a gender-blind comradeship at the core of the struggle.[42] Communist iconography tended to celebrate traditional gender roles as 'Many progressive women defined themselves and their interests around motherhood and the family and adopted a maternalist style of activism that valorized features of traditional femininity.'[43] In the 1930s the CPUSA encouraged rank-and-file women's efforts to organise councils and neighbourhood committees although it viewed a focus on women's issues as distracting from the priority of class struggle. Perceptions of women as different could potentially undermine legislative protection from oppressive employment practices that had been hard won, such as limitation on long hours and late nights.[44] Segal steadfastly asserted her independence from the official CPUSA organisation although she shared

---

40 Edith Segal, interview with author, August 24, 1989, see also NYPL ES Archives, uncatalogued photographs.
41 Victoria Phillips Geduld (2008) 'Performing Communism in the American Dance: Culture, Politics and the New Dance Group', *American Communist History*, pp. 46-47.
42 Michael Denning (1997) *The Cultural Front: the Laboring of American Culture in the Twentieth Century*, p. 137; see also Harvey Klehr (1984) *The Heyday of American Communism: The Depression Decade*, p. 163.
43 Kate Weigand (2001) *Red Feminism: American Communism and the Making of Women's Liberation*, p. 5.
44 Ibid. p. 24.

with pride a commendation letter from the New York District Bureau.[45]

The Chicago-based Communist Party newspaper, *The Daily Worker* provides glimpses of the kinds of spectacle that led to the formation of the Workers Dance League in 1932 when recreational dancers joined up with young modern dance professionals. Numerous events were advertised in the late 1920s, including social or folk dances as part of fundraisers or leisure gatherings. Worker group activities were established among national affinities, others sponsored through labour affiliations. Union newsletters also reported on dance offerings at summer camps, political party gatherings, member dance groups and children's classes. While the activities offered the basic physical benefits of dance, they also reinforced a variety of identities and values, depending on the context. The ideology of class conflict was central to all, however, underpinned by goals of reinforcing common bonds of working class membership. The proletarian cause was an international one, garnering support from around the world and legendary artists. In 1924, Anna Pavlova invited striking garment workers to attend a Chicago performance for free.[46] Gathering for diverse causes, musicians, actors and dancers shared stages with political speakers at fund-raising benefit events. In 1927, *The Daily Worker* relocated to New York, becoming a rallying point for the city's artists.

Soviet and German models

Connections to European and Soviet workers' theatre practices and the wider proletarian cultural movement were reinforced by links to Germany and the USSR. In 1931, Segal travelled to the Soviet Union as part of the American delegation of the Workers International Relief cultural department. The artist Maurice Becker, brother to Helen Tamiris, is among the group photographed on board the ship. In Berlin while on her way home, Harry Allen Potamkin, a co-founder of the John Reed Clubs of worker writers, asked Segal to return to the USSR and represent the clubs at a Workers International Relief (WIR) conference.[47] The John Reed Clubs provided a model of worker-artists groups named after the left-wing journalist who wrote *10 Days That Shook the World* and was buried in the Kremlin. Berlin-based, the WIR was a fund-raising organisation that also supported revolutionary film production and distribution, leftist theatre and the wider socialist arts movement. Created in response to the economic turmoil, drought and famine in the Soviet Union, WIR evolved into a complex

---

45 Letter to Segal, dated 4 February 1930. NYPL, ES Archives, file number 122-51.

46 Anon, 1924, 'Pavlowa (sic) Dances Indian Role Before Garment Strikers', *Daily Worker*, v. I, no. 365, 15 March, p. 4.

47 Edith Segal, interview with Bea Lemisch, 27 February 1981, Tape #1, U2W, Oral History of the American Left, Robert F. Wagner Archives, Tamiment Library, New York University.

international organisation. Instead of merely distributing documentaries and raising money, it began commissioning films and supporting Soviet studios, developing the propaganda potential of the medium. It presented films in union halls and other non-cinematic spaces, and its subscription funding enabled it to avoid government censors. Potamkin was also a co-founder of the 1930 American Workers' Film and Photo League, but the Comintern (the Communist International organisation in the Soviet Union) dissolved the organisation in 1935, coinciding with the implementation of Popular Front policies.[48]

During her travels, Segal studied with socialist actor and theatre director Senda Koreya (1904-1994),[49] the brother of Michio Ito. She learned about agit-prop theatre and the theatres of directors Erwin Piscator and Bertolt Brecht. Margarethe Wallmann (c.1901-1992) is also cited as a significant influence, reinforcing connections between German and American modern dance. Wallmann had studied and performed with Mary Wigman and taught at Denishawn schools in Los Angeles and in New York during a 1928 US visit.[50] She also taught at Wigman's school in Berlin, but broke away to develop choric dances, establishing with her own company a strong link between expressionist dance and activism. In 1931 Wallmann's large format productions aimed to combat unemployment, achieving a choreographic complexity with multiple layers of symbolic meaning.[51]

In Moscow, Segal heard Commissar for the Enlightenment, Lunacharsky speak. He advocated the retention of the old imperial arts, developing them into art for the proletariat rather than demolishing them as bourgeois forms and institutions. Segal's visit coincided with the emergence of a Soviet ballet style, encapsulated in *The Red Poppy* (1927). Watching the ballet, she recalled that the ballet mime 'looked so silly to me... they hadn't learned anything... I felt that they wanted to see, [they] wanted to sit in the same seats as the bourgeoisie sat in the Bolshoi Theatre with the hammer and sickle over

---

48 Vance Kepley, Jr. (1983) 'The Workers' International Relief and the Cinema of the Left, 1921-1935', *Cinema Journal*, pp. 7-23.

49 Ito Kumiyo changed his name to Senda Koreya after he was beaten up by a gang when it mistook him for a Korean. He spent four and a half years in Germany, learning agit-prop theatre techniques, returning to Japan in 1931. John Swain (2007), entry on Senda Koreya, *Columbia Encyclopedia of Modern Drama*, v. 2, M-Z, edited by Gabrielle H. Cody, New York: Columbia University Press, pp. 1208-1209. Koreya also became a prolific film actor, Abu Khattak, *Senda Koreya: Theater for Change*, summary of presentation by Thomas Rimer, delivered at UCLA, Terasaki Center for Japanese Studies, February 13, 2006. http://www.international.ucla.edu/article.asp?parentid=40075.

50 Andrea Amort (2005) 'Margarethe Wallmann', Jewish Women's Archive, http://jwa.org/encyclopedia/article/wallmann-margarete, accessed 15 October 2009.

51 Karl Toepfer (1997) analyses Wallmann's choric works in *Empire of Ecstacy: Nudity and Movement in German Body Culture, 1910-1935*, pp. 290-291.

UNIVERSITY OF WINCHESTER LIBRARY

the Czarist thing, so I forgave them in a way.'[52] Although uninspired by the Soviet professional dance performed during her visit, Segal found the idealised aims of proletarian art embodied in Pioneer children's dances in former palaces. Their ethos paralleled Segal's work with children's dance groups in New York which contributed to the choreography for the Red Dancers and the Communist Party pageants.

Class consciousness: Workers and children

The impulse behind Segal's 1924 Lenin tribute solo spread as she began teaching children under the auspices of New York trade unions and fraternal organisations, associations which would occupy a major part of her career as teacher, writer and choreographer. Many of those organisations celebrated national or ethnic identities, especially those of immigrants from Eastern Europe and Russia who had escaped pogroms and other forms of csarist persecution. Between 1880 and 1920 two million Jews had immigrated to the USA. The largest influx of immigrants in the first part of the 20th century arrived from Russia (a label which included people from new nations created in the aftermath of World War I), Austria-Hungary and Italy.[53] Yiddish theatre, choral groups and orchestra performances were advertised alongside folk dance events in the *The Daily Worker* newspaper. Social gatherings reinforced multiple identities -- local and global – including membership of a specific community of workers, an ethnic or national group, and membership in the international proletariat. Worker organisations grew in number as the effects of the Depression spread and the political became integrally interwoven with the quotidian. When asked what inspired Segal to 'mix dance with politics', she explained that they were not separate in her life – there was never any dichotomy between the two.[54]

As someone who grew up in the leftist cultural milieu, Robbie Lieberman analyses the left-wing folk song movement as reinforcing the totalising culture of the left, shaping a sense of community for its members rather than just their politics. It touched all aspects of their lives – fulfilling their social, cultural and educational needs.[55] *The Daily Worker* was as concerned with the mundane as it was the monumental, functioning as a conventional newspaper in many ways. Sewing tips and commercial film reviews were published alongside critiques of capitalism, reports on industrial accidents and racial intolerance, including front page coverage of lynchings in the American south.

---

52 Farlow, op.cit. pp. 45-46.
53 Epstein, op.cit. xiii, see also Ira Rosenwaike (1972) *Population History of New York City*.
54 Segal, interview with author, September 15, 1988.
55 Robbie Lieberman (1990) *My Song is my Weapon: People's Songs, American Communism and Culture, 1930-1950*, pp. 14-17.

The education of a new generation was crucial to the growth of the leftist movement, seen in the establishment of the Young Pioneers of America (YPA) in 1926 after the Communist Party became a legal political organisation. The YPA's ideology was evident in the ethos of its programmes, offering an alternative to the Boy Scouts and other mainstream children's organisations which were perceived as militaristic and perpetuating capitalist values. Modelled on children's groups in the Soviet Union and led by members of the Communist Youth League and the Communist Party itself, the Young Pioneers distanced children from parental control. Activities were aimed at developing future leaders and to awaken working class consciousness. Paul Mishler's account in *Raising Reds* highlights how Pioneers were educated in class tensions, encouraged to boycott school on May Day, support strikers by collecting money and attending picket line demonstrations.[56] Songs, games and dances were developed to reinforce Communist values, advocating equality and social justice. Some groups were formed around ethnic identities while others were affiliated to occupational groups, such as longshoremen, farmers or miners. Factional divisions in the 1920s were tempered by the breakup of groups that were organised by ethnicity or foreign language, a reorganisation that diversified local organisations, attracting African American members in the process. By the official start of the Popular Front period in 1935 and in line with Comintern dictates and policies in Europe, CPUSA ideology had moved away from Bolshevisation, a revolution modelled on the Soviet Union, to support for New Deal policies and working with rather than against Socialist and other leftist groups.

In 1924, Segal began working with left-wing children's groups. In 1927, the year she joined the Communist Party, Segal established the Pioneers, a dance group for children aged 11 to 14.[57] Segal's youth group exemplifies ties between radical organisations and the official Communist Party during the 1920s, revealing tensions that arose in consolidating Marxist ideology with life in America among a New York community comprised predominantly of children born to immigrant working-class parents. The Young Pioneers offered alternatives to the family structures, and used social and cultural activities to reinforce working-class identities and revolutionary praxis. A new identity was the goal, one that recognised ethnic heritage alongside American nationality while hopefully absorbing the radical politics of their parents. Activities initially reflected the cultural heritage of the immigrant communities that comprised their membership – the Finnish Pioneers had a Red Sewing Circle which were common in Finland while the Ukrainian group offered folk dance. Among Segal's archives is a photograph of the Ukrainian American Pioneer Dance Group which she directed. Five girls

56 Mishler, op.cit.
57 Lemisch, op.cit.

hold hands in a circle, moving around another girl in the middle whose right hand is raised in a fist. All wear a triangular scarf, the uniform of the Pioneers, also worn by children at the summer camp where Segal worked for decades. In contrast to the adult group pictures which depict a weariness or confrontational attitude, the Pioneer group image conveys a playful feeling. The YPA was disbanded in 1934, while the IWO Juniors continued on, reaching an overall membership of 20,000 by 1940.[58]

Segal also taught dance at the after school programmes run by the International Workers Order and at synagogues, or 'shules', reinforcing a working-class rather than a religious identity of its membership. By 1938, 4,000 students were attending the 53 Jewish children's schools in New York City.[59] Support for the Soviet Union and opposition to Zionist and traditional religious practices shaped activities that communicated Communist ideologies. Dance activities among other groups were led by members of the left-wing dance community, such as Nadia Chilkovsky, a member of the New Dance Group. Writing under the pseudonym Nell Anyon in 1933, she explained that the Pioneer motto, 'Always Ready' had become the title of one of their dances. The group's ideological foundations reinforced class conciousness: 'Our dance is not concerned with abstractions: it is not concerned with humanitarian generalities: WE ARE FOR THE WORKING CLASS, and we teach our children to grow into strong, able fighters in the interest of their class!'[60] Photographs of dances titled *Always Ready* and *Children in the Soviet Union* accompanied the article. An outline for Troupe 18 of the International Workers Order Pioneers (IWO) divided the dance session into a half-hour of technical exercises and a half-hour of dance. Basic movement skills and coordination exercises used folk dance forms and primary movement patterns. Arm and head movements were gradually added to travelling steps (runs, walks and leaps), followed by a focus on rhythmic work. The children's repertoire included 'Are you a worker or are you a banker?' and a simplified version of the New Dance Group's *Barricades*,[61] humanising the identities of picket line marchers.

Segal's work with children and young people was significant for the construction of identities that negotiated tensions between their heritage and American-ness. As Mishler explains, 'Children of radical immigrant parents needed a way not only to be involved in their parents' world but, somehow, to make it their own.... Segal's choreography offered an occasion for both children and adults to participate in a symbolic expression of their

58 Mishler, op.cit.. p.68.
59 Mishler, ibid. pp. 75-80.
60 Nell Anyon (1933) 'Workers Children Dancing', NDG first annual recital programme, p. 11.
61 Beate Narmot (1935) 'Children's Work', *New Dance* (Bulletin of the New Dance League, Anti-War, Anti-Fascist Issue), March, p. 13. Copy courtesy of Edith Segal.

common beliefs. These dances were not expressions of radical ideology, per se, but were the radical outlook distilled into action and gesture.'[62] Tensions emerged between policies of Americanisation as a way towards the spread of socialist and communist ideologies which came up against the desire to celebrate and perpetuate the ethnic roots of immigrants. Policy shifts are evident in the organisational structures which went to the extremes of requiring that meetings be conducted in English, despite the dominant language of the membership. The youth dance groups' activities conveyed strong ideological messages and for Segal, sowed the seeds for later performance material. Her Young Pioneers dance to the song 'Comrades, the Bugle is Calling' was developed into the Communist Party pageant section 'Revolution' for its 1928 Lenin Memorial.[63]

Communist Party Pageants

In addition to the small group and solo formats, mass spectacles at Madison Square Garden offered a vibrant forum for politically inspired dance, reaching crowds of up to 18,000. Segal choreographed for the Freiheit Jubilee in 1928 and Lenin Memorial Pageants sponsored by the Communist Party in 1928, 1930 and 1931.[64] While parades and historical re-enactments were already part of American civic celebrations, these mass communist spectacles transformed the standardised pageant form into a theatricalised mode of political expression. In the USA, the form was adapted by various groups to help fulfil what historian David Glassberg calls contrasting 'ideological projects'. Glassberg details how the pageant form grew in popularity, fulfilled the diverse agendas of sponsoring organisations and was shaped by contemporary events. Patriotic and hereditary groups, such as the Daughters of the American Revolution, used pageantry as 'a way to reinforce their particular definition of civic identity, social order and the moral principles they associated with the past – preserve Anglo-American supremacy in public life'.[65] Progressive educators and playground workers used the format as a democratic folk festival, its recreational activities celebrated Anglo-American traditions alongside immigrant cultural forms, leading to a 'ritual construction of a new communal identity and sense of citizenship anchored in the past, yet forged out of the underlying shared emotions generated in the

---

62 Mishler, op.cit. p. 93.
63 The scenes were Revolution, Memorial for Fallen Comrades, Reconstruction and Celebration, interview with the author, 15 September 1988. See also Edith Segal (1935) 'First Revolutionary Dance Group in America', *New Dance* Anti-War, Anti-Fascist Issue, pp. 16-17, courtesy of Edith Segal.
64 At the Freiheit Jubilee, the scene 'Struggle Between Red, Yellow and Black Forces' was danced and 'Strike' had some danced sections. Programme courtesy of Edith Segal.
65 David Glassberg (1990) *American Historical Pageantry*, p. 64.

present, in the immediate experience of playing together'.[66]

Local municipalities utilised pageants to advocate social reform, exemplified by *The Pageant of Thetford* (1911) in Vermont. Like the urban settlement houses, pageants reinforced social values. William Chauncy Langdon, one of the leaders of the movement and Director of the Thetford pageant, viewed it as a tool to reverse the economic and social decline of the small town and its surrounding locale. The community was the 'hero': the pageant took place outdoors with the town itself in the background. Episodes with 'abstract symbolic dancing' were interspersed with historical re-enactments of community ideals. Celebration of a locality was combined with the global, with the contributions of various ethnic groups acknowledged through folk dances performed in national costumes. Virginia Tanner, who taught dance in Boston settlement houses, choreographed sequences in a Duncanesque 'aesthetic dancing' style, providing continuity through the emotional imagery evoked in the different sections. Tanner appeared as the allegorical 'Spirit of Pageantry' to Dvořák's composition *Humoresque*, enticing a dejected 'Spirit of Thetford' to rise up and face the future with confidence.[67] Most American pageants of the early twentieth century looked to the past, their social reform agenda set out to instil hope in the future, and reinforce a sense of agency. Langdon's pageants, by contrast, portrayed a community adapting to new challenges over time – in the present and future rather than being chained to the past. The inclusion of dance marked a development away from the English version of the pageant format and was a prominent feature of the pageants produced at the Henry Street Settlement which Segal would have been exposed to during her childhood.[68]

A significant transition in the historical format occurred in 1913 with the production of three counter-hegemonic ideological pageants. The National Woman Suffrage Pageant was the first of these alternative events, occurring in Washington D.C. on 13 March 1913. Sarah J. Moore argues that the unprecedented gathering of women from across the nation succeeded in challenging dominant notions of female behaviour by moving women more visibly into a highly political and public arena. Held the day before the inauguration of Woodrow Wilson as President, the procession down Pennsylvania Avenue culminated in a tableau at the Treasury Building. Tensions between factions within the suffrage movement emerged when casting decisions were based in part on the presentation of a particular version of femininity shaped by fashion and behaviour. Key participants

66 Ibid.; also see Namia Prevots, (1990) *American Pageantry.*
67 Ibid. pp. 71-101. Another dancer named Virginia Tanner (1915-1979) contributed to the institutionalisation of dance at the University of Utah, the development of children's dance education and was instrumental in founding the Utah Repertory Dance Theatre.
68 Caroline Walthall (2011) *Dancing the Dialectics of Change: American Site-Specific Dance as Public History in the Twentieth Century.*

were chosen to help convey specific ideals of female beauty, challenging stereotypes of masculinised feminists which dominated negative representations of the activists. Female artists portrayed allegorical roles of Justice (played by classical dancer Florence Fleming Noyse), Charity, Liberty, Peace, and Hope. Floats were created on themes such as slavery, linking the women's cause to larger issues of human rights. Moore notes that while the use of pictorial representations in the pageant format was a standard practice, the Suffrage spectacle's political use of the allegorical characters marked a shift in the function of the pageant form.[69]

Supported by the radical International Workers of the World, the Paterson Strike Pageant had ideological roots closely linked to the aims and objectives of the workers groups – revolutionary praxis. John Reed received financial backing from philanthropist Mabel Dodge to produce a pageant to benefit striking silk workers in Paterson, New Jersey, notorious because of violent attempts to break the workers' actions. Premiering on 7 June 1913, in Madison Square Garden, the pageant evoked the closure of the mill by strike action which brings downtrodden workers to life, their revolutionary actions striving to improve working conditions. Symbolism evoked the international struggle against capitalism (May Day, the colour red, singing of the *Internationale*), offering a revolutionary spectacle which marked a collaboration between the arts and organised labour.[70] While the pageant's fundraising aims fell short due to production costs, the event gave a new performative voice to oppressed workers.

The Star of Ethiopia opened at the National Armory in Manhattan in October 1913. The pageant was written by W.E.B. DuBois as a vehicle to counteract the widespread racial stereotyping of blacks. DuBois was a leading African-American intellectual and activist, who worked to reverse widespread racial discrimination and prejudice. As with forms of cultural expression during the Harlem Renaissance that flourished throughout the 1920s, the pageant helped stimulate racial pride and foster a sense of black solidarity. It was created to celebrate the fiftieth anniversary of the signing of the Emancipation Proclamation that ended slavery, and its positive perspective of the black diaspora reinforced a statement of pan-African nationalism that also helped educate white audiences. Defeating

---

69 Sarah J. Moore (1997) 'Making a spectacle of suffrage: The National Woman Suffrage Pageant, 1913', *Journal of American Culture*, 20:1, pp. 89-103. I am grateful to Ellen Graff, Victoria Geduld and Lynn Garafola for alerting me to the alternative pageants discussed here.

70 Paterson Strike Pageant Program, available at the History Matters website, George Mason University, http://historymatters.gmu.edu/d/5649/ ; Frederick Boyd, ed. (1964) *The Pageant of the Paterson Strike*, (New York, 1913) and *Current Opinion* and *Survey*, June 1913, Reprinted in Joyce L. Kornbluh, ed., (1964) *Rebel Voices: An I.W.W. Anthology*, Ann Arbor: University of Michigan Press, pp. 210-214.

Italy's armies in 1896, Ethiopia was one of two African nations that resisted colonisation, a model of self-sufficiency, resistance and an icon of black nationalism. With scenes restaged as shorter pageants, *The Star* celebrated multiple economic, scientific and cultural contributions by Africans and African Americans. DuBois compared the folk-inspired creation to the African American religious 'Shout' in offering opportunities to develop a black American dramatic practice.[71] The ritualised movement of the Shout offered a means through which to subvert anti-dance restrictions under slavery, accepted as a performance of worship.

All three alternative pageants stimulated a sense of solidarity, issuing calls to action while being informative artistic events. The political impetus behind this type of performance necessitated a particular type of legibility, ultimately influencing the structure of movement components. A specific political agenda underpinned the Communist Party events at Madison Square Garden, staged when the Soviet Union was heralded as a model society. Thematic similarities such as the Soviet revolution and the construction of a communist nation to the seminal 1928 Lenin Memorial Pageant were seen as late as 1937. Topical concerns such as communist struggles in Europe (heroic individuals such as Karl Liebknecht and Rosa Luxemburg of the German Spartacus League) and the anti-fascist struggle.[72]

Communist Party pageants of the 1920s and 1930s echo historical pageant formats. However, instead of constructing a version of American history and a shared national identity, they preserved a mythic vision of the Soviet Union's recent past, interspersing historical re-enactment with music, drama and dance. In the Lenin Memorial Pageant of 1928, Lenin and Stalin replaced the allegorical figures of traditional pageants, with the proletariat as the hero.[73] Various pageant floor plans depict *Revolution*, *Memorial for Fallen Comrades*, *Reconstruction* and *Celebration* as dramatising visions of the past, the present and the future. There were 37 performers in the work developed from a children's dance. Segal described how the ten members of Artef were added to in the recruitment process: 'To these were added any individuals who seemed at all able to move correctly, recruited mostly from frequenters of the cooperative restaurant on Union Square'.[74] The neighbourhood was a hub of activism and creativity, a meeting point

71   David Krasner (2001) '"The Pageant is the Thing": Black Nationalism and the Star of Ethiopia', in Jeffrey D Mason & J. Ellen Gainor, eds., *Performing America: Cultural Nationalism in American Theater*, pp. 106-122.
72   See Barbara Stratyner (1998), '"Significant Historical Events...Thrilling Dance Sequences": Communist Party Pageants in New York, 1937', in Lynn Garafola, ed., *Of, For and By the People*, pp. 31-37.
73   Accounts are recovered from photographs, newspaper articles, interviews and floor plans drawn by Segal, and are acknowledged throughout the discussion.
74   Edith Segal (1935) 'First Revolutionary Dance', *New Dance Bulletin*, courtesy of ES, p.16.

for young radicals, artists and workers. Such an open audition of sorts hints at a limited dance competency, restricting the technical level of the choreography. *Revolution* was danced to Wagner's *Ride of the Valkyries*, adding another layer of symbolic power, a quite ironic one in retrospect, given the music's fascist associations.[75] A rehearsal photograph labelled 'Revolutionary Funeral March' depicts Segal as Lenin, standing strong in the centre of the performance space, surrounded by dancers as the proletariat leaning towards her as if drawn by her power.

A lengthy description of the Lenin Memorial Pageant in the *Daily Worker* by the *Morning Freiheit* editor Moissaye J. Olgin, provides the perspective of an ideologically committed spectator. He viewed the pageant as dramatising the radical change brought about by the Bolshevik revolution. Olgin wrote: 'Here is the mass of the Russian people, poorly dressed, bent-backed men and women of the Czar's empire. The crowd moves uneasily, the crowd is in deep despair. The Cossacks come. Lashes swish in the air.' Grotesque, cartoonish portrayals of the aristocracy and ruling class stirred a sense of anger amongst those in the Gardens: 'The huge gathering is one crouching monster, ready to leap. There is a stifled cry in the hall. When the young figures draped in red finally appear, driving away the apparitions, one greets them like a true liberating force. They are the purifying storm, there is abandon in their sweep...'[76] A letter to the editor by one A.B. Magil reinforced the positive accolades, declaring that the performance was 'an event of the first importance to the revolutionary movement, since it was the first mass cultural expression of the American workers, created from within of our own materials and with our own imagination and power, as a tribute to the greatest leader of the proletarian revolution.' For Magil, it was the first time American workers had 'achieved a unified artistic expression of their collective class spirit.' Problems such as lack of rehearsal time and technical difficulties were deemed 'healthy defects, resulting from unripeness, haste, lack of facilities. In them are the seeds of betterment.'[77] A common theme emerges from the written accounts – the possibilities of revolutionary praxis and the proletariat as an agent of change.

The portrayal of the Bolshevik leaders and the proletariat were achieved through broad characterisations. By contrast, complex concepts such as economic policies and topical events required the use of words or other unambiguous symbols. Placards with anti-capitalist slogans were used as sets, and there was a literal reading of words spelled out by the dancers'

---

75 I'm grateful to Joanna Harris for pointing out specific associations between fascism and the Wagner tune.

76 M. Olgin Describes Lenin Pageant', *Daily Worker,* 26 January 1928, clipping courtesy of Edith Segal.

77 A.B. Magil, 'Lenin Pageant', *Daily Worker,* 2 February 1928, clipping courtesy of Edith Segal.

bodies. In one instance, their floor patterns spelled out 'Five Yr Plan', referring to Stalin's economic policies. Floor plans for the 1928 pageant end with flag-waving participants forming the shape of a hammer and sickle. The mass gatherings at Madison Square Garden necessitated the use of vivid imagery and large movements to ensure legibility since small or subtle movements would have been lost to all but those sitting close to the stage. As Segal explained:

> The success of the pageant dances was possible because the dance patterns were constructed along big, thick lines, and the technique employed was based on simple movement. However, for more intimate performances on small stages, it was necessary to develop more complicated dance form and detailed technique... We have since learned that we must take the best of the existing bourgeois technique, that is, all that is vital and healthy. In the final analysis, what we have to say through our dance will determine the particular technique to be used and will lead us to the creation of new forms.[78]

In 1929 Segal established the Red Dancers. The group performed *The Belt Goes Red* at the 1930 Lenin Memorial Meeting, portraying machinery, the theme chosen because the assembly line offered a highly recognisable symbol of capitalism, through which workers were alienated from the object of their labour and thus from their essential humanity. Both the workers and the object of their labour were portrayed:

> Through the belt came parts of the machine being built, represented by dancers in stiff straight postures. When the 'parts' were assembled and the machine completed, through the belt came a bold of red material which was carried by the workers who surrounded the machine, indicating that they had taken possession of the machine being built.[79]

Analysis of a rehearsal photograph offers striking similarities to Soviet iconography and the machine dances of the brief period of the immediate post-revolutionary Soviet avant-garde. Nikolai Foregger had developed a series of exercises that celebrated abstraction and industrialisation of the new nation.[80] American workers did not destroy the instruments of capitalist production; instead, they assumed ownership, using a red cloth that evoked worldwide socialism. Segal told with pride how someone in the audience identified so closely with the portrayal of workers that he jumped up on stage to join in the action, carrying his union banner: 'Evidently he

---

78 Edith Segal personal correspondence with author, January 15, 1990.
79 May Day became a major international celebration with the red flag as a universal symbol of the movement, see Hobsbawm (1983), op.cit. p. 284. Edith Segal in correspondence to the author, 10 January 1990.
80 Mel Gordon (1975) 'Foregger and the Dance of the Machines', *TDR*, pp. 68-73.

was someone who didn't have any theatrical obedience, he thought that was the thing to do.'[81]

In the pageants, diverse theatrical modes conveyed mythical versions of the past. Theatre historian Mick Wallis notes how the historical pageant form, originally imported from Britain, exemplifies the invention of tradition linked to different international left political movements and constructs of national identity. Invented traditions, historian Eric Hobsbawm writes, 'seek to inculcate certain values and norms of behaviour by repetition, which automatically implies continuity to the past'.[82] Those dancing on the Madison Square Garden stage did not have a nostalgic past to look back upon. Paul Buhle distinguishes Jewish immigrants from other immigrants who envisioned a return to their native lands. Having no such illusions, the former looked to their new homeland as 'a place where a Jew could safely be a Socialist, and where a democratic culture with a permanent Jewish presence could be imagined'.[83] A revolutionary past was portrayed on the Madison Square Garden stage, a Russian rather than an American one. This was combined with an attitude towards industrialisation that linked technological progress to the pioneering American spirit at the centre of the construction of national identity. Historian Warren Susman posits that although the Depression evoked widespread mistrust in technology due to its failure to bring about an improved society, an underlying faith remained: 'A product of the machine age, the American did not surrender his faith in science and technology. Rather, he often attributed his difficulties to the failure to apply himself more rigorously to the creation of a culture worthy of such achievements in science and technology.'[84] As technological progress continued to modify workers' relationship to labour, the opportunity to return to nature offered restorative escapes.

Summer Camps

Segal developed some of the pageant choreography in summer camps, creating a structure for the longer productions. In writing about growing up as a 'red-diaper baby', the name given to children whose parents were part of the political and cultural left of the 1930s, Paul Mishler discusses how a utopian vision shaped American versions of Marxist thought, predicated on the belief that revolutionary praxis with societal transformation was possible through the power of the people. Crucially, this vision was manifest

81 Edith Segal interview with author, 15 September 1988.
82 Eric Hobsbawm (1983) 'Introduction', in Eric Hobsbawm and Terrence Ranger, eds. *The Invention of Tradition*, p. 1. Mick Wallis (1995) 'The Popular Front Pageant'.
83 Paul Buhle (1987) *Marxism in the USA*, p. 83.
84 Warren I. Susman (2003 [org.pub. 1973]) *Culture as History: The Transformation of American Society in the Twentieth Century*.

in leisure and educational activities after World War I, which shifted away from earlier experiments in communal living and property ownership.[85] Country retreats provided restorative time for labourers and their children just a few hours' drive from New York. A number of camps in relative proximity to the metropolitan area featured dance activities among a wide variety of classes. Camp Nitgedaigit (Yiddish for 'no worries') in Beacon, New York, was sponsored by communists, while Camp Midvale in New Jersey was affiliated with the Nature Friends organisation. This 'international hiking and cultural organization' was comprised of German immigrants drawn together by their political beliefs and love of outdoor activities. The Communist Party supported the International Workers Order's children's Camp Kinderland, established in 1923 on Sylvan Lake in Dutchess County, New York, with adults accommodated at Camp Lakeland nearby. The International Ladies Garment Workers Union (ILGWU) ran Unity House in the Pocono Hills in Forest Park, Pennsylvania, where Segal worked for a season. Summer resorts offered the ubiquitous activities of a holiday in the countryside, tinged with varying degrees of social consciousness. In another reflection written by a child of leftists, Robbie Lieberman recalls that the left-wing choral groups sang Soviet Red Army songs while slogans on athletic team uniforms at her camp read 'Free the Scottsboro Boys'.[86]

Segal's camp involvement dates back to 1921 when she was the only woman at the Cedar Lake Camp in Mt. Beacon, New York, much to her mother's consternation, according to the inscription on the back of a group photograph.[87] In 1924, Segal taught dance and exercise classes at Unity House, which went on to sponsor lectures and entertainment by prominent musicians and artists. For example, Unity House campers in 1933 were entertained by the Philharmonic String Quartet, the Mexican painter Diego Rivera, and the dancers Tamiris, Dorsha, Doris Humphrey and Charles Weidman.[88] Segal worked at Camp Kinderland for 35 years (with a break from 1936-1939 when she was in Detroit), guiding generations of young people in activities that linked creativity to social consciousness. Two photographs convey connections between the physical culture movement, the emerging modern dance and political ideologies. Taken in 1924 at Unity House, Segal is pictured outdoors leading exercises for a mixed gender group numbering over 35. The large trees in the background populate a landscape far removed from the Lower East Side tenements and sweatshops where many spent their working hours. Wearing skirts or shirt and knee-length trousers, the participants raise their arms upwards, reaching towards the sky, exuding a

85 Mishler, op.cit.
86 Lieberman, op.cit. p.17.
87 NYPL, ES Archives, uncatalogued photograph.
88 Jacob Halpern (1934) 'Unity House in 1934 Retrospect', *Justice*, October, p. 29); Anon. (1933) 'Unity House Has Great Season', *Justice*, 13 August, p. 8.

determination and gazing straight back at the camera. In contrast, another photograph shows 15 women plus Segal, barefoot, standing in a high *relevé*, arms softly raised and holding hands. A few of the dancers have a length of cloth draped across their torsos on top of their exercise outfits, softening the image. Some of them tilt their heads to the side with undefined focus away from their forward direction while those on the sides of the loose circle are in slight *epaulement*.

An undated set of photographs of the Nature Friends Dance Group provides a glimpse of that group's activities. Taken outdoors, presumably at Camp Midvale, the New Jersey rural escape, the photos depict clothing, cars and hair styles consistent with the late 1920s to early 1930s.[89] Sixteen young women are pictured in a grassy clearing with trees and wooden buildings in the background. They carry flags with hammers and sickles, held upright as they lunge forward in an array of formations, one arm thrust forward or held in front of the chest in a militaristic stance. The air of authority, of intense conviction, comes across even in the small black and white photographs. Back in New York, the Nature Friends Dance Group performed for a variety of other organisations in 'collective productions' during its first year in existence, including the 'Election Campaign, Lenin Memorial and May 1st pageants'. Their contributions to the 1933 Spartakiade dance competition included *Red Front* danced to music by Hans Eisler and *Dance of Today*, comprised of the sections *In the shop, Unemployed* and *Hunger March*.[90] Segal taught at two other camps, revealing further connections between leisure activity, politics and art. Artef and the campers performed at 'the First proletarian Nitgedaigit camp' on August 23 1928 with Segal directing dance movements for '"Turn the Guns" Anti-imperialist pantomimic spectacle' to a libretto by V Jerome and music by L. Adohmyan. Later pageants included one with a young woman dressed as the Statue of Liberty, reinforcing an all-American sense of community. Kinderland maintained close relationships to the city's *shules* and offered Segal opportunities to develop dance ideas performed at events in New York.

In addition to the work environment and socially conscious themes, Segal drew from a range of Yiddish and Jewish rituals and cultural practices in developing later choreography. Yiddish cultural activities were central to the camp's ethos, '*Foon shule in kemp, foon kemp in shule*' (from synagogue to camp, from camp to synagogue)'.[91] Dancers worked alongside actors,

89 The photographs are in an envelope from Dr Hertweck at the NYPL, ES Archives. The Nature Friends of America was designated as a subversive organisation in 1935 under Executive Order number 104450. http://www.nyu.edu/library/bobst/research/tam/summercamps.html, accessed on 6 November 2012.
90 First Workers Dance Spartakiade, programme notes, 4 June 1933, courtesy of Edith Segal.
91 Mishler, op.cit. p. 89.

singers and writers, reinforcing connections among existing artistic circles. Camp Kinderland integrated Yiddish language classes alongside pageants that taught children about their heritage and the potentialities for American democracy. Mishler highlights the close relationship between radical politics and Jewish culture at the camps: 'The Jewish Communist culture that was nurtured and expanded at Kinderland was historically grounded in the experiences of the Jewish working class of prerevolutionary Russia and of the New York City of the 1900s to the 1930s.'[92] Segal explained it as emphasising secular values through the focus on Memsher or heritage – 'the preservation of the best of secular Yiddish culture – from Isaiah's prophecy to the heroes of the Warsaw Ghetto, from Go Down Moses to We Shall Not Be Moved. Kinderland [was] a cradle of expressive, secular culture of the Jewish people and of their allies, first and foremost the Black people.'[93] The affinity between blacks and Jewish artists is evident in the continued focus on civil rights in Segal's choreography for campers and other groups in later decades. The injustices of slavery and its legacy in the USA were highlighted with a mixed race cast of dancers in *How Long Brethren* (1950) while *Freedom Train* (1961) was accompanied by a recording of Paul Robeson reciting a poem by Langston Hughes. Led by black communists, Camp Wo-Chi-Ca (short for Workers Children's Camp, established in 1936) in Port Murray, New Jersey, attracted Pearl Primus who appeared in camp fundraisers and was a camp counsellor in the 1940s. They espoused the Popular Front agenda, emphasising racial integration and harmony among the multi-ethnic working-class campers.[94] The actor, singer and activist Paul Robeson visited both Kinderland and Wo-Chi-Ca.

Union activities also took place at the camps, the thread to class conflict ever strong. In interviews and correspondence Segal spoke of altering a Swedish university 'hazing' dance she identified as the 'Oshen Tanz', by adding aggressive arm movements to the actions performed by two lines of dancers facing each other. They rhythmically alternated moving towards each other, developing arm gestures into playful slaps to indicate a fight in the ranks of workers.[95] Another union-related event occurred when the Furriers Union went out on a four-month strike in 1926. Segal joined a group of about 50 people from the camp where she worked who travelled to join the picket line. Although they did not dance on the picket line itself, an undated photograph taken at a camp show two lines of women facing each other, in poses close to Segal's description of the dance.[96]

---

92 Ibid. p. 94.
93 Farlow, op. cit., p. 12.
94 Mishler, op.cit.. and Peggy & Murray Schwartz (2011) *The Dance Claimed Me: A Biography of Pearl Primus*.
95 Edith Segal, correspondence to author, 10 October 1987.
96 Segal (1988), op.cit.

Red Dancers and the Workers Dance League

Segal formed the Red Dancers in 1929, one of the first and most prolific of the adult groups in New York. It fed into the Workers Dance League (WDL), a collective of soloists and workers dance groups drawn together by their activist concerns and a desire to raise class consciousness. They gathered for a mass dance at the Bronx Coliseum for the 1932 May Day celebrations. Eleven dance groups attended the conference on 13 November 1932 which established the WDL.[97] Precedents for a politically oriented dance existed in the proletarian writing and theatre groups, such as the Workers' Laboratory Theatre and John Reed Clubs, modelled on Communist Party ideals. Conflicting perceptions emerge about the relationship between the Communist International (Comintern) and workers' cultural groups in the US. Barbara Foley's re-examination of proletarian literature highlights the extent to which American writers were or were not constrained by dictates from Moscow. In contrast to standard histories of the radical arts movement, Foley argues the John Reed Clubs were effectively independent and that a fundamentally American worker-writer genre emerged. A definition of proletarian literature was predicated on shifting criteria, alternating between four fundamental questions of authorship, audience, subject matter and political perspective.[98] In dance, a worker-oriented practice also forged its own path, rather than turning to Soviet models for guidance.

Although the practice of an American, politically-informed dance developed independently, its debates paralleled tensions between bourgeois and proletarian ideals in other art forms. As stated in the WDL application form, the 'bourgeois' modern dance practiced by Graham, Humphrey, Weidman and Tamiris, was 'steeped in pessimism, mysticism, exoticism, diversified abstractions, and flights from reality'. The organisation's initial aims conformed to criteria for a proletarian art identified by Foley: turning workers into dancers, using themes drawn from their daily lives and performing in front of worker audiences. A political component was seen as implicit, for in striving to make workers the subject and object of dance in performance, its ideological content would be correct. In 1933 the qualities vital to a revolutionary workers' dance were spelled out: 'Clarity. We must take no chances of being misunderstood. Economy. We must never

---

97 Midi Gordon (1933) 'The Workers Dance League', New Dance Group, First annual recital programme, p. 6. In 'The Dance is a Weapon' essay in *Moving History/Dancing Cultures* (2003), Ellen Graff cites a *New Theatre* editorial which claims the WDL started in early 1933. My sources reinforce the 1932 date which is also supported by detail provided in Gordon's article, as well as archival sources presented by Victoria Phillips Geduld, op.cit.

98 Barbara Foley (1993) *Radical Representations: Politics and Form in U.S. Proletarian Fiction, 1929-1941*, p. 87.

be extravagant with our materials. Quantitatively large. This is necessary for our big informative subjects with sustained emotion. Swiftness of execution and intensity of emotion are necessary for our agitational bits.'[99]

It was a vibrant time, with the dancers performing at informal venues in front of audiences often gathered for other purposes such as strike meetings and rallies for causes such as the Scottsboro Boys and the *Daily Worker* or other union gatherings. When the WDL was established, however, workers groups also began appearing on the concert dance stage alongside more advanced groups and soloists, thus broadening their exposure to modern dance aficionados. This move opened them up to adverse criticism from knowledgeable viewers. Between October 1933 and April 1934, the WDL received 240 requests for groups to perform at workers' gatherings but limited availability of member groups meant that only 140 requests were filled.[100] League membership stood at 800 in 1934, growing to 2,000 by 1936 in 40 affiliated groups, 21 of which were located in the New York City area. The growth is attributed to the shift towards Popular Front ideologies and the change in name to the New Dance League.[101]

Edna Ocko was a founding member of the League, a dancer, musical accompanist, recital organiser, editor and a prolific writer. She explained that although the dancers used standard phrases drawn from a Marxist/Leninist lexicon, their analytical discussions were quite sophisticated. In one session, someone suggested that they should try living in a collective, stimulating 'a very serious political debate about whether the only way we could produce great dance was if we lived that way or work as workers'.[102] Aware of how they differed from their intended audiences – their days were spent in dance studios rather than on assembly lines or in garment industry sweatshops – they investigated ways of connecting to workers' experiences. Family connections offered insight to the proletariat, as many were second generation Jewish-Americans from the Lower East Side or other working-class neighbourhoods around the city. Ocko grew up in Harlem in a musical family, her father a left-wing activist and cigarmaker and she gained a degree in English which led her to work as a dance critic.

Segal's name dominates a 1934 WDL concert programme, appearing in seven out of 13 separate listings. In addition to the solo *Third Degree*, she directed six groups: two International Workers Order children's groups, the

99 Grace Wylie and David Nelson (1933) 'The Proletarian Revolutionary Dance', New Dance Group Annual Recital Programme, p. 7.
100 Edna Ocko (1934) 'The Revolutionary Dance Movement', *The New Masses*, p. 28.
101 Louise Redfield (1936) 'A Survey of the New Dance League', *Proceedings of the National Dance Congress*, New York, NYPL, ES Archives, file number 122-65, pp. 72-73.
102 Edna Ocko, interview with Richard Wormser, 1981, Oral History of the American Left, Robert F. Wagner Archive, Tamiment Library, New York University. See also Garafola, op.cit.

Nature Friends Dance Group, the Needle Trades Industrial Workers Union Dance Group, the Junior Red Dancers and the Red Dancers. The character of the dances was shaped by two factors: a Marxist vision of the function of art and the dancers' technical abilities. Readings of Segal's dances arise from contemporaneous reviews, some photographs of poor quality, and from comments from those involved in the Workers Dance League reflecting back on the period. Segal and the Red Dancers appeared at a range of leftist cultural functions, performing short dances on the workers' struggle and racial oppression prior to the formation of the WDL.[103] Between February 1930 and March 1931, Segal or one of the groups she directed performed at 19 events advertised in the *Daily Worker*. The dances ranged from the premiere of the inter-racial solidarity dance, *Black and White* which she created on herself and Allison Burroughs, to the Red Dancers, which identified itself as 'the first adult group to be organized in the revolutionary movement'. Burroughs was an African American dancer who trained at the Swiss institute of Émile Jaques-Dalcroze. The daughter of Charles Burroughs who directed the DuBois pageant, *The Star of Ethiopia*, Burroughs appears in a number of the early Red Dancer photographs, at times cast as the victim as discussed below, and as a member of the group in others.[104]

In addition to the main group, Segal established beginners and junior groups: 'Our aims are threefold: to bring to workers the message of the class struggle thru [sic] medium of the dance, to act as a center for workers interested in the dance as a cultural activity, and to develop leaders for new groups.'[105] Towards this end, according to programme notes, the three Red Dancers groups gave over 50 performances between January and June, 1933. Cora Burlar, Add Bates, Grace Weinstein, Sacha Pressman, Ethel Brohinsky and Syd Brohinsky are identified on the back of the *Hunger March* photograph, dated 1932.[106] Led by Bates moving towards the upstage right corner, the group of nine dancers embody the extremes of exploitation by bosses – the downtrodden, exhausted workers collapsed on the floor, with three dancers clenching their fists, arms out at right angles. Placing Bates, an African American dancer, in the position as leader conveyed a radical symbol of racial empowerment. Another dancer displays a powerful stance, her shoulders pulled back, captured mid-stride,

103 Ellen Graff, op.cit. pp.179-180.
104 Manning (2004) *op.cit.* pp. 71-73 for discussion of Allison Burroughs in the Red Dancers.
105 WDL Spartakiade programme notes, attributed to Syd Brohinsky, secretary, programme courtesy of Edith Segal, 4 June 1933.
106 Cora Burlar studied with Martha Graham and became a member of the Group Theatre. She went on to partner with Bill Baird in the renowned Bill & Cora Marionettes duet. See entry on Cora Baird by Peter J. Baird, in the Jewish Women Encyclopedia, Jewish Women's Archive, located at http://jwa.org/encyclopedia/article/baird-cora, accessed on July 20, 2010.

and a steely intensity emanating from her body.

These dances have lived on in memory, programme notes, reviews and the rare photograph until *Black and White* was revived in 1984. Dance critic Deborah Jowitt's review of the Frontline performance at P.S.1 offers a late 20th century perspective:

> Segal's duet, simple, minimal, and bold as newsprint, does have a message – one that was radical and much-needed back in 1930.... Serge St. Juste and Gary Onsum keep a clear boundary between them. They walk in circles around it. Even their first 'job', cross-cut sawing, enforces separate and balanced moves. Their push-and-pull goes awry, leads to trouble. So does their next task, assembly-line jobs that require more complex give and take. (I like this part a lot.) They fight. Then an invisible outside force pulls them together. At first back-to-back, they lock arms and rock; now the center line runs through their bodies. Finally, they break the pattern – both move together, support each other, march out linked.[107]

Susan Manning discusses the work in relation to 'interracialism' and interrelated concept of 'masculinism' where male performers represented all workers. A photo of the men – black and white – joined in solidarity, fists tightly clenched and impenetrable gaze towards the camera, has become iconic. Manning discusses the significance of its initial casting – Segal herself and Burroughs. Segal felt that the actions called for the dance to be performed by two men, starting with what she described as 'primitive work' (set out as hammering actions in her notes), joining efforts in a double saw action before moving on to meet in an assembly line which kept getting faster.[108]

Racism and the legacy of slavery inspired a number of Segal's dances such as the anti-lynching piece *Southern Holiday*. Burroughs initially portrayed the victim surrounded by her protectors who battled against dancers representing the Ku Klux Klan (KKK). Segal described the symbolism of the costume design: '...we didn't wear white robes, by any means, but they did suggest the KKK because they were tight, beige jersey dresses with long tight sleeves.'[109] Black stripes suggested the Klan's cross, with one stripe going from one wrist to the other across the chest, intersected by another stripe down the centre of the dress. The dance is pictured in programme notes for the WDL *Spartakiade*, an event modelled on the Soviet sports competitions offered as alternatives to the bourgeois-sponsored Olympic games. Three

---

107 Deborah Jowitt (1984) 'Dance', *Village Voice*, 10 July, p. 71.

108 Manning (2004) op.cit. pp. 68-75; Black and White Choreography Notes, ES Archives, file 122-36.

109 Lemisch, op.cit. Manning (op.cit.) discusses a review that refers to dancers 'blacking', or using dark make-up. I concur that there are no other references that would indicate the Red Dancers used make up to represent African Americans.

dancers in the tight dresses kneel, facing outward, around another dancer in black dress, protecting her against three ominous aggressors. *Southern Holiday* remained in performance for years, with Segal setting it on the Detroit New Dance Group.

Most photographs convey a sense of power and commitment, the dancers with strongly held torsos, one foot in front of the other, or in wide, weighted second position, with angular arms and clenched fists. Often one arm is held out in front of the body, tense and straight at shoulder height, the focus following the line of energy past the hand. Segal's *Black and White* with Add Bates and Irving Lansky was praised for its 'political clarity' while *Scottsboro* was said to convey 'a commendable political consciousness. With further working over, this dance will undoubtedly be a strong presentation, for it has within it the elements of "good dance"', inferring that it had a technical rigour combined with clear ideological proletarian message.[110] Questions over the relationship of artistic values and ideological clarity were debated in the *Daily Worker*, with A. Prentis challenging the positive praise for *Southern Holiday*, arguing that it and *War Trilogy* by the Rebel Dancers, 'while good ideology, were poor dance and their commendation isn't quite fortunate'. Segal received praise, however, for her 'good design and good dancing from every angle' in *Red Cavalry*.[111]

Ocko's insightful reviews constantly challenged all left-wing dancers, even questioning whether the workers' groups should continue to appear on concert programmes, deeming the agit-prop dances by the Red Dancers and the Nature Friends unsuited to the recital stage. Although commendable, their '... dramatic construction makes it appealing to the untrained eyes of thousands of people who have never seen dancing before, and its simple presentation of political ideas in dance form makes it comprehensible'.[112] The Red Dancers accused Ocko of placing 'the gratification of bourgeois-intellectual audiences' above ideological expression, arguing that the other dances should attain a higher degree of political expression in order to be legible to a wider audience.[113]

In 1934, dance 'scripts' were circulated to the member groups of the Workers Dance League, such as *War Trilogy*, originally set by Grace Wylie in 1932. Representative of agit-prop dances in its narrative structure and presentation of easily recognisable characters, it offers verbal descriptions and illustrated floor plans. The *Breadline* section presents the workers as 'tired, dogged, patiently waiting for their ration. Some are old, some young and sensitive, hardboiled – different types'. The opposing class

110 Ben Wolf (1934) 'League Recital', *Daily Worker*, 26 April, p. 4.
111 A. Prentis (1934) 'Takes Issue with Dance League Recital Review', *Daily Worker*, 15 January, p. 5.
112 Edna Ocko (1935) 'Anti-Fascism', *Dance Observer*, November, pp. 93-94.
113 Grace Sosin (1935) 'From the Red Dancers', *New Theatre*, March, p. 27.

is represented by two 'jingoistic' characters: 'America's sweetheart type dances in sharp satiric form-affected sweetness – "almost" jazz'.[114] Agit-prop dances represented workers through naturalistic and vernacular movement, performed with exaggerated dynamic qualities to emphasise their weariness, oppression and resignation. The provision of storylines and movement guidance moved away from creative approaches associated with modern dance. Jeanette, the secretary of the Needle Trades Workers Dance Group explained: 'Some people dance like birds or flowers, they call this Nature. Others try to dance like the Greeks or the Egyptians two thousand years ago. They call this classical dancing. We, young workers, try to perform revolutionary dances.'[115] Revolution took prominence over individual expressivity.

Union Dance Groups

Affiliations with labour unions and workers' cultural organisations broadened accessibility to cultural expression for those on assembly lines and in the garment industries, although the level of political engagement varied. A member of the Martha Graham 'group', Lily Mehlman, recalled that her classes for the socialist International Ladies Garment Workers Union (ILGWU) were non-political.[116] *Justice*, the union's newsletter, announced a series of eight dance recitals held at Washington-Irving High School during 1933-1934. The ILGWU newsletter featured a number of cultural and health activities – mandolin orchestra, sports groups and drama groups, part of a larger initiative to make education accessible. Eventually led by women and comprised of female workers, the union activities gained prominence as a Broadway hit musical later in the decade with *Pins and Needles* (1937), originally created for striking workers.[117]

Classes at the communist aligned Needle Trades Industrial Workers Union (NTIWU) functioned on two levels, one emphasising the physicality of dance and the other emphasising politics: 'We are striving not only to express the struggle of the workers in their spirit of revolt against the miserable working conditions caused by the exploitation of the bosses, but we are attempting to uplift our spirits in an expressive manner'.[118] A union

114 Anon. (1934) 'Anti-war script', *WDL Bulletin Anti-War Issue*, p. 4, courtesy of Edith Segal.
115 Bella Hearst (1933-1934) 'With the Needle Trades Workers Dance Group', *The Needle Worker*, December-January, p. 35.
116 Lily Mehlman, telephone interview with the author, 28 March 1990.
117 Mark Franko (2002) discusses the garment industry worker-performers and the ILGWU production *Pins and Needles* in *The Work of Dance: Labor, Movement, and Identity in the 1930s*.
118 Estelle Weiss (1933) 'The Needle Trades Dance Group, *Needle Worker*, March-April, 4:3-4, p. 14.

representative offered 'ideological guidance', with narrative scenes based on 'the daily drudgery of the assembly line and movements derived from actions performed on the factory floor'.[119] The Needle Trades Workers Dance Group members were encouraged to attend weekly open forums at Segal's studio at 77 Fifth Avenue while the regular Friday class was led by Irving Lansky of the Red Dancers under Segal's guidance. In the union publication *The Needle Worker*, Bella Hearst described how after warming up, the worker-dancers moved to 'the serious business of walking like a boss... This way and that way, our bodies dance, backs arched inwards, stomachs out...Our hands are stretching out, grasping, desiring everything'.[120] The group also gathered on Sunday afternoons for 'creative work and folk dancing' and explained that men perceived the activity as a 'form of play' so were not inclined to participate.[121]

By the middle of 1934, the Sunday sessions were led by John Bovingdon (1890-1973) and held at the Neighborhood Playhouse. One of the few male dancers involved in the left-wing movement, Bovingdon emphasised coordination of breath with movement. His history is elusive although a 1928 profile in *The American Dancer* magazine mentions dance classes in Seattle and he drew on an eclectic combination of mind-body techniques, variously described as rhythmic gymnastics, forming the basis of his 'mono-dramas'. His movement philosophy was influenced by his time in Japan when he was an economics professor at Keio University in Tokyo. A Harvard graduate in 1915, he later lectured in psychology in Boston. His wife and dance partner, Jeanya Marling, was photographed with Segal in Berlin on her trip to the USSR. Bovingdon spent time in Moscow as a journalist and dance teacher as part of a 'radical arts colony' and at the International Theatre.[122] Accounts of his activities are rare but paint the picture of a bohemian lifestyle. During the 1920s in Los Angeles he was part of a 'free-spirit' artistic group that included composer John Cage, novelists Theodore Dreisler and Aldous Huxley. At parties to raise money, Bovingdon danced nude around the gardens of the modernist Schindler House, occasionally accompanied by a young 'bare-breasted woman in performances of Balinese folk dance'.[123] Back in New York, a solo performance in 1936 led critics

119 J. Singer (1934) 'The Needle Trades Dance Group', *Needle Worker*, 13 August, 1:8, p.4.

120 Hearst, op.cit.

121 Weiss, op.cit.

122 Anita Spizer (1928) 'An Explorer in Dance Thought, The art of John Bovington', *American Dancer*, 10, 11, 23, 31. Bovingdon is mentioned in Arnold Rampersad's 2001 book *The Life of Langston Hughes, Volume I, 1902-1941, I too Sing America'*. Langston met the dancer in Moscow, p. 247. Barbara Naomi Cohen-Stratyner, (1982) 'John Bovingdon', *Biographical Dictionary of Dance*, p.116.

123 Mathis Chazanov (1987) 'The Living Wasn't Easy but House is Worth Saving', *Los Angeles Times*, September 17, p. AN1.

to challenge classification of Bovingdon's work as dance. Introduced by speeches, a series of portraits evoked characters and contexts such as *Red Army Speaks, Peasant Comes of Age,* and *Legend of the Rice Workers,* comprised of 'illustrative semi-rhythmic gestures accompanying the spoken phrase'.[124] His *Underground Printer* was an experimental film directed by Thomas Bouchard. Bovingdon performed in the second New Dance League Men in the Dance recital and wrote about dance in the Soviet Union for the 1936 National Dance Congress Proceedings.

Detroit

Although there were artistic tensions between the rising professional modern dancers and the proponents of a workers dance, Segal remained active as a Field Organiser for the New Dance League. In 1936 she moved to Detroit and was paid a $5 weekly salary for working with the New Dance Group (co-directed by Fey Arnold and Ann Blanc). The Detroit branch initially gathered together for folk dancing, eventually performing modern dances on socially conscious themes. Segal choreographed *Ivory Tower* which set out to challenge the isolated individual: 'Our purpose is to work out a dance to show that these people must inevitably be affected by the same economic forces which face the workers'.[125] *Anti-war cycle: Industrialism; war, Fraternization* was performed by 18 dancers at the Dance Festival for the Cause of Peace at the Detroit Institute of the Arts, to commemorate America's entry into World War I. The NDG shared the stage with the Rebelarts (sic) Dance Group, Olg Fricker and Dance Group, the Theodore J. Smith Dance Group and the Wayne University Dance Group, encompassing styles as diverse as 'ballet, Spanish, toe, neo-classic and modern forms'.[126]

When the dance salary ceased after a few months, Segal decided to join the Federal Theatre Project (FTP) but she was required to be unemployed in order to be hired. National Director Hallie Flanagan wrote a letter supporting Segal, praising the duet *Black and White* which Flanagan saw as a Spartakiade judge in New York. As choreographer, actor and dancer, Segal worked on the productions ranging from *Let Freedom Ring!* (1937) to the living newspaper *One Third of A Nation* (1937) based on President Roosevelt's inaugural address.

124   Edna Ocko (writing under the pseudonym of Elizabeth Skrip) (1936) 'John Bovingdon', *New Theatre,* June, p. 32; See also John Martin (1936) 'Bovingdon Gives Recital, *The New York Times,* 30 April, p.16.

125 Pre-Congress report, 1936, NYPL ES Archives file number 122-65; The cast included Frances Brines and Rose Menacer as Middlemen and Rose Savage and Al Sniderman as Financiers.

126 Anon (1936) 'Detroit Studios to Hold Festival', *Detroit News,* 29 March, Home and Society section, 10 and Russell McLaughlin (1936) 'A Modern Dance Festival Hails the Cause of Peace', *Detroit News,* 6 April, p. 20.

Rather than the limited resources of a recreational dance group, Segal had new production opportunities and worked with actors rather than dancers and advocated for movement training on a regular basis. The production report on *The Tragic History of Dr Faustus* (1937), directed by Verner Haldene, indicated that Segal was the only performer with dance training. Main challenges were 'trying to get rhythm, flexibility and the feeling for line, as well as the actual dance figures and execution'. Performed to a recording of Stravinsky's *Firebird Suite,* Segal created six dances including solos for herself as a 'Devil-wife' and a Faun, with the pantomimic choreography for Darius, Alexander and the unmasked Paramour section deemed the most successful. Haldene reported that a scaled-down version of *Dr Faustus* toured community centres, churches and schools, bringing its running costs out of the red.[127]

Some problematic relationships dogged the Detroit FTP, delaying its opening production and generating a 'tug of war over grass-roots principles' about aesthetic preferences and the involvement of non-local professionals.[128] Further controversy arose when allegations of Communist influence on the organisation came from within. Magician and FTP employee John E. Matthews set out a series of allegations and Segal was one of those singled out as an activist, accused of maintaining a Communist Party noticeboard and urging members to become involved in outside United Auto Worker union events. She was called to testify at a City Council hearing which also highlighted long-standing tensions between responsibilities of the professionals, volunteers and relief workers on the project.[129] In order to increase the involvement of unions and attract more workers to the shows, Segal attempted to sell blocks of tickets to worker groups as was the practice in New York City. Her Communist Party membership was openly admitted and she also sold copies of the *Daily Worker.* Outside the FTP she helped create something theatrical for the Detroit cigarmakers when they went on strike. While it was not a FTP-related activity some fellow project members were involved. The charges were deemed to be malicious and went no further than the local hearings. Segal garnered the support of Herbert Ashton, WPA Regional Director who described her as a valuable member of the FTP and explained that the political activities were undertaken during her personal time.[130]

While in Detroit, Segal met and married her second husband, Lawrence Emery, who wrote for the *Daily Worker.* She was in the city at a crucial time

127 Segal, Edith (1937) Choreographer's Report and Verne Halden, Director's Report, Library of Congress, Music Division, Federal Theatre Project Collection. p. 2.
128 Paul Sporn (1985) *Against Itself,* p. 173.
129 *Detroit News,* 26 June 1938, part 3, p. 8.
130 Donald Slutz (1938) 'Branded Red Unit, Detroit Actor Makes the Complaint', *Detroit News,* 26 June, part 2, p. 8.

in labour history, situated at the home of the automobile industry when the struggle to establish the United Auto Workers (UAW) Union reached its height. It involved a significant challenge to the exclusivity of the American Federation of Labor organisation and was a hard-fought campaign. Sit-down strikes enabled workers to seize control of the factory by sitting down on the job which prevented the use of strikebreakers. The longest sit-down strike occurred at the Fisher Body plant in Flint, Michigan, when 2,000 workers occupied their factory for 40 days.[131] Segal recalled participating in the picket lines in front of a General Motors (GM) Factory where she directed simple rhythmic steps that helped the strikers keep warm in addition to reinforcing solidarity. They marched in circle and grasped the waist of the person in front of them with legs 'extended sideways so that we rocked side to side as we advanced'.[132]

> We were part of each other, you know. There was no separation and we moved, instead of walking forward with each foot, we moved from side to side as we moved forward. We were physically connected with each other. It was like a dance in a way. It was solid. So, we kept warm and we made the line impenetrable.[133]

The auto workers strikes were led by communists and peppered with outbreaks of violence, including an attack on the Women's Emergency Brigade who came to picket in support of their striking husbands, friends and family members. Segal is photographed singing at a Women's Brigade rally after one violent event. Other contributions include working on *Million Dollar Babies Sit Down*, a musical skit created for protesting Woolworth employees in Detroit in February 1937 and inspired by the Flint GM action. Although the Woolworth show was never produced, theatre historian Paul Sporn establishes stylistic links to representational strategies of the working-class theatre movement, including 'mass stage action, the use of ritualized chorus effects, the adaptation of popular songs to comment on social issues'. Rather than conveying a message to viewers, the show functioned as a 'political divertissement, providing the relaxation of humour without losing sight of the fight workers are engaged in'.[134]

---

131 Zinn, op.cit. p. 129.
132 Farlow, op.cit.
133 Paul Sporn (1979) transcript of oral history interview with Edith Segal, Federal Patronage of the Arts in Michigan during the Great Depression Project, Wayne State University, November 13, Tape 2, p. 7, NYPL, ES Archives, 122-71.
134 Paul Sporn (1985) 'Working-Class Theatre on the Auto Picket Line', in Bruce McConachie and Daniel Friedman, eds., *Theatre for Working Class Audiences in the United States*, pp. 157-158. Mary Heaton Vorse (1937) 'Youngstown, Girdlerism: An Eyewitness Account', 19 June 1937, reported on a Women's Brigade rally after previous violence that killed two and injured 17, clipping from Edith Segal Archives, uncatalogued box of photographs.

With the demise of the FTP in 1939 and to help care for her husband who had been in a car accident, Segal returned to New York and immersed herself in teaching, writing and marching for various causes. The combination of activism in lobbying for union organisations, dancing on picket lines, with recreational groups and involvement in the Detroit FTP led Segal to declare that her time in Detroit came closest to achieving long-held goals of engaging with the workers through art. While there she 'saw class struggle in the raw',[135] later reflecting on how she felt part of the union movement, in solidarity with those working to consolidate labour power in the United Auto Workers Union. Segal: 'I knew when I got back to New York, I wouldn't have the connection with the unions that I had before. There wouldn't be the connection between art and work and workers.'[136]

Coda

With Segal's move to Detroit, the impetus behind the New York workers dance groups as expressions of revolutionary consciousness was taken by others. She continued to create dances from the heartfelt concern for the dispossessed, exploited or discriminated against. Despite her declared atheism, Segal was active in helping to perpetuate Jewish culture, working in *shules* and creating dances that celebrated Jewish rituals. As a poet of numerous children's books, she advocated cross-cultural understanding. Her civil rights advocacy is evident in the dances she created at Camp Kinderland, and she spoke to me with pride about the one performed in front of Paul Robeson. She also took great pride in recounting her conversations with Igor Mosieyev, when the Soviet folk dance company tour during the Cold War years helped people perceive those from a communist nation as human beings. Her group comprised of Jewish High School of Bronx and New York students and graduates performed with the Harvesters, a leftist musical group in a series of dances ranging from an *American Medley* of folk dances to *Sweatshop, Warsaw Ghetto Memorial,* and *Nigendl/Family Portrait* (1958), based on Jewish folk songs, stories and poems. Although readings of her choreography taken from faded photographs may evoke calls for simple clarity, they cannot convey the vibrancy of moving bodies and the deep commitment of the performers captured in written accounts.

Many years later, Segal mused that 'It's becoming harder and harder not to be accused of being a propagandist but to find a medium that reaches people.'[137] For years, however, dance was Segal's medium, with poetry and songwriting gaining prominence after her choreographic creations for worker groups had ceased. She leaves a unique historical account of

---

135 Farlow, op.cit. p. 11.
136 Sporn (1979), op.cit.
137 Farlow, op.cit. p. 147.

someone who crossed over dance genres at a vibrant time in New York and remained open about her political convictions in the face of years of government surveillance.

Anti-communist sentiment hit the headlines years before the infamous hearings by Senator Joseph McCarthy began. In 1943 Bovingdon was hired by the Office of Economic Warfare as an economic analyst. Shortly afterwards Representative Martin Dies, Chair of the House Committee on un-American Activities, named Bovingdon as a government employee with left-wing sympathies. Described in an article in *Life* magazine as a 'cultist', Bovingdon's 'record and career as a ballet dancer is well known', and he was pictured in a loincloth with his wife. He was asked to resign from his job and was fired when he went public with his refusal, drawing the attention of journalists in the *New York Times* and other weekly news journals. Articles in *Time* magazine also inferred that his double life as an academic and 'esthete' contributed to his termination. Bovingdon defended his artistry, asserting that he 'was not a ballet dancer, only seeking after health through scientific bodily movement'.[138]

Segal's career as a freelance dance teacher meant she escaped the scrutiny of the mainstream press although in 1953 she was called to appear before the State of New York's Joint Legislative Committee on Charitable and Philanthropic Agencies and Organisations. Witness testimony reveals leading questions that probed whether Segal and other camp employees were propounding explicit communist ideology. Segal was called in to respond, but claimed the fifth amendment 30 times, refusing to answer questions about whether she spoke to the campers about her campaign work for Ethel and Julius Rosenberg who were executed as Soviet spies.[139] Years later, Segal explained to me that she kept silent about her political affiliations while at camp, but that the values of equality and justice underpinned her creative work with campers.

When I first interviewed Segal, the Berlin Wall was still standing and the Soviet Union was still a major superpower with missiles aimed at the USA – and vice versa. I only asked her directly about her membership in the CPUSA once the tape recorder was turned off, not realising she had been so open about her membership in previous oral history interviews. FBI Records obtained through the Freedom of Information Act reveal the extent to which her life was under official scrutiny for decades. Initial reports summarise her activities during the 1930s and early 1940s with the first requests for information starting in 1949. Informants' details are redacted but they detail activities as diverse as social events to listing her teaching activities,

138 Anon. (1943) 'The Strange Case of John Bovingdon', *Life*, 16 August, p. 34.
139 Transcripts of the investigations of communist activities, New York area, Part 5 (summer camps), Hearings on Un-American Activities, House of Representatives, 84th Congress, First Session, 25, 28, 29 July and 1 August 1955.

identifying who paid the rent, and reporting on membership fee payments for a range of front organisations. There are also lists of Christmas cards sent to people incarcerated under the 1940 Smith Act, which criminalised people who advocated change that was perceived as calling for the overthrow of the US government. Letters were intercepted and files contained reprints of her poetry advocating peace and racial harmony. Like a scene out of a 1950s black and white film, one can visualise FBI agents knocking at the door and yelling to be allowed entry, with Segal on the other side refusing to open up and answer questions, as recounted in one report. She was described as a 'watchdog' for the Party while in Detroit, but another informant explained that 'she never attained the status of functionary'. One of the reports was 41 pages in length, written at the height of the Cold War in 1956.[140]

Geduld discusses how some of the left-wing dancers paid a hefty price for their political and cultural associations during the 1950s. The lives of Jane Dudley, Anna Sokolow, Edna Ocko and Martha Graham dancer Bonnie Bird were affected in different ways. The fear of recrimination was strong even to those who were open about their affiliations, leading Segal to cut off the top of a 1931 photograph of the Red Dancers in 'Flag Dance to Soviet Song'. The interracial group brandished flags with the hammer and sickle although the photographic remnant leaves the semi-circle of 11 women holding chopped off banners. The sentiment is clear, the dancers lunge forward with strong purposeful gazes, one arm at their sides, the other bent in front of the chest with elbow perpendicular to the floor, ready to lash out.[141] Segal's activism and artistry touched multiple generations, her Communist Party membership may be incidental as the true political power of the party is relatively minimal. She stands as an example of a female dance activist, strongly committed to advocating racial equality and workers' rights which fed into changing ideals of freedom that would see her onstage with fellow leftist musicians Pete Seeger and Woodie Guthrie, and marching in opposition to the Vietnam War and for a nuclear free world.

---

140 FOIPA file number 1080924-001

141 Geduld (2008) op.cit. In the copy Edith Segal gave the author in 1989, the photograph is labelled 'Flag Dance to Soviet Song' and dated 1931, but in her papers at the New York Public Library, the photo refers to 'Victory Dance' and is located in the 1950s photograph folder. The costumes appear identical to the ones taken outside the Bronx Coliseum for May Day, 1932.

Chapter 2

Dancing on the Left in Britain in the 1930s

*A new orientation of the dance is being achieved in England today by
various maturing labour groups. It springs from a desire to re-establish the
lost contact of the art with the objective conflicts, both class and cultural,
of everyday life. Although by no means a popular idiom, Dance-Drama
represents the form that is being used almost exclusively in this country for
the expression of a social ideology.' * Leslie Daiken, 1936

Despite an enthusiastic 1936 report about English workers dance groups
published in the American *New Theatre* journal, little is known about their
existence. Britain's political and economic conditions during the 1930s
provided a fertile atmosphere for the emergence of a revolutionary dance,
however, multiple factors inhibited its development. Substantial research
gaps remain, but sufficient details have emerged to sketch out a modern
dance practice premised on Marxist principles with ties to the Co-operative
movement, the left-wing theatre movement and occasional appearances at
political events. This chapter examines a politicised dance in multiple guises:
one striving for professional status, recreational agit-prop proponents and
pageant dancers. A strong movement component in left-wing theatre
productions is evident, with close ties between drama groups and dancers
which may have shifted energies away from dance activities.

Difficulties encountered in the historical recovery of a British workers
dance are due in part to its size; it was not widespread enough to claim it as
a *movement*. Only a few groups with the moniker 'workers dance' have been
traced, emerging later than the left-wing American groups and abruptly
ceasing by 1939. In 1934, two unnamed groups 'specialising in the
Revolutionary Symbolic dance' were announced in the Workers Theatre
Movement Monthly Bulletin.[1] Leslie Daiken's article in the US *New Theatre*
publication lists four political dance groups: Margaret Barr's Dance Drama
Group, the Workers' Propaganda Dance Group, The Workers' Ballet Group
using music composed by Alan Bush and the Workers' Dance-Drama
Group. According to the report, the Workers' Dance Drama Group drew
its membership from trade unions, factories and Co-operative societies
in London.[2] Significantly, the development of a movement was hindered
by where the modern dance practitioners were situated in relation to

---

1 Workers Theatre Movement Monthly Bulletin, 'News from our Groups', March 1934,
p. 16, Unity Archives, THM 9/5/3
2 Leslie Daiken (1936) 'English Letter', *New Theatre*, June, p. 30.

institutionalisation of theatre and recreational dance practices, alongside ballet and standardised training systems of diverse dance styles for both professional and recreational enthusiasts.

An absence of published material prohibits the ability to recover a comprehensive picture of the dances although some personal accounts exist in archival sources, enabling a partial reading of a British workers dance. Archives from two prolific writers has been valuable – dance critic Fernau Hall and the composer Alan Bush – providing different perspectives of the personalities and performances. A Canadian who immigrated to England in the 1930s, Hall (1915-1988) took great interest in all dance that came through London, studying a diverse range of styles to increase his understanding.[3] Drafts of an unpublished autobiography and early versions of a 1950 book are among the boxes of his papers at the National Resource Centre for Dance at the University of Surrey. The composer Alan Bush (1900-1995) made carbon copies of correspondence, now housed at the British Library, which offer crucial ideological and aesthetic detail as well as insight into personal politics and creative processes of the groups he worked with. A widespread policy of anonymity in cast lists, seen as a challenge to theatre hierarchies, also inhibits the recovery of details.[4] The abrupt end of British revolutionary dance was prompted by the outbreak of World War II and the departure of a key figure, Margaret Barr, who moved from England to New Zealand and when Bush was conscripted into the military. The left-wing dance history is intertwined with influences from two strands of modern dance – an American style influenced by Martha Graham and the Central European *Ausdruckstanz* version. This chapter also draws on recent scholarship about the dance scene in Britain in the early 20th century, to identify the challenges of situating a left-wing dance practice that did not fit within emerging dance institutions.

Setting the Context

The year 1926 provides some markers on which to establish a sense of the socio-political climate that fed into the emergence of workers dance groups in the early 1930s. High unemployment levels and labour unrest were rife in Britain even prior to the onset of worldwide economic Depression in 1929. The 1926 General Strike marked the height of a period of labour tensions, when an eight day strike was taken by three million workers who came out nationwide in support of striking miners. Rather than achieving their aims, the workers' actions resulted in the passage of a restrictive Trade Unions Act in 1927. Despite the failure, versions of socialist and communist ideologies

---

3 Mary Clarke (1988) 'Obituary – Fernau Hall: Dance critic who tried all the steps', *The Guardian*, 12 August.
4 Martin Bauml Duberman (1989), *Paul Robeson*, pp. 223-224.

influenced Britain's mainstream economic and political framework to an extent. The complexities and strength of class divisions were not ultimately challenged, however, and multiple left-wing parties divided energies and loyalties within the workers' struggle. The Communist Party Great Britain (CPGB, formed in 1920) refused to align with other left-of-centre political organisations, arising out of policies set by the Communist International in the Soviet Union. Two distinct ideological phases occurred which impacted upon politicised cultural activities, a 'class against class' struggle which shaped policies in the late 1920s and early 1930s, and the Popular Front period starting around 1935 which instituted socialist alliances.[5] Attitudes towards the use of arts as a political tool shifted between the late 1920s and 1930s, opening the way for a range of socially conscious productions and practices to develop.

Historian James Hinton's detailed account of labour history highlights the extent to which a British trade union history is distinct from a history of its working class. This is most evident in the hierarchies deeply embedded between skilled and unskilled labourers. Trade union organisations from the Victorian era were modelled on old craft guilds which privileged skilled labourers or artisans due to their specialised knowledge. A 'labour aristocracy' shaped in the early years of the Industrial Revolution resulted in a stratum of workers situated between the emergent middle class and unskilled labourers, privileged in terms of respectability, higher income and specialised employment skills.[6] The emergence of a new trade unionism in the early 20th century shaped a strong working class solidarity with clear hierarchies of power and rooted in 19th century conditions. As historian Eric Hobsbawm establishes, there was a perception that capitalism was a national and permanent state of economic and social affairs, with hierarchies established both between and within the different classes. Workers in relatively privileged employment positions emerged as leaders and organisers of collectives, including trade unions and co-operative societies, reinforcing their exclusivity from other manual labourers. The stratified working class created unions that were unresponsive to those with greatest need – the less skilled, poor and women – undermining the development of cohesive and unified labour front.[7] During World War I, exclusive power was challenged when women and unskilled labourers replaced many skilled men, gaining knowledge previously learned through specialised training and developing skills that had empowered individual workers during the Victorian era.[8] Significantly, women were excluded

5 Matthew Worley (2002) *Class against Class: The Communist Party Between the Wars.*
6 James Hinton (1983) *Labour & Socialism: A History of the British Labour Movement, 1867-1974.*
7 Eric Hobsbawm (1984) *Worlds of Labour: Further Studies in the History of Labour.*
8 Hinton, op.cit., pp. 2-3.

from many trade unions, in part because their jobs in domestic service and the numbers working in cottage industries were difficult to organise while there was also deep seeded hostility from male trade unionists.[9]

At the height of the Great Depression in 1933, a quarter of the workforce was unemployed, as the nation's manufacturing industry suffered a significant decline in traditional exports (such as cotton, shipbuilding and mining). New industries centred on technological advances such as cars, aeroplanes and electrical engineering, contributing to the rise in numbers of white collar workers. Hinton draws on George Orwell's prose to describe contrasts between the two Englands that resulted: the 'half-empty satanic mills of the depressed North with the "glittering white structures of concrete, glass and steel, surrounded by green lawns and beds of tulips" which passed for factories on the Great West Road'.[10] The skilled, white-collar workers remained largely unorganised until late in the 1930s. Overall, CPGB membership remained small with few women recruited and by the late 1920s its membership was largely comprised of unemployed. Retention was poor while expectations of member commitment and responsibilities within the organisation was high. By the end of the 1930s more members were employed, increasing the CPGB's influence on trade unions which they had refused to work with earlier in the decade.[11]

On the wider political front, the aims and objectives of many workers' organisations involved strategies of accommodation within existing capitalist structures rather than fulfilling a revolutionary impetus. Hinton argues that 'what the labour aristocracy sought was not escape from its class situation, but rather the establishment of an acknowledged status for itself within the existing social order'. Socialist principles aimed to address social and economic imbalances instead of idealised goals of overthrowing capitalism, emerging in the early 20th century as the fight between '"the people" and landed wealth' rather than labour and capital.[12] Segregation between the working class and a rising middle class was evident across all aspects of social life, resulting in standardised expressions of working-class identity with clear distinctions apparent in housing, education, and significantly, life expectations. Fredrick Engels' 1844 seminal study of industrialisation, *Condition of the Working Class in England*, documented what emerged as characteristic aspects of workers' lifestyles, some of which

9 Gil Kirtin (2006) *The Making of Women Trade Unionists*, p. 28; Irene Osgood Andrews & Margaret A. Hobbs (2008) *Economic Effects of the War upon Women and Children in Great Britain*, pp. 87-89. See also Claire A. Culleton (2000) *Working-Class Culture, Women, and Britain 1914-1921*.

10 Hinton, op.cit., pp. 120-121.

11 Andrew Thorpe (2000) 'The Membership of the Communist Party of Great Britain, 1920-1945', *Historical Journal*.

12 Hinton, op.cit. pp. 9-10.

remain today.[13] E.P. Thompson's 1963 study, *The Making of the English Working Class*, provides an even more comprehensive genealogy of the construction of class identities, ones that are always in creation and brought to consciousness through the cultural superstructure. Class associations were evident in choices of leisure time activities and clothing, with football emerging as a unifying sport and the flat cap recognised as a male working-class uniform.[14]

During the Second International of 1890-1914, shaped by an organisation of socialist and labour parties, cultural forms came to be conceptualised as an escape from everyday drudgery, asserting an artistic autonomy while envisioning a socialist future. Pictorial representations of pastoral landscapes offered a vivid contrast to industrial workplaces and factory town life, exemplifying one aspect of a larger movement informed by socialist principles. Designer and poet William Morris led the Arts and Crafts movement which set out to regain a lost quality of life linked to a celebration of artisan skills diminished by the mechanisation of work begun in the Industrial Revolution. The quotidian existence of workers was deemed to be enriched by the artisan designs that surrounded them while May Day pageants and festivals offered brief respites from work routines while reinforcing class and community bonds. Until World War I, symbolic representations of socialist ideas eschewed 'the proletarian fist', instead imagined visually

> by the flowing robes of the indeterminately medieval peasants, artisans and goddesses of Walter Crane's engravings. Beauty comprised both *nature* and *culture*, the unspoiled and the innocent – the simple home, the dignified work, the craft that was 'true to materials' – but also the highest products of literature, music and the fine arts. It was a unifying, integrative principle, a way of restoring wholeness to the World.[15]

Numerous socialist cultural activities – choirs, orchestras, educational associations and theatre groups – also broadened access to 'high culture' although ideological content was not dictated.[16] Andy Croft highlights an ideological contradiction, with light entertainment, folk songs and Beethoven's music sitting alongside 'old time music hall' at Communist Party events. 'For all the talk of culture as a "weapon in the struggle for socialism", the Communist Party also contained another, utopian, sense that socialism

---

13 Hobsbawm, op.cit.

14 E.P. Thompson (1980) *The Making of the English Working Class*, org. pub. 1963.

15 Raphael Samuel (1985) 'Theatre and Socialism in Britain (1880-1935), *Theatres of the Left, 1880-1935*, pp. 5-6. Visual artist Walter Crane was attracted to socialist principles, illustrating and writing about idealised visions of society while his style helped to shape trends in children's illustrations.

16 Raphael Samuel (1985) 'Introduction: Theatre and Politics', op.cit., pp. xvii-xviii.

was a weapon in the fight for an enriched and democratic human culture'.[17]

A grassroots socialist organisation, the Co-operative Movement, sponsored diverse educational, arts and recreation activities for its members. Socialist principles of joint ownership were seen as early as 1760 when a co-operative flour mill opened on the outskirts of London. During the 19th century short-lived experiments in housing and shops laid the foundations for the Rochdale Pioneers which became the Co-operative Wholesale Society, later to feature as a significant sponsor of workers' dance activities. After World War I the organisation expanded to fulfil diverse needs of its membership at national and local levels, moving beyond its original roots as a wholesale organisation. Aligned with the Labour Party and in some areas, emerging as a political party in its own right, the Co-operative movement emerged as a mainstream organisation which gained strength throughout the early 20th century. It was multi-faceted, offering its members everything from a share in the profits of its retail outlets, manufacturing, banking, education, trade unions, in addition to establishing social and cultural networks, reinforcing community bonds and class solidarity. Between 1914 and 1938 its international membership rose from over four million to 71.5 million individuals and their families.[18] The support of socially conscious dance practices by Co-operative societies is explored in detail later in the chapter.

Left-wing theatre groups of the inter-war years were established upon a foundation of politicised theatre dating back to the 19th century, with performances in working men's clubs. Both entertainment and social commentary were seen in plays about themes such as the women's suffragette movement and new labour policies.[19] Despite the resonance of topical issues, a cultural hegemony existed with plays created to appeal predominantly to middle to upper class audiences. Drama groups and choirs began to establish clear ties to workers and socialist organisations and by the late 1920s, new plays with strong class themes were being written for amateur worker productions. A new cultural emphasis emerged, informed by post-world war and post-Bolshevik revolution perceptions of the socialist movement and its cultural manifestations. Marxist historian Raphael Samuel described: 'It was a self-consciously proletarian aesthetic, of a futuristic dream in which socialism was no longer an escape from the proletarian condition but rather

---

17 Andy Croft (1998) 'Introduction', in Andy Croft, ed., *A Weapon in the Struggle: The Cultural History of the Communist Party in Britain*, p. 1.

18 *International Co-Operative Day Souvenir Programme*, 2 July 1938, p.11, from the personal archives of John White. Four Principles of Co-operation underpinned the Pioneers of Rochdale organisation: Open membership, democratic control, dividend on purchase, limited interest on capital. (p.3) Also see Johnston Birchall (1994) *Co-op: The People's Business*.

19 Richard Stourac and Kathleen McCreery (1986) *Theatre as a Weapon: Workers' Theatre in the Soviet Union, Germany and Britain, 1917-1934*, p. 192.

a realisation of workers' power. Instead of the deference to high culture, there was an iconoclastic desire to break with it...'[20] Labour choirs and brass bands provided opportunities for artistic participation alongside ideological enlightenment, drawing people into political meetings with the promise of entertainment. Both elements – a proletarian aesthetic and 'high art' themes and music – are echoed in the dances although the full propaganda potential of the arts was neglected by the Labour Party which came to full power with its first Prime Minister elected in 1924. The rift between Labour, a socialist ideology in the Co-operative movement and the revolutionary rhetoric of the Communist Party meant that the latter held little power within Parliament but was influential, nonetheless.

Returning to events in 1926, the year marked the first performance of the Hackney Labour Dramatic Group, a cornerstone of the Workers' Theatre Movement (WTM). Productions emphasised the representation of class struggle on stage, out of which a new agit-prop style emerged in improvisational sketches integrating music, song and cabaret stemming from music hall traditions.[21] Within the WTM, workers' theatre groups were established independent of labour institutions, but aligned with communist ideologies. A primary aim among British recreational groups was involvement in something that expressed workers' existence, yet conveyed a spirit of hope. Struggles occurred between those advocating agit-prop formats and those who felt that workers' art should be uplifting, not merely didactic, but of sufficient quality and entertainment value to draw in the unconverted.[22]

Until the emergence of the Popular Front in 1935 the Communist Party perceived cultural activities as a distraction from political priorities although some prominent theatre leaders were party members, as explored below.[23] Left-wing performances were rarely reviewed in the communist *Daily Worker* periodical although event notices regularly appeared. A fundamental disconnect between the cultural organisations and the Communist Party stemmed in part from a perception that Labour and Conservative Parties were part of the same problem.[24] As noted above, there was a disparity between the political representation of labour and its rank and file, with many of the

---

20 Samuel, op.cit. p. xix.
21 Stourac and McCreery, op.cit. p. 201, See also Samuel, ibid.
22 Jon Clark (1979) 'Socialist Theatre in the Thirties', Jon Clark, Margot Heinemann, David Margolies and Carole Snee, eds., *Culture and Crisis in Britain in the Thirties*, p. 219; Anthony Jackson (2007) *Theatre, Education and the Making of Meanings: Art or Instrument?* Jackson asserts that this relationship changed with the implementation of Popular Front policies. See pages 67, 75-83 for a discussion of agit-prop aesthetics.
23 Stourac & McCreery, op.cit. pp. 206-207.
24 James Klugmann (1979), 'Introduction, The Crisis in the Thirties: A View from the Left', in Clark, et al. op.cit. p. 23.

poor and unskilled remaining outside its organised party structures. Samuel argues that Labour Co-op drama functioned to provide 'access to a higher culture, elevation to a spiritualised plane – in brief – *emancipation from the working class's condition of existence*'.[25] A range of classes in the arts and general education sponsored by the charity organisation, the Workers Educational Association, offered avenues for personal development rather than prioritising awareness of class consciousness although working-class solidarity was reinforced through the time spent together.

Dance in Britain

The wider dance field in 1926 held the seeds of a distinctly English ballet with the expansion of a professional field supported by a range of organisations. The left-wing dancers examined below worked outside of the young institutions, striking out on their own in paths by drawing inspiration from American and Central European modern dance innovators. Class issues in the dance world shifted with a gradual acceptance of performance as a career for respectable women, in contrast to past perceptions of dance as immoral. The 'English school' of training was a 'combination of step-dancing and skirt-dancing'.[26] Subsequent to the arrival of Diaghilev's Ballets Russes in 1911, ballet was taken out of music hall venues, leading to the decline of an established professional stage dance that populated music halls and variety shows. By 1926, multiple dance styles were being institutionalised, utilising set syllabi and an examination system to mark progression and encourage standardisation.

Dance historian Geraldine Morris provides a detailed genealogy of various pedagogic systems, noting that professional dancers embodied a mixture of styles rather than studying with a single teacher or style.[27] Training systems emerged that evolved out of the practices of foreign performers and teachers who sought to replicate their own backgrounds during their time in England. Seraphine Astafieva, for example, was a Russian ballerina who opened a school in Chelsea in 1915. Anton Dolin, Alicia Markova (née Alice Marks) and Margot Fonteyn trained with her, and African Caribbean dancers Berto Pasuka (who went on to establish Les Ballets Nègres) and Richie Riley arrived from Jamaica to study with her. Eduardo Espinosa (1871-1950) worked to codify a ballet training system, establishing the syllabus for The British Normal School of Dancing which integrated English terminology drawn from social dancing and setting the foundations for the Royal Academy of Dancing (established in 1935 from the Association for Teachers of Operatic Dancing founded in 1920). As Morris chronicles, the

---

25 Samuel, 'Theatre and Socialism', op. cit. p. 29.
26 Geraldine Morris (2012) *Frederick Ashton's Ballets*, p. 39.
27 Ibid.

UNIVERSITY OF WINCHESTER
LIBRARY

range of classes provided a foundation in the *danse d'école* to such a level that some of Britain's indigenous ballerinas such as Markova were of a standard high enough to dance with Diaghilev's Ballets Russes.[28]

The Imperial Society for Dance Teachers (established 1904, with the name change to the Imperial Society of Teachers of Dancing in 1925) continued to expand its stylistic foundations, offering an Imperial Ballet syllabus based on training in Paris and a Classical Ballet Cecchetti syllabus. These joined other 'faculties', including Opera, General, Modern Ballroom Dancing; Classical; Greek Dance – Ruby Ginner Method; and Natural Movement – Madge Atkinson Method. In 1931 a Stage branch was implemented, providing a syllabus for training in specialist commercial dance styles, reaching an overall membership of 4,000 by 1938.[29] Independent teachers taught classes in the various syllabi, often with a selection of styles at a single school. There was a diverse range of schools and informal training spaces in London, each advertising their certification of teaching status with the various dance organisations.

Interrelationships between choreography and technical training meant they developed alongside each other. In 1926 Marie Rambert and Ninette de Valois each established their first ballet companies on foundations that drew from classes taught within the Cecchetti and Espinosa approaches.[30] De Valois opened the School for Choregraphic Art [sic] which became the Sadler's Wells School a few years later. Rambert started the Rambert Dancers which became the Ballet Club in 1930, performing on the small stage of the Mercury Theatre. Frederick Ashton premiered his first ballet, *A Tragedy of Fashion* for Rambert in 1926.

Able to draw on her own choreographic talents, de Valois's school fed into the Vic-Wells Ballet in 1931, affiliated to the long-established Sadler's Wells Theatre and the Old Vic Theatre under the leadership of Lillian Baylis. Ashton began working with de Valois's Vic-Wells Ballet in 1935, while Rambert continued to mentor young choreographers such as Antony Tudor to create for the Rambert Ballet Company. The 1930s decade was a vibrant time for dance in London, a period of amazing growth with a critical mass of gifted leaders, teachers, young choreographers, dancers and support from a variety of sources – subscription bookings, enthusiastic balletomanes and the occasional contributor such as the artist and photographer Cecil Beaton. A sense of tradition was shaped by this group of young dance professionals who worked between companies which were able to sustain their innovative paths through a network of support at a crucial time in their existence. Fears that the entrepreneurship which supported the Ballets

28 Ibid.
29 'About Us: History', Imperial Society of Teachers of Dancing (ISTD) website, http://www.istd.org/about-us/history/, accessed online 20 April 2013.
30 Morris, op.cit. p. 43.

Russes would not survive after Serge Diaghilev's death led to the formation of the Camargo Society (1930-1933). P.J.S. Richardson, the editor of the *Dancing Times*, and British dance critic and balletomane Arnold Haskell commissioned choreography, music and design that helped establish the Vic-Wells Ballet repertoire. De Valois's company became the Royal Ballet in 1956 and Rambert's company underwent a stylistic change from ballet to contemporary dance, both remaining a significant presence in Britain's dance landscape.[31]

Modern dance precedents

Natural dance styles offered alternatives to ballet and vaudeville style music hall entertainment, inspired around the world by Isadora Duncan and in Britain by innovators who looked to ancient Greek aesthetics and ideas about nature for inspiration. Aesthetic shifts occurred in reaction to rapid changes arising from the growth of capitalism, technological advances and the rise of modernity that altered perceptions of nature and society.[32] As dance historian Alexandra Carter argues, the codification of natural movement dance practices offered transferable dance systems aligned to perceptions of dance as art, reinforcing relationships between movement, expression and music. Proponents of natural dance styles established pedagogic approaches structured to develop transferable knowledge of the craft of dance, drawing from a physical culture movement as well as an expressive performativity. Madge Atkinson's Natural Movement and Ruby Ginner's Classical Greek Dance were comprehensive movement systems, with Ginner emphasising a link to classical aesthetics while Atkinson reinforced concepts of nature.[33]

Although there were non-balletic forms in the examination systems of training spreading throughout Britain, two styles dominated the offerings from Central Europe. The *Ausdruckstanz* became established through the lineage of Rudolf Laban, through proponents of the Viennese dancer and choreographer Gertrud Bodenwieser and German Mary Wigman, who opened schools in the 1920s. Based in Devon, Kurt Jooss and Sigurd Leeder from the Laban lineage also came to be a significant presence in the dance landscape. In the early 1930s, a group of English dance students

---

31 Beth Genné discusses how a dance canon was developed during this time and the details behind some quite strategic decisions. See Genné (2000) 'Creating a Canon, Creating the 'Classics' in Twentieth Century British Ballet', *Dance Research*. See also Morris, op.cit.

32 Rachel Fensham (2011) 'Nature, Force and Variation', in Alexandra Carter and Rachel Fensham, eds., *Dancing Naturally: Nature, Neo-Classicism and Modernity in Early Twentieth-Century Dance*.

33 Alexandra Carter (2011) 'Constructing and Contesting the Natural in British Theatre Dance', in Carter and Fensham, eds., ibid. See also Richenda Power (1996) 'Healthy Motion, Images of "Natural" and "Cultured" Movement in Early Twentieth-Century Britain', *Women's Studies International Forum*.

travelled to Germany to study Laban's 'expressionistic' dance, with Jeanette Rutherston and Trudl Dubsky opening the Dubsky-Rutherston School of Dance in London. Another proponent was Leslie Burrowes, a practitioner of Margaret Morris Movement (another non-balletic dance style) before studying with Wigman in Dresden in the early 1930s. Returning to London, she commented on the disparity in national temperament, an English preference for virtuosity and controlled displays of emotion that hindered the spread of Wigman's style.[34] This is reinforced in a *Dancing Times* survey of Central European dancers in England which classifies the style as 'difficult to accept', asserting that dance was 'the most conservative of the arts'.[35] The article focuses on the differences in teaching approaches, the use of music, issues of self-expression, and philosophical approaches to technique. An intellectual component in the work of Bodenwieser-trained Dubsky and Helen Elton was deemed to be not overly heavy, but the author warned against placing too much emphasis on self-expression at the expense of technical ability. Criticism extended to a London teacher's failure to train dancers 'with anything approaching the perfection of the classical training from the foot and leg point of view; on the other hand, the arm and body training does produce great suppleness and strength, and every muscle has attention paid to it'.[36] Distinct differences between pedagogic approaches are evident in how Central European styles emphasised improvisation and individual creativity in contrast to the syllabus-led learning that shaped the teaching of even the 'free' styles of modern dance in England.[37]

By late August 1935, Laban-trained German dancer Kate Eisenstaedt had moved to England because of her Jewish heritage.[38] The European imports complemented the British systems, with classes structured on set syllabi, evaluated by examinations with certificates of achievement awarded. Some classes were taught at schools that also taught the syllabi for the Imperial Society (Operatic Association Branch). The May 1935 issue of *Dancing Times* pictures students at the height of a jump, front arm and head thrown up with a sense of abandon. The caption identifies it as a 'Central European Class' taught by Eisenstaedt at the Noreen Bush School.[39] British dancer,

34 Larraine Nicholas (2010) 'Leslie Burrowes: A Young Dancer in Dresden and London, 1930-34', *Dance Research*.

35 Jeanette Rutherston (1934) 'The Central European Dance in England', *Dancing Times*, December, no. 291, p. 313.

36 Ibid. p. 315.

37 Fensham, op.cit. p. 5.

38 Rutherston, op.cit. An advert in the February, 1934 *Dancing Times* lists Kate Eisenstaedt from Berlin as teaching at the Rutherston Dubsky School of Rhythmic Movement in Great Ormond Street, London. Jeanette Rutherston was affiliated with the Bodenwieser School in Vienna. A notice in the April 1934 *Dancing Times*, p. 57, gives details of a performance-demonstration by Eisenstaedt and students from the Rutherston-Dubsky School.

39 Anon. (1935) *Dancing Times*, May, no. 296, p. 189.

teacher and choreographer Elton studied with Bodenwieser in Vienna in 1927, inspired by movement that was 'flowing, light and at one with the music'.[40] She taught the Bodenwieser Method at the Brooke-Elton School, contributing choreography to one of the pageants discussed below.

Other proponents of Central European modern dance conveyed an intense expressivity in photographs, a three-dimensionality of the torso with sculptural arm shaping, and usually in a grounded stance that contrasted to the uplift of ballet, musical theatre styles and ballroom dancers that populated the pages of *Dancing Times*. Another innovative style was influenced by American modern dancers, with Margaret Barr among the few in Britain at the time.

Margaret Barr and the Dance Drama Group

Dance history's grand narrative has emphasised the institutionalisation of American modern dance in Britain in the late 1960s when Graham technique became the cornerstone of the new London Contemporary Dance School and Ballet Rambert became a contemporary dance company. Yet as Larraine Nicholas establishes, Margaret Barr (1904-1991) provides a much earlier link to the formative American model, although she did not leave a lasting influence.[41] The child of an English mother and American father, Barr moved between India, England and the USA. Graduating from high school in Santa Barbara, California, Barr and her sister studied Denishawn style dance with Martha Graham's sister, Geordie. Other key components of Barr's aesthetic were instilled in her at seminal institutions which helped shape an emergent American avant-garde in theatre, dance and production. At the Cornish School in Seattle in 1925, Barr studied ballet with Russian émigré Adolph Bolm and Dalcroze eurythmics that emphasised a musical expressivity with Louise Soelberg. The institution is significant for its faculty which included composer John Cage and Bonnie Bird a former Martha Graham dancer and teacher. Knowledge of theatre lighting and a dramatic sensibility were honed through a summer school course in Carmel, California with director/producer and actor Maurice Browne of the San Francisco Little Theatre. During the 1910s the Little Theatre movement was comprised of small experimental theatre spaces which survived with little funding for extravagant designs, relying instead on realistic sets when they were used at all and avant-garde advances in lighting.[42]

---

40 Helen Elton (1998) 'Vienna Revisited in Memory', in Bettina Vernon-Warren and Charles Warren, eds., *Gertrud Bodenwieser and Vienna's Contribution to Ausdruckstanz*.

41 Larraine Nicholas (2007) *Dancing in Utopia: Dartington Hall and its Dancers*, especially chapter 2, 'Dance-Mime for the People'.

42 On the significance of the Cornish School, see Karen Bell-Kanner (1998) *Frontiers: The Life and Times of Bonnie Bird: American Modern Dancer and Dance Educator*. For a

Barr and her sister Betty started a dance school in Santa Barbara, but a career-changing move occurred when they relocated to New York City in 1927 and studied with Graham. Although accounts of her career indicate that Barr deputised for Graham's classes this was at an early point in the development of Graham technique.[43] While in New York, Barr created *Hebridean Suite*, a dance which remained in her repertoire across continents for decades. As analysed below, Barr's core principles correlate to Graham's in multiple ways, significant differences, however, existed between their choreographic philosophies. Barr's choreography was influenced by her training in acting and theatre production which contributed to a strong narrative impetus and use of task-based movement motifs based on everyday actions. Nicholas notes that the phrases dance-drama or dance-mime were integrated into the title of the various groups Barr formed in England.[44]

According to biographer Caryl Von Sturmer, a desire to create her own dances prompted Barr's return to England from New York in 1929. She set up the short-lived 'Workshop of Modern Dance' in Sloane Square with Joyce Peters. The advertisements reveal qualities associated with Graham's style, focusing on bodily dynamics such as 'the breath pause, relaxation, muscular control, percussion and release – and dance forms: lyrical, dramatic, stylisation and group movement.'[45] However, as Nicholas argues, in Barr's stylisation of mimetic movement 'her foregrounding of content would not allow her to take the abstraction process further in the direction of pure dance'.[46] Her early work reinforced connections to drama and her American mentors facilitated professional theatre opportunities in London. Barr set the movement for Maurice Browne's 1930 London production of *Othello* directed by his wife Ellen van Volkenburg which featured African-American singer and activist Paul Robeson as Iago. The controversial production was deemed uneven, with unwieldy costumes that were a source of a dispute, restricting the movement Barr created. Until the last scene, Robeson was in 'unsuitably long Elizabethan garments (including tights, puffed sleeves, and doublets), instead of Moorish robes which would have naturally enhanced the dignity of his performance.'[47]

Van Volkenberg was instrumental in arranging for Barr to meet

---

summary of the Little Theatre Movement, see David Blanke (2002), *The Nineteen Tens: American Popular Culture through History*. The Provincetown Players in New York was one of the most influential Little Theatres of the period.
43 Garry Lester (1997) 'Margaret Barr: Epic Individual and Fringe Dweller', *Proceedings: Society of Dance History Scholars*; Nicholas (2007), op.cit.; Von Sturmer, op.cit.
44 Nicholas (2007), op.cit. p. 63.
45 Von Sturmer, op.cit. p. 16. Some accounts of Barr's contact with Graham are not able to be independently verified, according to Larraine Nicholas, op.cit. p.61.
46 Nicholas, (2007), op.cit. p.75.
47 Duberman (1989) op. cit. p. 136. See Von Sturmer, op.cit. for discussion of Barr's disagreement with the director,

philanthropists Dorothy and Leonard Elmhirst who established Dartington Hall, a centre for educational, scientific, agricultural and artistic study in Devon. In 1930 Barr began teaching and choreographing at the rural idyll which offered opportunities to develop artistically with a repertoire linked to a programme of educational outreach to the surrounding communities, a connection integral to the institution's philosophy. It was a magnet for artists and writers of all types, attracting an international who's who of artistic and intellectual innovation over the years: sculptor Henry Moore, writer Aldous Huxley; philosopher Bertrand Russell; Russian theatre practitioner Michael Chekov; Indian poet, painter, educationalist Rabindranath Tagore, and American composer Marc Blizstein, whose musical 'The Cradle Will Rock' came under fire for its politics in the Federal Theatre Project in 1939. Two artists based at Dartington became fundamental to Barr's aesthetic – composer Sir Edmund Rubbra and designer Peter Goffin who collaborated with Barr in the production of dances that critic Fernau Hall praised for their theatrical spontaneity and variety in tackling new themes. Soelberg, Barr's eurhythmics teacher from Seattle, was instrumental in creating the strong dance ethos at Dartington, working with Barr creatively and in an administrative position in the School of Dance-Mime.

Within such a rich and artistically sympathetic environment, Barr's dance philosophy continued to take shape and her dances were performed locally from 1931 to 1934. The choreography ranged from 'dance-dramas' to more entertainment oriented fare such as the 'Jabberwocky Dance' and 'Lobster Quadrille' for a local Alice in Wonderland production. Inspiration from the local environment and community shaped a choreographic path for Barr's London years. *Colliery*, a 1933 dance about mining, was created with the Liverton Village Players – farm workers, labourers and foresters – drawn from the surrounding neighbourhood.[48] A strong social consciousness was evident in thematic choices and in her personal activism. Although Barr was used to a certain level of privilege, having grown up with servants in India and attended private school in England, her father's poor health eventually impacted the family's financial situation. Accounts of her life are peppered with anecdotes of events that broadened her awareness of social inequalities and political oppression. For example, Barr befriended Sinalese revolutionaries on her way back to London which landed her in trouble with the authorities.[49] At Dartington, the 1933 production of *The People* encapsulated Barr's politically informed approach and hints at ideological tensions that may have arisen between the choreographer and her employers, who were among the class criticised by the narrative.

---

48 Fernau Hall (1950) *Modern English Ballet*, pp. 140-141; von Sturmer, op.cit. pp. 17-20.
49 Von Sturmer, op.cit. p. 27.

The characters included industrialised oppressed workers, a Visionary and Patriot, and a Capitalist. [50]

In 1934 the School of Dance-Mime at Dartington was replaced by the Jooss-Leeder School of Dance, formed when Kurt Jooss's company emigrated due to Nazi oppression in Germany. Although it was envisioned that the two groups would work alongside each other, the plan proved unfeasible. Barr left while Jooss remained in Devon until his internment during World War II. The change of personnel at Dartington marked a shift in overall institutional aims, moving dance away from a community-based form towards a more professionally-based education and training institution. [51]

Back in London in 1934, Barr taught classes advertised to develop 'vitality, exhilaration and body loveliness', working in studio in Soho. [52] Two strands emerge in her work after leaving Dartington – recreational classes and a loyal core of more experienced performers. It would have been a significant shift – moving from the Devon landscape to central London; from a foundational role in a significant institution, with expansive dance studios and financial support, surrounded by students, colleagues, collaborators and artists from other disciplines to a more tenuous economic and artistic position. She went from a studio designed to accommodate her dance style to working on an uneven floor above a Greek restaurant in Soho, an area populated at the time by foreign residents and their restaurants alongside artists, new film companies and theatre. [53] Money was a constant struggle, and her work increasingly reflected the economic and social turmoil of the Depression era and rise of fascism in Europe. Her replacement at Dartington, the Kurt Jooss Ballet, received constant mention and half-page advertisements in the influential *Dancing Times*. Barr's press coverage was rare and awareness of her professional circumstances tinged perceptions of her work in one unsigned review: 'MB is obviously going through a period of transition and search in her work, but though bearing a certain relation to real life, Miss Barr entirely ignores the fact that however grim the surroundings and circumstances in life are, there is always a spark of light to be found somewhere'. [54] The review sat alongside notices of amateur fare that included George and Ira Gershwin's *Funny Face*, musical farces and romantic-comedy operas. Between 1934 and 1938, Barr's Dance-Drama

50 See Nicholas (2007) op.cit. pp. 75-79.
51 Nicholas, ibid. Also see Victor Bonham-Carter (1958) *Dartington Hall: The History of an Experiment*. Pages 126-130 refer to tensions between Louise Soelberg, Barr and Jooss, as three different dance groups were essentially competing with each other at Dartington.
52 Von Sturmer, op.cit. p. 25.
53 F. H. W. Sheppard (General Editor) (1966) "General Introduction," *Survey of London*: volumes 33 and 34: St Anne Soho, British History Online, http://www.british-history.ac.uk/report.aspx?compid=41022, accessed 4 May 2013.
54 Anon. (1935) The Dance Drama Group, *Dancing Times*, March, no. 294, p. 713.

Group (DDG) appeared in diverse venues – town halls, small theatres and studios – in dances chosen from an equally wide range of themes. Support came from political groups and avant-garde theatre, the latter significantly with the leftist actor-director-producer André van Gyseghem (1906-1979). In one of the earliest documented London performances, the DDG shared the stage for the premiere of van Gyseghem's Experimental Theatre's production of Aubrey Menon's *Pacific* (1934). Trained at the Royal Academy of Dramatic Art, Van Gyseghem performed at the First International Workers Olympiad in Moscow in 1933 and worked at the Embassy Theatre School where Barr taught movement classes. Van Gyseghem's multiple trips to the Soviet Union shaped a theatre aesthetic informed by socialist realist approaches. A member of the Communist Party, he was part of a network of artists who were at the forefront of leftist theatre and pageant performances in London.[55]

While Barr almost vanished from pages of the *Dancing Times*, she continued to create dances for political events. Her political views were influenced by her husband, Bruce Hart, a pacifist Communist Party member, an activist and occasional performer in her works. Cultural offerings dominated the Political and Social Evening programme sponsored by the Epsom-Ewell Branch of the Communist Party, with only one speech embedded between musical offerings, a mass recitation and two plays by the Banstead Left Theatre Club (including George Bernard Shaw's 'Augustus Does His Bit'). Barr's 'Physical Exercise and Dance Technique Demonstration' preceded the Dance-Drama Group's *Red, White & Blue: Women of Britain* (*Imperialism, Pacifism and Militant Labour*), in which 'revolution won out over conservatism'.[56] Other shows were performed in non-commercial venues such as the Unity Theatre's Britannia Street studio and in town halls throughout London.

Dance suites explored different aspects of the same theme, using mime alongside formal movement patterns often with a strong narrative thread. *Medieval Suite* (1934) presented a satirical view of historical class divisions comprised of *The Hunters, The Falcon Ladies, The Crusader* and *The Amorous Bailiff*. Other light-hearted class depictions were seen in *Saturday Night* about an evening out at the pub. *The Three Sisters* (1932) couched an anti-war statement within Anton Chekov's literary structure and was among one of Barr's strongest works. Performed repeatedly for six years, *Three Sisters* presented 'the reactions of three women of different character to the circumstances of war', as summarised in a programme note. The five scenes centred around the strong characterisations of the Spinster, the Prostitute (danced by Barr), and the Young Girl developed through 'stylized versions of naturalistic movement and creating dramatic patterns of contrast and

55 Colin Chambers (2006) *Here we Stand: Politics, Performers and Performance*, p. 223.
56 Von Sturmer, op.cit., p. 30.

repetition out of these key dance images'.[57] Barr combined accessibility of meaning through mimetic gesture within a modern dance movement vocabulary. A socially conscious impetus resonated throughout, seen in *Routine* which ridiculed military rituals, while *Sketches of the People: Eviction, Breadlines* (1935) critiqued economic policies.

A *Times* critic defined Barr's style as being 'only one degree more abstract than the spoken drama...The central point from which each piece starts is an idea or story; movement is devised solely with the object of bringing this to life.'[58] Hall, a devoted follower of her work, in a 1938 *Dancing Times* article comments on Barr's blend of characterisations, abstracted gestures and formal patterns, with themes dictating the degree to which she relied on each of the elements. Although professing a preference for 'formal beauty', Hall praised the interplay between naturalistic gestures and what he described as a Graham-based technique. A 1938 version of *Hebridean* which had premiered in New York interwove various movement styles, including folk-based forms in its evocation of daily dramas in a Scottish fishing village as detailed in Hall's lengthy description:

> In the first scene, 'At the nets', we see three Scots girls standing together with their backs to the audience and mending imaginary nets on the back wall. The pattern of the hands as they cross and uncross, and their lovely flexible movements, represent something quite new to ballet, and wholly delightful. Later there were some almost equally fine triangular patterns of straight arms and bodies, when the girls turn to face the audience. The next dance, a jig, is executed with fire and a fine sense of style. The steps are mainly traditional, but presented with a sure feeling for theatrical effect. The last scene, 'The Storm' contains some rather obvious mime that any ballet mistress might have invented. The ending, however, when we are left with one of the dancers looking out at the sea, is magnificently successful. Her expression of utter desolation remains in the memory long after the end of the ballet.[59]

In terms of narrative development, the blend of mimetic, stylised movement with formal components that emphasised spatial and rhythmic qualities, *Hebridean* ranks as a well-crafted and richly complex dance, its premiere praised by Graham.[60] A musical score by Rubbra replaced the folk songs that initially accompanied the dance.

Other Dartington dances were restaged in London, such as *The Miners* (1936), a version of *Colliery*, to a score by Michael Tippett. The integration of diverse modes of symbolic expression – text, chorus, music and movement –

57 Fernau Hall undated draft of 'The Modern Scene in Ballet', 2, F. Hall Archives, NRCD.
58 Anon. (1935) The Arts Theatre, Dance-Drama Group, *The Times*, 12 February, p.12.
59 Fernau Hall (1938) 'Modern dancing at King's Cross', *Dancing Times*, p. 527.
60 Von Sturmer, op.cit.

portrayed a mine explosion and the devastating aftermath on survivors and the local community. Accounts of later lecture-demonstrations emphasise the same core principles advertised in 1930, focusing on the breath as the movement impetus. Set exercises used the barre in contrast to the work of Graham's floor series, however, for Hall, Barr's dancers 'avoided the spins and beats of classical ballet, they used the top half of their bodies with exceptional flexibility; instead of seeking to defy gravity, their movements were often directed down into the ground.'[61] While comparisons to Graham were often made by Barr and Hall, *New York Times* critic John Martin's 1932 review honed in on Barr's reliance on mimetic gesture, emotionally charged movement which he felt overpowered phrases of 'excellent design.'[62]

Barr's attempts to establish a permanent professional company were thwarted by financial hardships. The generosity of its 15 members subsidised company productions and rehearsal costs, as the dancers undertook jobs in pubs and even the zoo to contribute to a communal fund while South African dancer Teda de Moor drew from her family fortune.[63] In 1938 de Moor wrote to composer Alan Bush for financial assistance to help bring Barr's choreography 'to a standard which would enable us to dance to the "unconverted"... Now, our standard never rises as our people cannot afford to work for nothing so we keep losing the members just as they get fairly well trained.' De Moor outlined an annual budget of £500 that included studio rental charges, pianist fees and £200 to sustain five dancers.[64] Dances were produced on a financial shoestring, with handmade musical instruments used for accompaniment (including potato casks transformed into drums, topped by dried raw hides cleaned and prepared by a group member). Cymbals were made from second hand circular cattle drinking troughs suspended from an iron frame. Tippett's score for *Dance for Two with Chorus* utilised tin cans and wooden blocks.[65]

Décor was kept to a minimum for financial and aesthetic reasons, inspired in part by socialist realist theatre practices. At the monthly studio performances at Unity Theatre's Britannia Street site 'there were no curtains, exits, entrances or proscenium arch: only an imaginary line separated the audience from dancing area. Though some backcloths were used, décor was generally three-dimensional: solid ramps and platforms over which the dancers moved. Décor and lighting were changed in full view of the audience – and sometimes with their help.'[66] Lighting stood on equal footing

---

61 Fernau, 'The Modern Scene in Ballet', op.cit.

62 John Martin (1932) 'The Dance: In England', *New York Times*, 14 August, p. x5.

63 Kaye Russell (1938) 'Dancing for Progress', *The Millgate*, no. 391, April, pp. 407-408.

64 Teda de Moor letter to Alan Bush, 13 April 1938, correspondence file, Alan Bush Collection (ABC) BL, MS Mus 453, v. 128.

65 Russell, op.cit. p. 408.

66 Hall, op. cit. undated draft of Modern English Ballet, p. 296

with décor, contributing to a dramatic intensity. Years later an Australian critic observed that in Barr's dances, 'lighting has always been regarded by her as a third actor or mover. Even the shadows danced'.[67]

Barr worked with amateur dancers, offering classes through the left-wing Unity Theatre and co-operative society groups. The desire to involve the lay dancer in her Dartington productions remained, working with two constituents within one group – the young dancer with professional aims and the recreational performer. Accessibility to all was stressed in 1937 advertisements describing her style 'based on the natural laws of life. Thus it appeals to "lay" people, for the pupil does not need to start at seven years of age [in contrast to ballet]. It is not full of centuries of tradition, but is modern – interested in the ordinary movements of life drama'.[68] Some dances appear to have a more agit-prop function and aesthetic. Industrial workers inspired *Factory* (1934), which was labelled as a 'dramatic improvisation' which evoked 'Clocking in, idle chatter, levers, clattering machinery, the accident, back to work again'.[69] Critics saw in the dance 'the throb and thump and whirr of machinery [produced] by purely human means', and 'gyrating arms and rhythmic hand stamping'.[70] Amongst the praise there was resistance to the use of text, with one critic objecting to the shouting of "Swine!" "Slaves!" and "Unite!"', while another commented on the 'emotive function' of words which were not adequately integrated with the movement.[71]

Daiken's 1936 article on English workers' dance reported that the Workers' Dance Drama Group was distinguished from Barr's main group by the absence of professional dancers. After 18 months' training, the WDDG toured through London and its suburbs, its repertory placed the labourer centre-stage in dances such as *Factory* and *Mills*'.[72] Programme notes for a performance of *Mills* at a benefit performance for the Friends of the Soviet Union in 1935 describe the work as 'an experiment based on integral sound rhythm'. Sections titled 'The Factory Gate', the 'Speed-Up' and 'Loom Wrecking' explore class tensions where a 'fine' lady is mocked with a 'dance of the ragged shawls' in the 'Speed-Up' section. Dehumanisation of the workers results in 'Revolt', which ends with the mill 'hands' taking possession of the factory. These dances contrasted to the broader repertoire of Barr's advanced group in which class-based issues were seen in easily recognisable class characters or literary themes devoid of such agitational

67 'R.R.' quoted in von Sturmer, op.cit p. 128.
68 Margaret Barr quoted in anon. Nov. 1938, 'Ourselves' [Co-operative Wholesale Society Newsletter], November.
69 Quoted in Nicholas (2007), op.cit. p. 73.
70 Anon. (1934) 'Van Gyseghem's Experimental Theatre', *The Era*, 14 November.
71 Anon, quoted in Nicholas (2007) op.cit. p. 113; Anon. (1935) 'The Arts Theatre', *The Times*, 12 February, p. 12.
72 Daiken, op.cit. p. 30.

impetus. Parallels can be drawn to the multiple styles evident in left-wing theatre performance where individual character development was perceived as 'bourgeois' while didactic aims dictated easily recognisable archetypes to facilitate a narrative exploration of class-based relationships.

In working more with recreational dancers, Hall noted that:

> the apparent content of dance dramas acquired much more individuality and social realism... *Means Test* [1937] for example, dealt with the tragic break up of families produced by the brutally inhuman assistance regulations. But there was no enrichment of her form to cope with this new content. The movements tended more and more to abstract patterns, and in the absence of any comprehensible dance images the content was completely obscured.[73]

An increasing didactic tone and, according to Hall, a decline in standards resulted in the dissolution of the professional group in 1938. In scrutinising Barr's dances, Hall remarks on the significance of her work in relation to the labour movement, her use of contemporary themes, and collaborations with experimental and contemporary composers such as Rubbra and Tippett. A lack of technical development was attributed to Barr's isolation and the absence of a traditional dance form to underpin her style.

Barr left for New Zealand in 1939, eventually settling in Australia. She revived early dances in the 1950s such as *Breadline* from the 1930s and continued to choreograph in response to contemporary events such as the threat of nuclear destruction and the Vietnam War. A strong advocate of Barr's choreographic and political convictions, von Sturmer felt that Barr was in a 'no-win situation', considered too 'arty' by radicals in Australia. He explained '...they wanted *Breadline* to end in revolution. It just would not have worked.' For Barr, the need to retain a connection to reality meant a different outcome: 'Because people with muscles weakened by hunger cannot move far and rise only to collapse, the dancers hardly moved from the spot... Margaret always stressed to her dancers the need to return to scientific fact. "What is going on in the body in this situation?"'[74] Accounts of the dance stand in sharp contrast to the American dances where an optimistic revolutionary outcome was indicated by dancers wearing red surging onstage to rally the masses. Years later, Barr reflected that the name 'total theatre' was a more accurate description of her style than dance drama because of interdisciplinary qualities which left her outside distinct theatre and dance classifications.[75] Although a strong political ideology informed her work, the unwavering commitment to her vision for a physical basis for dance, seen in *Breadline*, distinguishes Barr's dances of social protest

73 Von Sturmer, op.cit. pp. 297-298.
74 Von Sturmer, op.cit. p. 58.
75 Margaret Barr quoted in von Sturmer, ibid. p. 14.

from the agit-prop style seen in the USA which ended with the oppressed emerging victorious, as analysed in the previous chapter. Further examples of Barr's activism through dance are analysed below in her pageant work.

Alan Bush, the Workers' Ballet Group and Unity Theatre

Other workers' dance groups found their genesis outside the dance community, demonstrating associations with socio-political organisations. Composer Alan Bush was a catalyst behind the London-based Workers' Ballet Group and the Workers' Propaganda Dance Group which became the Unity Dance Group. While studying in Berlin in the late 1920s, he met the influential director and playwright Bertolt Brecht and the left-wing composer Hans Eisler. Bush grew up in a prosperous family, initially attracted to spiritualism and theosophy after the death of his brother during WWI. In Berlin Bush studied with pianist Arthur Schnabel, spending hours on intensive training, attending operas and concerts, and composed the string quartet *Dialectic* in 1928. Exposed to the writings of Lenin, Marx and Engels while studying philosophy and musicology at Berlin University (1929-1931), Bush also witnessed the rise of anti-Semitism first-hand. His correspondence does not mention attendance at any dance performances, but he was living within a closely interrelated arts scene and was friends with left-wing theatre practitioners and musicians at the time.

Bush's music took on a political impetus when he was elected as the Assistant Musical Advisor to the London Labour Choral Union from 1926 to 1940 (when it was replaced by the Workers' Music Association Singers). He joined the Communist Party in 1935 and from 1936-1941 was Chairman of the Workers' Music Association which is still in existence as an international organisation, working to promote peace and the ideals of the labour movement.[76] Compositions for choral groups included *Song for Labour* and he was politically active on a personal level. Bush canvassed for parliamentary elections and became involved in hunger marches, composing *Hunger Marchers Song* in 1934. His musical style in the 1930s style was defined as more 'European', influenced by formalist and avant-garde aesthetics, while later compositions were of a more 'popular, folk-related idiom' to help appeal to the working class.[77] Marxism underpinned his creative approach, he wrote: 'For me, as a musician and as a man, Marxism is a guide to action. It challenges me to express through musical art the feelings of men and women, above all in their struggles to create a condition

---

76 See Nancy Bush (2000) *Alan Bush, Music, Politics and Life*; and Rachel O'Higgins (2002) 'Rhapsody in Red' summary of BBC Radio 4 programme, July, www.alanbushtrust.org. uk. American musician-activists such as Pete Seeger are also members of the group, see the WMA website, http://www.wmamusic.org.uk/index.html, accessed on 4 May 2013.
77 Duncan Hall (2001) *A Pleasant Change from Politics*, p. 134.

of social organisation in which science and art will be the possession of all and in which they will themselves be no longer exploiters nor objects of exploitation.'[78]

He was a prolific correspondent and his letters to other artists reveal debates about the relationship between art and society based on Marxist principles and the manifestation of class issues in dance and music for the workers. The Workers' Ballet Group (WBG), grew out of the 1934 Pageant of Labour at London's Crystal Palace. As a catalyst behind the group's creation, it brought to fruition Bush's long-held idea of combining 'a ballet with orchestra and choral commentary which should symbolise the upward struggle of the working class'.[79] Although the workers' dance did not receive the press coverage seen in the USA, similar debates took place in private. The aim of the WBG was 'to develop a dance style which workers of England could feel themselves at home in... no difficult steps – no jazz about it. But neither does it derive from folk dance. What we try to do is to set forth the various burning questions of the day, the situation of the workers in the economic system, the causes of war, etc., in our dances...'.[80] The grand visions for choreography created to communicate political content are analysed below in relation to specific works often referred to as ballets. Bush essentially functioned as artistic director, composer-accompanist and musical director for a couple of dance groups, thus helping to establish a more complex music-movement relationship than one might anticipate in such an amateur performance group. However, the extent to which his ideals as set out in correspondence were accomplished in performance remains unknown. Dance compositions include *His War or Yours* (1935) for the London Workers Ballet, *Mining*, and incidental music for *The Star Turns Red* (1940) a play by Sean O'Casey for Unity Theatre.

Details of the dance group membership during its first year have not been uncovered, however, correspondence establishes connections to Europe. In a letter to Eisenstaedt who was working with the group after arriving from Germany, Bush outlined timing indications so she could start choreographing a new four act dance prior to having the music. He explained: 'The third [section] is a kind of saddened repetition of the first and might have some related music. The second could be an agitated triple time, the finale a graceful one.'[81] A summary in the *New Theatre* article describes an untitled dance which may be the dance Bush was discussing:

The theme is a demonstration of the unity between the British working-

---

78 Alan Bush (1980) from *In My Eighth Decade & other Essays*, p. 20.
79 Alan Bush letter to Edward P. Glenn (Pageant Director, Festival of Labour Pageant), 2 February 1934, February-July 1934 correspondence file, ABC BL, MS MUS 450, v. 125.
80 AB letter to Editor of *Railway Times*, 6 August 1935, ABC BL MS MUS 451, v. 126.
81 AB letter to Kate Eisenstaedt, 31 August 1935, ABC BL, MS MUS 451, v. 126.

class with the workers in the colonies, and conflict between these joint forces and the capitalists. Through the conflict of war, and the misery of its aftermath, comes the determination to seek power by driving the capitalists out of control. This movement is a rhapsodic treatment of power. Next comes the primitive illustration of how the proletariat can, and does, engage in the business of Production, Distribution, and Consumption. The ballet concludes with a mass dance celebrating the idea of Holiday.[82]

With his musical commitments requiring extended periods of time away from London, Bush wrote letters to convey his ideas about the dance, asking for a close movement-music correspondence: 'every particularity of the rhythm should be accompanied by a suitable rate of step or movement.' He wanted a pianist to accompany rehearsals on a regular basis so he could 'take part in the dancing or at any rate not be worried all the time with playing' although there is no evidence he joined in the dancing. Other visions for the group include inviting Barr to participate, expanding the membership to twenty dancers and including gymnastics to attract young men.[83]

In 1938, Bush wrote to Eisenstaedt with suggested alterations for the WPDG's *Anti-Fascist Ballet* which articulates a more complex narrative than seen in the American workers dances. The six scenes set out the rising tide of oppression in Germany: 1) Jewish shopping scene in which a Jewish woman is turned away, 2) Young Jew helps Gentile girl (who has fallen and injured her leg; 3) The coffin scene depicts a family in mourning over the death of the young Jewish woman; 4) Women's scene; 5) Armament factory scene with depiction of a strike and starvation of the women and children factory workers; and 6) Concentration camp scene. Bush repeatedly emphasises that non-naturalistic movement should be used and called for the addition of episodes such as 'the burning of books and a ritual dance more desolate than before' in the coffin scene. He mentioned that he lost his copy of the words, indicating that there was some verbal accompaniment to the dance.[84]

Extensive debates about choreographic structure and the need to raise technical standards emerged. A seven page letter from Gertrude Watts, the dance group secretary, was sent to Bush in August 1938. A schism threatened the existence of the group with tension arising from differing levels of technical competence and ambitions. As one dancer reflected: 'The two elements are those who like myself believe in mass effects; and those, who... want more individual technique developed. I consider that [our]

---

82 Daiken, op. cit.

83 AB letter to Theresa Gorringe, 26 December 1934, BL; AB letter to Kate Eisenstaedt, 31 August 1935; AB letter to Edward Caine, 5 November 1934. ABC BL MS MUS 453, v. 128.

84 AB letter to Kate Eisenstaedt, 6 January 1938, ABC BL MS MUS 455, v. 130.

propaganda could be more direct, more subtle and more telling if we each didn't hamper the other.'[85]

Bush's group developed close ties to Unity Theatre, co-founded by Van Gyseghem who became president of the highly influential theatre collective. Formed in 1936 by members of the Rebel Players, Unity attracted politically engaged professional actors, directors and associate amateur members. Its productions encompassed Soviet theatrical techniques such as montage from film director Sergei Eisenstein, emphasis on body movement from avant-garde theatre director Vsevolod Meyerhold and minimalist approaches to realist aesthetics from Nikolai Pavlovich Okhlophov, director of the Realist Theatre in Moscow from 1930-1937. The early repertoire of American one-act left-wing plays was supplemented by contributions from British worker-playwrights, such as *Where's That Bomb?* (1937) written by two taxi drivers. During its initial year, agit-prop formats dominated tours to the provinces while experimental theatre productions were performed at Unity's London home in Britannia Street. The site also became Barr's base for weekly classes and rehearsals, augmented by monthly studio performances in 1938.[86]

Goldington Street Theatre, Unity's new home, opened on 25 November 1937, seating 323 people, and remained the group's base until destroyed by fire in 1975. A gala event featured the Workers' Propaganda Dance Group (WPDG) and the London Labour Choral Union. The evening centred around a production of Clifford Odets' *Waiting for Lefty*, a significant American play which transformed the audience-performer relationship, breaking through the fourth wall with the audience yelling 'Strike!' at the end and agitating for the taxi drivers to take action. Paul Robeson sang Negro spirituals, modifying the words to make them more topical. The WPDG contributed *A Comrade has Died*, a dance about Spain which conveyed 'the brutality and inhumanity of fascism and the inevitability of its overthrow in the workers' revolution.' In addition to providing rehearsal space and performance opportunities, links between the dance and theatre groups were strengthened when the WPDG was renamed the Unity Dance Group in early 1938.[87] Barr's Dance-Drama Group alternated appearances

85   GW letter to AB, 20-4-38, MS Mus 453, Alan Bush Collection, vol. 128. Correspondence in the file identifies other group members as George Cossey, Ann Lepper, Jimmy Turner, David Goodall, and Molly Myrtle. Dorothy and Buffy were also discussed in the correspondence at this time, however, their surnames are omitted. A letter from Goodall to Bush on 7 May 1938 indicates his plans to withdraw from the Co-operative Pageant due to the expulsion of Dorothy, and that four people had also left the group due to the internal tensions.

86   Hall, 1938, op.cit.

87   According to Colin Chambers (1989), Paul Robeson sang 'Ol' Man River', changing the words 'tired o' livin' and scared o' dyin'' to 'must keep strugglin' until Ah'm dyin'', finishing off with the '*Internationale*. See anon., 'The Workers Theatre Opens' *New Theatre*,

with Bush's group during the three week run of *Where's That Bomb?* in February 1938. Barr's group danced *Three Sisters, Hunters* and *Eviction,* while Bush's newly named Unity Dance Group performed *A Comrade Has Died, His War or Yours* and *Miners.*

Choreography in Unity Productions

Dance critic Fernau Hall was also active in Unity Theatre as a performer, including a role in the highly popular *Waiting for Lefty.* Hall documents the extent to which a movement component was integral to various Unity Theatre productions, revealing a close relationship to ideas about a socially conscious dance practice. While Barr's and Bush's groups performed separate dances, actor and folk dancer Margaret Leona helped shape a strong movement component within Unity Theatre performances which included musicals, pantomimes and mass declamations which mixed speech with movement.[88] Hall performed in *Defend the Soviet Union* (1937) and *Agony of China* (1938) and recalled Leona's stagings as 'stylised movement': 'It would not be true to say that her movements and groupings were *added* to the voices – the former were conceived by her as an integral part of the complete effect she desired, sometimes lending emphasis to the words and sometimes building up an effect of their own.'[89] A specific propaganda purpose underpinned the mass declamation form, offering a performance opportunity to non-dancers that blended simplistic movement with an oratory structure. For example, Charles Mann's detailed production notes for the play *Meerut* were circulated, revealing a strong rhythmic impetus behind the delivery of a simple text, with a small cast of six people who remained stationary in a makeshift cell until the very final moments of the action.[90]

Hall explained how Leona's production of *Defend the Soviet Union* utilised a movement component by assigning 'to each passage a definite mood and corresponding vocal colour, and [she] kept these contrasts distinct by always rehearsing them separately... We were collective farmers gathering grain, the rotors of a giant turbine ... or partisans attacking... each step and gesture had to be firmly stylised and exactly in rhythm with the words.'[91] The dynamics

no. 3, January 1938, p. 1, THM/9/3/1, also quoted in Clark, op.cit. p. 226. See *The Story of Unity Theatre*, p. 117. anon., 'What Unity is Doing' New Theatre, February 1938, p. 4, THM/9/3/1

88 Jenny Pearson, 'Obituary, Margaret Leona', *The Independent*, 13 February 1995, http://www.independent.co.uk/news/people/margaret-leona-1572846.html (Margaret Helen Gertsley).

89 Fernau Hall, undated, unpublished autobiography, p. 137, F. Hall Archives, NRCD

90 Charlie Mann (1933) 'How to Produce *Meerut*', in Samuel, et.al., eds. op.cit., pp. 106-108.

91 Hall, undated, unnumbered manuscript, chapter 15, 'Unitarian Salute', F. Hall Archives, NRCD

and rhythms of the text were broken down and set line by line, using musical indications such as *crescendo* or *decrescendo*. *Agony of China* developed the form even further, reinforcing the role of movement in creating the dramatic action: 'Margaret [Leona] set out to find a combination of spoken word and stylized movement that together would create the precise effect of feeling required at each moment... where the words suggest the bombing of an open town, she arranged a series of sweeping movements representing the effect of the explosions on different groups of people.' Movement was set individually then groups rehearsed until 'all the groups were dove-tailed together in a fine contrapuntal effect by a system of word-and-action cues.' Ironically, the existence of the mass declamation format, offering recreational performance opportunities combining stylised movement and speech, may have impacted on the attraction of a workers dance. As theatre historian Colin Chambers notes, mass declamations enabled performers at all levels of capability to participate.[92]

Hall performed the role of Joybell in Sean O'Casey's play *The Star Turns Red* (1940), with movement to Bush's score set by Soelberg who had come via Dartington. Hall enthusiastically recalled: '...the crisp overarm sweep of men throwing hand grenades, and Red Jim's posture at the window with his right arm up beside his head furnishes a brilliantly effective focus for the whole tableau towards the end of the scene.' In another scene, Red Jim '...leaps to the centre of the stage and scuttles on bent knees across to the windows...' The limitations of working with non-dancers was overcome by mixing direct music-movement relationships and choreography departing from the score to fulfil the requirements of the dramatic action.[93] Soelberg also created the movement for *Busmen* (1938), a living newspaper combining documentary and fictionalised action to highlight topical issues, the form codified by the American Federal Theatre Project.

Recreational Dance and Pageants

Where the unions and Communist Party were major sponsors in the American left wing dance, the Co-operative movement took on the task in England. Co-operative organisations provided folk dance classes for young people in the Woodcraft Folk which was founded in 1925 as an alternative to the Boy Scouts. Co-founder Leslie Paul was influenced by the political element in Boy Scout leader Ernest Thompson Seton's writings: 'Seton taught us to detest the greedy industrial society which had destroyed a whole people in order to steal their land. So that from the beginning "woodcraft" had political and social meanings for us – it was not just a romantic escape, but a

---

92 Colin Chambers (1989) *The Story of Unity Theatre*, p. 82.
93 Fernau Hall, 'The Star Ballet', F. Hall Archives, NRCD. A rehearsal schedule also shows eight dancers listed for each cast of the work.

form of opposition to society.' The very title referred to an old craft – working with wood – and activities reinforced a respect for and harmonic relationship with nature, exemplified by Native American and tribal traditions. On a more political tone, a primary principle laid out in its charter evokes Marx: 'We further declare that the welfare of the community can be assured only: when the instruments of production are owned by the community, and all things necessary for the good of the [human] race are produced by common service for the common good.' With the rise of fascism in Europe, a new banner was adopted: 'Join the Woodcraft Folk to work for world peace and fight war and fascism.'[94]

John White, a long-time member of the Woodcraft Folk from the 1930s, recalled that the political element of activities such as music, dancing, art and poetry was implicit rather than explicit. Divided into groups by age, weekends were spent camping, reinforcing a bond with nature. Upon joining the Folk, members took on a name drawn from the outdoors such as an animal, bird or tree. White sees the renaming and use of uniforms as a means of equalisation, a way in which deeply rooted class boundaries were erased, at least temporarily.[95] The Woodcraft Folk had links to the Co-operative Movement, which initially funded its activities and was also advertised as the children of the Labour Party for a period. The Co-op organisation had a number of auxiliary groups and created its own folk dance structure in 1938. Dance was also taken to 'the workers' in recreational dance classes that emphasised keeping fit rather than political activism.

Politicised dance was also found in mass pageants, utilising large casts in highly simplified movement patterns. A pageantry movement swept across the country in the early 1900s, based on the work of the English director of music at Sherborne School, Louis Napoleon Parker, as exemplified in his 1905 *Sherborne Pageant*. Significant historical events were re-enacted to celebrate the 1200 year history of the English town, with 900 participants drawn from the local community. An ideological agenda existed in Parker's pageants, tinged with an anti-modernist nostalgia through which 'the moral principles of the past could reach a wider audience.'[96] The pageant form became codified and replicated by numerous villages and towns across the nation. Theatre historian Mick Wallis's analysis of the Parkerian pageant highlights the form's educational function while reinforcing a sense of community, establishing symbolic and often mythic representations of the past. Wallis identifies them as 'ideological projects', in which class divisions dissolve but only temporarily.[97]

---

94 Leslie Paul (1980) *The Early Days of the Woodcraft Folk*, Woodcraft Folk, 3, from the personal archives of John White, quotes pp. 9 and 24.
95 John White, interview with author, 11 August 2005.
96 David Glassberg (1990) *American Historical Pageantry*, p. 44.
97 See Mick Wallis (1994) 'Pageantry and the Popular Front: Ideological Production

The Parkerian form was transformed into a tool of the political left in the 1930s. In contrast to a local community as hero, a generic version of 'the people' emerged as heroes who ultimately rise up in revolt. Wallis examines episodes where the workers are transformed from happy peasants to downtrodden factory labourers. Left-wing pageants essentially functioned as a 'mass medium', bringing together amateurs and professionals, committed communists and fellow travellers, endowing those involved with a sense of historical agency and offering opportunities for audience participation.[98]

Between 1934 and 1939, at least three left-wing pageants integrated dance as part of the visual spectacle. Produced on a grand scale with large budgets and casts, their political agendas were aimed at a broader audience than seen in the New York Communist Party pageants of the 1930s. Bush took on various roles in all three, with ballet and folk dance in the first pageant and choreographic contributions from Barr, Eisenstaedt, Leona and other dancers associated with the workers dance groups. Bush composed incidental music for the 1934 Pageant of Labour at Crystal Palace in London which ran for five days, sponsored by the Women's Trade Union Council. A complex narrative drew from fictionalised episodes and factual moments to depict the history of the Trade Union movement, beginning with 'the enslavement of the worker by capital' in pre-industrial England, as described in the programme.[99]

The Pageant of Labour was an enormous undertaking, with 1,500 performers, 200 dancers and the 'London Labour Choir of 100 Voices'. Dance episodes were choreographed by ballet teachers Sybil Spencer, Margaret Irwin and Mary Clifton-Haddon, folk dancer Mary Bult, and Bodenwieser dancer Helen Elton. They created a Pastoral Ballet, Children's Ballet, Machine Ballet, Ballroom Ballet, International Ballet and Finale.[100] The titles denote a wide range of themes, while the label 'ballet' indicates a movement sequence rather than a specific dance genre. The Children's Ballet represented 'the degradation, the slavery and misery of childhood under the factory system....The movements of the ballet suggest dull, mechanical obedience to an awful task-master'.[101] In Elton's choreographic plans for *The Triumph of the Machine*, one group would move mechanically, 'gradually

in the 'Thirties', *New Theatre Quarterly*, p. 18; (1995) 'The Popular Front Pageant: Its Emergence and Decline', *New Theatre Quarterly*; and (1988) 'Heirs to the Pageant: Mass Spectacle and the Popular Front', in Andy Croft, ed., *A Weapon in the Struggle: the Cultural History of the Communist Party in Britain*.

98 Wallis (1988) op.cit. p. 50.

99 London Pageant of Labour present "The Pageant of Labour" at the Crystal Palace, 15-20 October 1934 Scenario in the Lord Chamberlain's Plays archive, British Library Department of Manuscripts, ref. L.C.P. 13140.

100 Alan Bush, Pageant of Labour Correspondence file, ABC BL. The programme also lists Peggy Goulding as Ballet Mistress along with the choreographers.

101 London Pageant of Labour Scenario, op.cit.

gathering more and more groups as they go on, until they build one massive "Machine"'.[102] A Strauss waltz accompanied the Ballroom Ballet in the episode 'London Receives the Chartists', using social dance forms such as the quadrille.

Letters from Sybil Spencer to Bush reveal her perception of thematic and stylistic constraints in the International section. The use of movement in relation to words in a choral ballet troubled her 'as there is no doubt that the dancing side is bound to suffer', and she asked Bush to provide two to three minutes of 'soft, lyrical music' to conform to the balletic training of her dancers. Grand plans for the dance had to be scaled back as the cast was reduced from 150 to 23 dancers at one point. Spencer initially envisioned different groups representing the nations of the world, through the use of 'mime or...stationary movements characteristic of their particular country'.[103] A *Dancing Times* report declared that Bush's music 'was by no means easy for the dancers or the choreographers'.[104] Bush's style at the time integrated contrapuntal compositional strategies 'allied to serialism but based on tonality'.[105] Whilst Spencer's letters revealed tensions between her balletic style and the organisers' visions, the event put Bush in contact with others who shared his beliefs in a Marxist function for art, leading to the first incarnation of the Workers' Ballet Group.

Towards To-morrow Pageant

Bush was on the planning committee and composed music for the 2 July 1938 *Towards To-morrow: a Pageant of Co-operation*, part of the Festival of Co-operation held in London's Wembley Stadium. The pageant was one aspect of a day-long event celebrating the international organisation. Sixty thousand people attended as participants and spectators, with clowns, bands and community singing. Sheepdog Trials evoked rural labour while a Mass Woodcraft Folk Display included 'Tent Pitching', folk dancing and games. Two hours were allotted for the pageant, commemorating the growth of the Co-operative Movement in relation to the rise of the working class, from feudal times to the aftermath of World War I. The £15,000 pageant budget was overrun, generating resistance to proposals for later grand pageants.[106] London area Co-operative Societies drew on the energy and enthusiasm of

102 Helen Elton letter to Alan Bush, May 16, 1934. Pageant of Labour Correspondence file, ABC BL.

103 Gudrun Hildebrandt, a Central European dancer, was initially co-choreographer for this section. She resigned in disagreement with Spencer over the choreography. Letter to ADB, 27 June 1934; SS letter to AB, 25 June 1934; SS letter to AB, 26 June 1934.

104 anon. (1934) *The Dancing Times*, November, p. 138.

105 Sadie quoted in Richard Hanlon and Mike Waite (1998) 'Communism and British Classical Music' in Andy Croft, ed., *A Weapon in the Struggle*, p. 75.

106 Van Gyseghem, André (1979) 'British Theatre in the Thirties: an autobiographical record' in Clark, et al., eds. op.cit. pp. 209-218.

their membership to create a cast of 3,000. A forty-minute commercial film and extensive coverage in various co-operative society publications facilitate a rare vision of pageant performance. Unless otherwise noted, the following analysis is based on a viewing of the film, supplemented by a 56 page souvenir programme.[107]

Eight episodes chronicled a history of industrialisation and struggles between workers and owners, evoked through text, symbolic imagery, movement and song. An opening procession led by the Dagenham Girl Pipers was followed by 'a laughing merry crowd of country folk of Merrie England, minstrels, morris dancers, gypsies, clowns and peasants'. Harking back to a pre-industrial rural existence, a village fair ensued, complete with a Punch and Judy puppet show and children interweaving streamers around a maypole. The picture of the past necessarily drew from a limited nostalgia to reinforce perceptions of the evils of industrialisation symbolised by two large effigies of capitalism – ubiquitous top-hatted, cigar-smoking fat cats wheeled on by masked overseers with whips. The mechanical age and its devastation of the idyllic community were represented metaphorically and figuratively. Four groups of machine men marched on, their costumes more than their movement evoking robots. They divided into 'factories' in four corners of the field, marching in set floor patterns. Special effects included smoke bellowing from a tall smokestack which arose out of an ivy bush, a vivid image of the transformation from nature to machine. Villagers were forced into factories, their early attempts at revolt crushed by the capitalists' intimidating henchmen. Echoes of the narrative can be seen in the pageantry of the 2012 Olympic Games Opening Ceremony, as explored in Chapter 4.

Mass movement accompanied simple passages of text. A line of overworked children trudged up to a central platform to the cries 'We want work. We want bread.' The capitalists responded with 'We want more children. Fewer men and women and more children. For our factories we want more children.' Actors portrayed prominent figures in the international struggle for democracy such as Thomas Paine, joined by portrayals of William Cobbett and Robert Owen, founders of co-operative groups. Owen's short-lived co-operative community at New Lanark in Scotland during the early 19th century included a school where children wore Greek-style simple white cotton tunics and the curriculum included music and dance. New Lanark was symbolically evoked to symbolise co-operative efforts with a crowd of children performing group exercises and demonstrating their education by forming themselves into numbers in mathematical problems and spelling out words with their bodies. The factory children who had collapsed with exhaustion were revived, their rags abandoned to reveal tunics as they joined the others from the utopian experiment.

107 I am grateful to John White who retained his copy of the souvenir programme and shared it with me.

New Lanark's principles paved the way for the international co-operative movement which followed later. Groups processed in line behind banners commemorating visionary forerunners, from the 1844 Rochdale Pioneers to the various Co-operative societies. The display of unity temporarily thwarted capitalism's advance, but it gathered strength only to return to cries of war. Mounted horsemen – 'the four horsemen of the apocalypse' – scattered the crowds as troops and 'tanks' surged forward behind smoke screens and fake guns.

Dance segments were most prominent in the final representations of death, grief and the power of unity, advancing the narrative of the last three episodes. Following the onslaught of war, darkly cloaked figures interlinked arms in a march towards the central platform. Wearing helmets with small skulls dangling from their garments enhanced an oppressive atmosphere. Eisenstaedt's basic movement motifs in *The War Ballet* were necessitated by the scale of the venue, and possibly by the technical skills of the dancers. Once the figures of death mount the two levels of a circular stage, they lunge from side to side, facing inwards with arms held shoulder height. Forward steps flowed into a low turn with outstretched arms, flaring out capes attached to their wrists. Moving out of the turn, the dancers crouch down, arms thrust forward to hide their faces, the phrase repeated as they circle the platform. In another phrase, unison steps travel forward, followed by a backward lean with head and arms suddenly thrown back as if reacting to a gunshot. Although the visual and audio are not synchronised on the film, a close movement-music relationship can be inferred from Bush's notes.

The *Ballet of Mourning Women* opened the seventh episode, choreographed by Barr and danced by her Workers' Dance Drama Group. Brief close-up shots facilitate a more extensive movement analysis. As with other characters, the costumes enable easy recognition by spectators even in the farthest seats in the arena, reinforced by the choral lament which starts:

> We are women. Is to weep
> The last privilege we keep?
> We are women, and we bore
> All the fighters in your war[108].

Additional stanzas convey their various roles as nurses, mothers, lovers, and wives. The dancers kneel down with bowed heads, hands crossed over their chests, then cover their faces. Mounting the platform, some collapse to the floor, while others stand with arms raised, creating a spatial arc of colour and bodies, shaped by the contrasting black cloaks and glimpses of long grey dresses underneath. The women gather strength from each other, as the words shift from the questioning of loss to a defiance found in unity:

---

108 Festival of Co-operation Souvenir Programme, p. 37.

We are women and proclaim
This is the accepted time
Nations, people, men and women,
Children in the glowing morning
Make a ring around the aggressor;
Dispossess the dispossessor.
Build the warm alliances,
Of Humanity for Peace.[109]

To the strands of the *Marsaillaise*, the Well Hall Dance Drama Group portrayed a group of workers (identified by overalls and carrying red scarves) process in to choreography by de Moor, Barr's assistant. The mourning women's capes are removed and used by the workers to topple the effigies of Capital. After the ominous figures are destroyed, the choreography builds to a celebratory and unified climax as the mourners and workers intermingle, waving scarves in set patterns. Barr's dancers separate, encircling the workers standing on upper levels of the platform. Facing outwards, they repeat a simple side-to-side swinging pattern, one hand holding the long skirt, the other a scarf, their arms moving in a lateral figure eight path. Close-ups reveal a more sophisticated dance sequence than seen in earlier sections. A strong attack at the start of the swing sets the impetus travelling sequentially up through the torso to the head in a full body wave. Some of the women then kneel, facing each other in pairs, swinging flags overhead as the workers stop in powerful poses reminiscent of Soviet socialist realist statues. Proud and strong, their heads held high, they look out to the audience. One account of the pageant told of Barr's transformation of forty 'girls', 'of whom the majority knew nothing of movement and dancing, and made them proficient in three months by weekly lessons!'[110]

A procession of nations celebrated the international strength of the movement. The four countries of the British Isles were represented separately – England (men in overalls and women representing leisure in tennis whites) Scotland, Wales and Ireland – rather than Britain as a nation. Banners announced each group dressed in 'national' costumes – Hungary and Romania evoked a peasant past while black-wigged women in kimonos represented Japan. A woman dressed as the Statue of Liberty was followed by frontier icons for the USA contingent – Native Americans and cowgirls – presumably due to the preponderance of female participants. Groups representing Spain and the USSR broke from this pattern, their military style uniforms referencing armed struggles of the Spanish Civil War and the Soviet Revolution. Their entrance into the arena raised loud cheers of salute

109 Ibid.
110 Anon. Nov. 1938, 'Ourselves' *CWS newsletter*, Co-operative Archives v. 14, no. 8, pp. 1-2.

from the audience.

Two chariots enter, bearing the allegorical figures of Peace and Prosperity who climb onto the stage. Barr portrayed Peace, clothed in a diaphanous long white dress, long hair flowing loose, bearing a palm branch. Photographs of Barr reveal a contrast between the image of peace, as her right arm is held aloft in a clenched fist – a worker's salute. She recalled the criticisms to such an overt aggressive gesture (suggested by van Gyseghem) performed by the personification of Peace.[111] Prosperity was represented by a man, holding aloft the striped flag of the Co-operative movement. Male and female spirits of co-operation joined together as the lower levels of the platform circle around them, with a unified honour guard of workers and women, freed from their cloaks of grief. To close the event, Co-operative President R.G. Gosling read out a resolution renewing 'Faith in the Principles of Democracy, Freedom and Peace...', and the release of white pigeons carried the message of peace and freedom across Britain.

Festival of Music for the People, 1939

A five day Festival of Music for the People in 1939 included the last of the large pageants involving Bush and the dancers. On 1 April in the grand expanse of the Royal Albert Hall, Leona directed the Woodcraft Folk in the independently produced Music and the People Pageant. Bush was chairman of the festival committee, with directorial support from John Allen, one of Unity Theatre's directors. Following the modified Parkerian formula, episodes integrated spectacle, music, song and movement with fictional narrative interspersed with historically authentic moments. Mixing past and present, actors portrayed classical composers Handel and Beethoven, while artist and activist William Morris was followed by Paul Robeson singing spirituals with John Payne and his 'Negro Choir'. Such a mixture reinforces the perception among proponents of a British leftist culture that the workers, the people, should share the cultural heritage attributed to the bourgeoisie. Bush was particularly concerned to broaden workers' exposure to classical music,[112] commissioning scores from contemporary British composers.

Episode 1 introduced Singers, Dancers and Players as each proclaimed their links to the past through social dances, reinforcing communal bonds in the present:

> We are the Dancers. Today we provide
> The Lambeth Walk and the Palais Glide;
> Yesterday the Barn-Dance, the Polka and the Waltz,
> And earlier still, in the streets and fields,

---

111 Von Sturmer, op.cit., 31, see also Nicholas (2007) op.cit. p. 114.
112 Richard Hanlon and Mike Waite (1998) 'Communism and British Classical Music' in Andy Croft (ed.) *A Weapon in the Struggle.*

The Furry, the Maypole and the Hobby-horse.
Do you remember, as you tread the floor,
How your fathers danced it long before
And their fathers' fathers, and what it was for?...[113]

Accompanying the dances invoked in the text, a rural past destroyed by industrialisation was represented in movement by Woodcraft Folk dancers in Leona's arrangements of traditional choreography. Although there is substantial documentation of festival planning, the involvement of the Unity Dance Group is unclear. Payment was made to Kate Eisenstaedt and programme notes list the Unity Dance Group in Episode 6, the French Revolution, however, the group is not mentioned in published accounts of the performance. Ruby Ginner's assistance in staging the original form of the *Carmagnole* was acknowledged in the programme. Earlier letters to Bush reveal deep divisions amongst Unity dancers, with four resigning just prior to the pageant.[114] There is the possibility that the entire group disbanded.

Hall's unpublished autobiography described the dances viewed in rehearsal. He found the folk dances 'almost unbelievably dull – English folk dances would break the heart of any choreographer'. In contrast, Leona surpassed herself in the *Carmagnole* which Hall describes as a vigorous circling section with contrast between the 'regular rhythms of the outside groups and the wild irregular rhythm of the central circle'. The Woodcraft Folk dancers performed with precision and rhythmic sensitivity, 'fierce enough to frighten any aristocrat',[115] highly appropriate for an episode about the French Revolution that ends with the *Marsaillaise*.

Representations of 'the people' in Britain

The creation of dances influenced by ideologies tinged with Marxism and visions of art as a political tool necessitated a particular type of legibility with diverse modes of symbolic expression. Pageants such as the *Festival of Labour* and *Towards To-morrow* offered nostalgic images of the mythical 'merrie England', followed by the symbolic destruction of the tools of industrialisation. The pageants Bush helped stage occurred just prior to and during the Popular Front period, sponsored by organisations with broader socialist ideals despite having Communist Party members at their organisational helms.[116] Deeper

---

113 Scenario for Pageant, Music and the People, LC Plays, List 1, Vol. 10, British Library
114 Letters to Alan Bush from David Goodall, 5 May 1938 and George Beard, 7 May 1938. ABC BL MS MUS 453, v. 128.
115 Hall, unpublished autobiography, op.cit. pp. 137a and 138b.
116 In *Towards Tomorrow*, Bush, pageant director André van Gyseghem and the author of the script, Montagu Slater were all members of the Communist Party, as was the author of the Music for the People Pageant, Randall Swingler. See Wallis (1998) op.cit., pp. 54, 59.

schisms emerge through closer analysis of the dances, traceable to class divisions and national attitudes towards modernisation's impact on society.

In London, the workers in *Towards To-morrow* metaphorically destroyed the bricks, mortar and metal of factories, revealing significant differences in attitudes towards industrialisation, the past and the future. Later episodes portrayed a return to the idyllic past of village life, embodied in the utopian co-operative experiment of New Lanark. An organic community emerged out of the bonds of working together on the land, one which vanished with industrialisation. A nostalgic and sentimental identity was constructed that permeated cultural representations during the interwar period, conveying longing for a utopian countryside, with the BBC reinforcing perceptions of the national character through its broadcasts. The evocations of pastoral and non-industrial landscape were also taken up by the left, in opposition to the evils of capitalism arising from advances in technology.[117] In 1935 a London *Times* critic proclaimed Barr's work as 'essentially original and essentially English'.[118] Significantly, reviews and articles constantly stressed how Barr's work encapsulated and dramatised aspects of the *English* workers' existence.

Overt symbolism conveyed through various theatrical modes represented mythical versions of the past. Wallis notes how Parker's pageant form exemplifies the invention of tradition linked to different international left political movements and constructs of national identity.[119] The Music for the People Festival in 1939 provides an example of 'ideological production' during the Popular Front period, just prior to the outbreak of World War II. This period witnessed a celebration of the 'folk' as 'the People', the dance themes evoking rural labourers rather than those affected by technological advances of modernity.

By the late 1930s, classical ballet was praised for its socially conscious possibilities. Unity Theatre Weekly Bulletins in 1938 contained notices about Antony Tudor's London Ballet and there were hints about potential involvement of ballet and opera groups with Unity's activities.[120] Antony Tudor's *Dark Elegies* (1937) was praised for its theme, the tale of loss and hopes of a fishing village equated with the everyday, particularly England's 'island race': '*Dark Elegies* is valuable because it is a revelation of human nature, and hence a protest against every kind of inhumanity'.[121] This perspective signals a shift from 1933 when the British delegation of the

117 Martin J. Wiener (1981) *English Culture and the Decline of the Industrial Spirit, 1850-1980.*

118 Anon. (1935) 'The Arts Theatre, Dance-Drama Group', *The Times*, 12 February.

119 Wallis (1995) op.cit.

120 Anon. (1937) New Theatre, no. 2 Unity Theatre Collection, THM 9/3/1, box 1

121 Lawrence Gowing(1939) 'Ballet: A Choreographer to Watch', *New Theatre*, August, 1:1, p. 22.

Workers' Theatre Movement travelled to the USSR for the First Olympiad of workers' theatre. Their first exposure to proletarian culture was a classical ballet performance in Leningrad: '[it] came as quite a shock because the WTM had been expelling members for such major transgressions of the revolutionary cultural code as using props. To have suggested producing anything as traditional as the equivalent of a classical ballet would have been heresy.'[122] The retention of ballet in the Soviet Union was a surprise to American visitors as well, as explored in Chapter 1.

A fundamental difference between the American workers dance movement which flourished during the early 1930s and the London-based groups was the former's proximity to a unique period in which major modern dancers codified their movement philosophies in techniques still taught today, integrally linked to their choreography. British modern dancers faced a different artistic milieu, without the broader institutional structures supporting left-wing American dancers. After Barr left Dartington, the Co-operative Society and Unity Theatre appear to be the only organisations consistently linked to left-wing dance. The Dance Drama Group's diverse repertory meant that Barr could structure performances to suit different audiences, whether at venues such as Steiner Hall, at Communist Party social events in town halls, or at Unity's Britannia Street studio and their Goldington Street Theatre.

Critical scrutiny was extremely limited in British specialist journals and mainstream periodicals. Coverage of performances was rare, and the level of analysis often superficial. Hall's writings proved an exception, but the most revealing of these remained unpublished. Workers' theatre bulletins functioned more as member notice boards than circulating the level of critical debates seen in American publications. A British *New Theatre* (the Official Organ of the Unity Theatre Club and Left Book Club) commenced publication in 1937, and sporadically appeared during the war under the title *The Call*, however, a full run has not been located. Post-war issues of *New Theatre* began to address critical issues at the level seen in the American journal of the same name.

Extensive research into a British workers dance uncovered only a handful of dancer-choreographers, each working in different styles. Barr's American dance training occurred at an early stage of Graham's development after breaking away from Denishawn. At the time Graham was working towards developing the dramatically dynamic attack and economy of gesture seen in *Heretic* (1929). Although the Workers Dance League was formed after Barr left New York, there is a possibility she was aware of early agit-prop dances. Writing in 1950, Hall compared Barr's technique to the level of Graham's in the early 1920s and a lack of

---

122 Chambers (1989), op.cit. p. 32.

grounding in dance traditions (presumably technique), contributed to her isolation from other choreographers working at the time.[123]

Two London-based choreographers were from the Central European strand of modern dance which brought *Ausdruckstanz* principles of expression and movement to England: Eisenstaedt studied with Laban and pageant choreographer Helen Elton with Bodenwieser. They were working apart from their mentors, except for Bodenwieser's brief period of teaching in England during 1934. Others involved in pageants had international roots, such as American Louise Soelberg as noted above, while Margaret Leona was a folk dancer and vocal coach in Unity productions. Recreational dance classes taught by Eisenstaedt and Barr were heralded as a leisure activity instead of an overtly political tool. Rather than emphasising the dance's potential to express a working class consciousness, the focus was on the health benefits of dance-drama, its accessibility to all in addition to a creative component. Advertisements were aimed at the converted – as members of a co-operative society or linked to Unity Theatre. A women's health movement was publicised in the *Dancing Times* and an article about Barr's Dance Drama dance style was sub-titled 'A Creative Expression of Physical Fitness' in the journal for the Co-operative Wholesale Society employees.[124]

The Co-operative Movement provided opportunities for performing politicised modern dance in pageants in addition to sponsoring folk dance groups. Bush held strong opinions about movement-music relationships, with themes inextricably bound to his political beliefs. Crucially, he appears to have left the dance component to the dancers: the creation of movement itself. His assistant, Michael Tippett who also composed music for Barr, reflected that 'The Pageant of Labour must clearly be the high-water mark of the movement, which Alan to a considerable extent initiated to provide music with left-wing texts for performance by sympathetically inclined amateur choral societies. This movement was, more or less, swept aside at the outcome of war, simply because so many other concerns unified the nation.'[125]

John White, a member of the Woodcraft Folk during the 1930s and for years afterwards, reflected on the period and the extent of the group's political agenda. The Woodcraft Folk offered an alternative to the Scouts, for boys, girls and young people, with folk dance featured among its activities. Its founding principles reflected a broadly socialist ideology: one of equality regardless of class, joint ownership of the means of production, and

---

123 Hall, Draft, 'The Modern Scene in English Ballet', F. Hall Archives, NRCD.
124 Anon. (1938) 'Dance Drama: A Creative Expression of Physical Fitness', *Ourselves*, 14:8, August, pp. 1-2;
125 Alan Bush (1980), *In My Eighth Decade & other Essays*, p. 106.

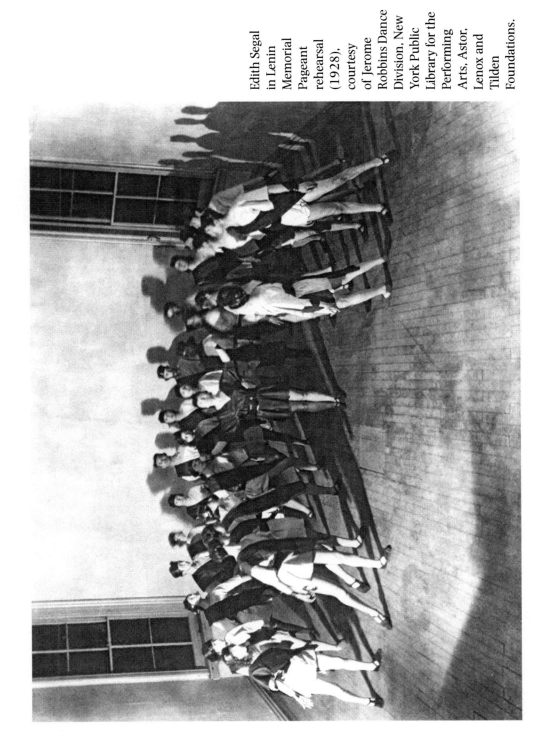

Edith Segal in Lenin Memorial Pageant rehearsal (1928), courtesy of Jerome Robbins Dance Division, New York Public Library for the Performing Arts, Astor, Lenox and Tilden Foundations.

Edith Segal, Lenin Memorial
Pageant (1928), Madison
Square Garden, courtesy
of Jerome Robbins Dance
Division, New York Public
Library for the Performing
Arts, Astor, Lenox and Tilden
Foundations.

Edith Segal, undated, courtesy of Jerome Robbins Dance Division, New York Public Library for the Performing Arts, Astor, Lenox and Tilden Foundations.

Nature Friends
Dance Group,
undated.
summer camp
at Lake Midvale,
New Jersey,
courtesy of
Jerome Robbins
Dance Division,
New York Public
Library for the
Performing Arts,
Astor, Lenox
and Tilden
Foundations.

Edith Segal, *The Belt Goes Red* (1930) Lenin Memorial Pageant at Memorial Square Garden. courtesy of Jerome Robbins Dance Division, New York Public Library for the Performing Arts, Astor, Lenox and Tilden Foundations.

UNIVERSITY OF WINCHESTER LIBRARY

Helen Elton c. 1934, photo by Yvonne Gregory, courtesy of Camera Press.

Kate Eisenstaedt's Central European dance class (1934), photo courtesy of Dancing Times.

War Dance, choreography by Kate Eisenstaedt. Towards To-morrow Pageant of Co-operation, 1938, photo by R Fox Ltd.

Ballet of
Mourning Women,
choreography by
Margaret Barr,
Towards To-
morrow Pageant
of Co-operation,
1938, photo by R
Fox Ltd.

Robert Henry Johnson and Amara Tabor Smith in *Sailing Away* (2010). photo by Anthony Lindsey, courtesy of Zaccho Dance Theatre.

Mira II: Norman Rutherford, Keith Hennessy, Jess Curtis and Kim Epifano in Contraband's *Mira II* (1994), photo by Marty Sohl, courtesy of Sara Shelton Mann.

Jules Beckman,
Jess Curtis and
Keith Hennessy
in *Ice, Car, Cage*
(1997/98),
photo by
Ray Chung,
courtesy of
Keith Hennessy.

Debby Kajiyama and Lena Gatchalian in the Dance Brigade's *Cave Women... The Next Incarnation!* (2003), photo by Andy Mogg, courtesy of Krissy Keefer.

Anusha
Subramanyam
in classical
bharatanatyam
choreography.
Murugan
(2001),
photo by Vipul
Sangoi.

Anusha Subramanyam in her own choreography, *From the Heart* (2010), photo by Vipul Sangoi.

Mavin Khoo in *Sufi:Zen* (2010), choreography by Gauri Sharma Tripathi with Khoo and Jonathan Lunn. Akademi production at the South Bank Centre, photo by Vipul Sangoi.

Sapnay/Dreams (2005) choreography by Mavin Khoo and Gauri Sharma Tripathi, dancer facing camera, Rachel Waterman Akademi production, Trafalgar Square, photo by Peter Schiazza.

Awaz/Voices (2006), choreography by Chitra Sundaram, dancers (left to right) Divya Kasturi, Amina Khayyam and Prarthana Purkayastha, Trafalgar Square, photo by Vipul Sangoi.

significantly, the potential for communal agency to affect social change.[126] White was a backstage volunteer at the Festival of Music for the People, assigned to assist Paul Robeson, and has vivid memories of Unity Theatre productions, attesting to the links between the left-wing organisations and the more mainstream Co-operative Movement. Unity Theatre emerges as a key institution in the brief history of a British workers' dance. Soelberg and Leona created choreography for living newspaper and mass recitation productions. Ironically, the close relationship between the left-wing theatre group and the politically informed dance could have thwarted dance's ability to gain a foothold. Rather than evolving as separate entities, Unity productions integrated set movement for non-dancers, usurping the development of agit-prop dance groups.

To what extent can the British dances be considered 'workers' dance? Alan Bush, Margaret Barr and Teda de Moor were from relatively privileged backgrounds unlike many of their American dance counterparts who were born to immigrant factory workers. Significantly, Barr's group is only listed as the *Workers'* Dance and Drama Group in the Co-operative Movement's *Towards To-morrow* pageant programme. In this instance Barr's professional group was augmented by workers – or at least members of the co-operative movement. Writing about the left-wing theatre movement, Jon Clark distinguishes between labels, arguing that perhaps 'socialist' theatre is a more accurate term than 'workers' theatre, the former emphasises political aims rather than participants' origins'. The significance of Unity Theatre also lies in the working relationship between amateurs and professionals.[127]

The dissolution of the short-lived left-wing dance groups in the UK has clear markers. In 1939 Barr emigrated to New Zealand and Bush's musical work took him away from London for much of the year, a time marked by internal tensions in the Unity Dance Group resulting in the resignation of some of its members. The last of the pageants occurred prior to the outbreak of World War II in 1939 with the involvement of the Woodcraft Folk. Once war was declared, the ideological imperatives shifted, as they did among the American radical dancers.

---

126 John White, interview with author, 15 August 2005.
127 Clark (1979) op cit. fn. 9, p.236.

Chapter 3

Politics, Dance and the Personal: Redefining Performance in the San Francisco Bay Area

'*Contraband is art made into life, life made into ritual; and ritual made into therapeutic healing. Contraband is exactly what our present age requires.*'
Eric Hellman, 1990[1]

'*No one in the dance scene touches the ugly pus-filled truths of politics with the irony and fury of Ms Keefer, and Mr Hennessy and company make ritual inseparable from a sexy life-affirming corporeality.*'
Ann Murphy, 2004[2]

As a confluence of factors made New York City home to a revolutionary dance movement in the 1930s, a unique environment exists in San Francisco, shaping it into the bastion of postmodern dance theatre and performance rich in political and social themes. Whereas earlier manifestations of political dance drew from Marxist tenets with aims of raising class consciousness, the San Francisco strand embodies broader sources of inspiration, expanding conceptualisations of 'the political', reinforcing communal identities and highlighting a range of topical issues and race and class based inequities. The California city evokes diverse iconic images ranging from its landscapes (natural and manmade) to its ideological and cultural symbols. Its dramatic geography creates fog that rivals the legendary London haze of Charles Dickens' novels. It is a city of hills, breathtaking vistas, crowded skyscrapers juxtaposed against the expanse of the bay. It is the birthplace of numerous alternative trends in lifestyle and philosophy and their intersections with art and politics. North Beach, once home to Italian immigrants, still boasts the City Lights Bookstore and Vesuvio's bar, frequented by writers and cultural icons Jack Kerouac, Allen Ginsberg and Lawrence Ferlinghetti. The corner of Haight and Ashbury Streets remains a popular destination for tourists in their search for remnants of the 'Summer of Love' of 1968 when sex, drugs and rock 'n roll were freely available. The city hosts the world's largest and most openly gay, lesbian and transgendered population. Influences from Asian and Hispanic cultures permeate the architecture, food and philosophy towards life. Recurring threats of earthquakes, mudslides, and fires attest to the inability to fully control nature, despite continued attempts to do so. Life is often lived on the edge, attracting a rich mix of migrants in quests for intellectual, spiritual, artistic and political answers.

---

1 Eric Hellman (1990) 'Raw Emotion,' *S.F. Weekly*, 4 April, p. 18.
2 Ann Murphy (2004) 'The Spin Room,' *Dance View Times*, 2, no. 40, 25 October, http://www.danceviewtimes.com (accessed on 5 March 2005).

The area's vibrant dance community has a long history, encompassing all genres of the art form. Isadora Duncan is heralded as a San Francisco native, her innovative and rebellious art laid the foundations for succeeding generations who established modern dance traditions. In contrast, the San Francisco Ballet, established in 1933 as the San Francisco Opera Ballet, contributed to the emergence of a national classical ballet canon, premiering the first full-length *Nutcracker* in the USA in 1944. Under Ronn Guidi's directorship between 1965 and 1998, the Oakland Ballet's reconstructions of seminal works by Bronislava Nijinska came to be considered international masterpieces. In the immediate period after World War II, new opportunities opened to train in dance, from recreational and folk dance styles to classes aimed at a working class clientele. The Oakland Parks and Recreation Department dance programme opened in 1947, headed by Ruth Beckford who performed with Katherine Dunham. East coast modern dance styles which had roots in the west through the influence of Ruth St Denis, Ted Shawn and Denishawn alumni, were re-established in the Bay Area during the 1940s. Carol Beals brought Martha Graham's technique classes to the Peters Wright Creative Dance School, founded in 1912,[3] while Graham-trained Welland Lathrop also settled in the area in 1946, later teaching at San Francisco State University, reinforcing a creative flow between east and west coast dance centres.

The intersection between dance and social issues has deep roots. In 1937, members of the San Francisco Dance Council premiered a collaborative piece, *Changing World*, accompanied in some sections by avant-garde composer Lou Harrison's music. Lenore Peters-Wright, of the Peters Wright Creative Dance School, choreographed the *Women Walk Free* section, with others entitled *Town and Country, All Women are One,* and *Life, Liberty and the Pursuit of Happiness*.[4] During the years Bennington Summer School decamped from Vermont to Oakland's Mills College, José Limón premiered *War Lyrics* (1940). His first group dance integrated text by William Archibald in an indictment of the devastating impact of war on women.[5] Dance classes taught by Bonnie Bird, Lenore Job and Gloria Unti (who went on to become a dance advocate and teacher to marginalised young people) were also offered at the California Labor School, linking the art form to union activities. The 1947 schedule entitled *Education for Peace and Security* offered Mimi Kagan's dance classes based on her training with Hanya Holm.[6]

From the late 1950s, Bay Area choreographers began to re-define dance through movement explorations with a spirit of experimentation and

---

3 Joanna G. Harris, email to author, 25 March 2007.
4 Joanna G. Harris, emails to author, 25-27 March 2007.
5 Margaret Lloyd *The Borzoi Book of Modern Dance*, [orig. pub. 1949], pp. 204-206.
6 Joanna G. Harris, email to author, 25 March 2007; interview with author, 18 October 2005. See also Joanna Gewertz Harris (2009) *Beyond Isadora: Bay Area Dancing, 1915-65*.

innovation, led by Anna Halprin. A dance boom in the 1970s attracted numerous dancers and choreographers from New York's dance mecca, drawn by the climate and artistic freedom. Dance was already institutionalised in higher education (Mills College, San Francisco State, and the University of California at Berkeley) while at the grassroots level, numerous studios established a wide variety of styles. Small performance venues provided choreographic platforms for the burgeoning alternative dance community, its practitioners encompassing African-American specialisms, non-western styles, contact improvisation, as well as modern dance and ballet. Existing autonomously and at times in precarious financial conditions, independent dancers, teachers and choreographers created their own organisational structures and support systems, such as the Bay Area Dance Coalition, further reinforcing a sense of community among the disparate artists. In 1977 a defining characteristic was noted which continues today: 'Dancers here expect to merge lifestyle with dancing, dancing from the self, for the self and for and with the community'.[7] As detailed later in the chapter, Dancers' Group and CounterPULSE exemplify institutional networking and funding which helps sustain the field. As the economic decline of 2008 devastated federal and state funding sources, private finance, philanthropic grants and social media fundraising campaigns are increasingly vital. Volunteer and bartering systems, support from within the dance field itself, also underpin an exchange network.

Rather than providing a comprehensive history of the alternative dance scene, I focus on significant practitioners with longevity as performers, teachers and choreographers, some of whom moved from the margins into the mainstream. Others have regular international teaching and touring commitments, influencing dance practices in Europe, Asia and Central and South America. Their iconoclastic aesthetic styles explore a myriad of social and political themes. Representative works exemplify the trajectory of a socially or politically inspired postmodern dance and performance in the 1980s and 1990s that moved into the 21st century. Creative relationships with musicians, vocalists, writers, designers, visual and media artists, shape collective and multi-disciplinary approaches in works that reflect upon the body, the meanings it carries and exploring its boundaries.

Reviewing the rich sources of dance criticism in the years since I initially wrote about the scene, many new names, venues and festivals attest to the continued vibrancy of the field, reinforcing the need for an account of 21st century dance in the Bay Area to come from within, from someone with a more immediate perspective than I can offer. This chapter offers a partial update, however, emphasising vibrant collaborative relationships and creative processes that distinguish the area's community. Dance critic

---

7 Eleanor Rachel Luger (1977) 'Taking Care of Business,' *Dance Magazine*, January, p.26.

Rita Felciano's regular column in the *SF Bay Guardian* offers snapshots of select performances, an overview of 2011 highlighting how dancers have managed to survive despite diminished public funding. Increasing numbers produce works outside performance venues, moving into galleries, museums and back into their own studios with informal showings as well as utilising more of the Bay Area's iconic public spaces in site specific work.[8] Interactions between scholar-practitioners at universities and the wider dance community are helping to shape a more publicly accessible intellectual critique.

The foundations of the contemporary dance ecology reveal a defining community ethos and collaborative impulse. Within the larger Bay Area, 799 organisations exist 'that create, foster, teach, promote, present or in other ways, either wholly as their mission, or for a majority of their activities', as recorded in a partial census of activities in 2013.[9] The analyses that follow here draw on my own performance viewing over an eight year period and during repeated visits, supplemented by reviews, archival material and video recordings of some productions. Margaret Jenkins' dances subtly embed topical themes through an intellectually rigorous dance formalism supported by design, music and occasionally text. Joe Goode constructs non-linear narratives and strong characterisations drawn from popular culture, often using subversive humour. Joanna Haigood's extensive research shapes theatrical representations of the past linked to social histories of specific sites focusing on discrimination and oppression, using aerial techniques or exploring the pedestrian on city streets. Jo Kreiter's site dances focus on aspects of female empowerment, the local community and the environment. Sara Shelton Mann links the personal, the political and the mythical in dances drawing on a range of physical and theatrical techniques. Mann has been a catalyst behind multiple manifestations of the group Contraband, out of which a number of performer-creators have followed their own paths. Keith Hennessy's eclectic collaborations and confrontational solos politicise the body in unique ways. The experience of immigrants from the Philippines inspired the work of Pearl Ubungen in the 1990s while the larger diasporic and ethnic dance community requires a chapter (or a book) of its own. Feminist principles inform Krissy Keefer's dances in which a strong polemic is blended with high production values and a vibrant physicality. For many in the area, utopian impulses are mixed with a belief in the ability to change society, informing a perception of art as cultural activism which shape provocative and entertaining performances. Key words recurred in interviews and publications that distinguish San Francisco's blend of

8 Rita Felciano (2011) 'Top flight: Year in Dance 2011', *SF Bay Guardian*.
9 See the Dancers' Group report by Wayne Hazzard, Michelle Lynch, Laurie MacDougall and Kegan Marling, *Dance Activity in the San Francisco Bay Area: A Report on Key Benchmarks*, which drew information from the California Cultural Data Project.

politics, social issues and dance from New York's earlier manifestation: spirit, soul, ritual, myth, tribal and multifarious communities. The eclectic mix of aesthetic styles and themes evident in the early 21st century dance scene arose in part out of the paths laid by those examined here.

Staging the environment

San Francisco's reputation as a hotbed of liberal radicalism is so pervasive that it was frequently evoked by ultra-conservatives in scare tactics during the 2006 national mid-term elections. Advertisements warned that voting Democrats into power threatened to spread the city's values into America's heartland while the San Francisco Democrat Representative Nancy Pelosi is a magnet for Republican and right-wing vitriol. The poet Kenneth Rexroth observed that San Francisco 'is the only city in the United States which was not settled overland by the spreading puritan tradition.... It has been settled mostly, in spite of all the romances of the overland migration, by gamblers, prostitutes, rascals and fortune seekers who came across the [Panama] Isthmus and around the Horn. They had their faults, but they were not influenced by [Puritan leader] Coton Mather....'[10] On this foundation, a rebellious outpost was transformed over the years into a cosmopolitan site where tolerance for difference and progressive politics are perceived to reign. The Gold Rush of 1848, an influx of Asian immigrants, and arrival of refugee activists from unsuccessful revolutions in Europe, all contributed to the area's rebellious and non-hegemonic ethos.

Essays in the anthology *Reclaiming San Francisco: History, Politics, Culture* detail the myriad forms of activism and resistance that lend credence to the city's reputation. The local historian and activist Chris Carlsson charts the significant rise and decline of organised labour power, detailing how the General Strike of 1934 resulted in an unusual relationship between labourers and their employers. Unionisation of workers reached unprecedented proportions, extending to all areas of blue collar employment, with restaurants achieving almost complete unionisation by the 1950s. Such collective power and resultant stability was welcomed for a time by the ruling elite; however, workers' power was gradually chipped away with the rise of the Cold War, the decline of shipbuilding and associated industries, and technological advances that fundamentally altered manual working conditions and the employer/employee power relationship. In addition, the financial cornerstone of the area shifted towards a service-based economy, as the power brokers proposed to transform the city into a homestead for globalised corporate businesses. A belief in collective power remains, however, as activists battle to resist the 'Manhattanisation' and 'touristification' of

---

10 Kenneth Rexroth quoted by James Brook (1998) in 'Preface', in Chris Carlsson and Nancy Peters, eds., *Reclaiming San Francisco: History, Politics, Culture*, p. x.

the city.[11] The historian Richard A. Walker argues that in order to protect their urbanity, San Franciscans tend to 'move in counterflow to mainstream ideas of modernity... they never bought wholeheartedly into the ideology of progress'.[12] In the wake of World War II, extensive redevelopment plans were set into place. Although not completely successful in all its challenges, a revolution of the local populace succeeded (at least temporarily) in restricting the extent of urban regeneration which saw over a thousand working-class homes demolished, limited freeway construction and saved some historic buildings and iconic cablecars.

The gap between rich and poor has increased exponentially with the economic surge accompanying the dot-com boom in nearby Silicon Valley. An influx of wealth resulted in a middle-class exodus to more affordable suburbs while the percentage of the population in lower and upper income brackets has increased. The 2010 census also reveals significant demographic shifts with a decline in white and African American populations and increases in Asian and Hispanic/Latino numbers living in the Bay Area.[13] Interrelationships between class and racial inequities exist, as feminist bell hooks asserts:

> Class matters. Race and gender can be used as screens to deflect attention away from the harsh realities class politics exposes. Clearly, just when we should all be paying attention to class, using race and gender to under-stand and explain its new dimensions, society, even our government, say let's talk about race and racial injustice. It is impossible to talk meaning-fully about ending racism without talking about class...[14]

Those who keep the city functioning through their manual labour – such as cleaners, shopworkers, food service staff – resist being priced out of their neighbourhoods by gentrification, which takes its toll on the racially and economically marginalised. The rise of the computer and internet industries and the increasing prominence of the city as a Pacific Rim financial centre have led to new tensions between financially secure newcomers and established communities whose livelihoods and homes are threatened.

A history of progressive politics and collective action was consolidated with the emergence of the 1960s counterculture movement. At the University of California at Berkeley, the Free Speech protest movement of 1964-65 spurred on a decade of national student anti-establishment and

11 Chris Carlsson (1998) 'The Progress Club: 1934 and Class Memory'; Randy Shaw (1998) 'Tenant Power in San Francisco'; Rob Waters and Wade Hudson (1998) 'The Tenderloin: What Makes a Neighborhood', *Reclaiming San Francisco*, ibid.
12 Richard A. Walker, 'An Appetite for the City,' ibid. p. 13.
13 Tyche Hendricks (2006) 'Rich City, Poor City,' *San Francisco Chronicle*. Bay Area Census, http://www.bayareacensus.ca.gov/bayarea.htm, accessed 12 October 2013.
14 bell hooks (2000) *Where We Stand: Class Matters*, p. 7.

anti-war demonstrations, inspired by the achievements of the Civil Rights movement. According to James Miller, the impact of McCarthyism during the 1950s had silenced leftist activists, but new voices emerged in the 1960s, in which revolutionary praxis had moved away from the concept of the 'proletariat', shifting towards a belief in 'students as an agency of change'.[15] Dissatisfaction with society, economic shifts and the rising de-personalisation of corporate life has made San Francisco a strong magnet for migrants. Activists and artists looked to the creation of new senses of community and political ideals, searching for answers to existential questions that shaped a generation's outlook in the face of mutual annihilation nuclear threats between the West and the Soviet Union.

By the mid-1980s, California's relatively rich funding environment was diminished by the passage of Proposition 13 in 1978, which capped increases in property tax. Over the years a reduction in tax revenues has chipped away at the state's infrastructure with arts funding taking a heavy toll. The 'trickle-down economics' of Reaganomics and the 'moral majority' political and social agenda were highly divisive. A rise in AIDS-related deaths hit the local dance community hard, and identity issues moved to the fore of artistic agendas, firmly linking the social and political with the artistic. Out of this fervour emerged expanded visions and functions for dance: as ritual; as the expression of gender, ethnic and sexual identities; as a mouthpiece for the disenfranchised; and as hegemonic critique. The choreographed protests that Susan Leigh Foster analyses continue to take place, as activists protested about civil rights, war, economic and social inequalities, and environmental damage. Civil disobedience strategies involve different levels of bodily control and collective movement, ranging from ACT UP events of the 1990s to the more recent Occupy SF and Occupy Oakland protests of the early 21st century.[16]

Dance forerunners: Anna Halprin, Mangrove and Tumbleweed

Although New York City is generally hailed as the birthplace of the postmodern dance movement, Bay Area practitioners also forged influential paths. Anna Halprin is known for her use of dance as a healing art, although reappraisals of her early innovations note the extent to which she presaged new approaches to dance as a social and community art form. Moving to the Bay Area at the end of World War II, Halprin worked in conjunction with Graham-trained Welland Lathrop in their San Francisco studio from 1948 to 1956. Movement experimentation blossomed beyond codified vocabularies, with such seminal choreographers as Merce Cunningham, Trisha Brown,

15 Quoted by James Miller (1987, 1994) *Democracy is in the Streets: From Port Huron to the Siege of Chicago*, p. 87.
16 Susan Leigh Foster (2003) 'Choreographies of Protest', *Theatre Journal*.

Yvonne Rainer, and Steve Paxton travelling west to participate in Halprin's workshops on the wooden dance deck of her Marin County home.

The formation of San Francisco Dancers' Workshop in 1955 saw the transformation of movement experiments into performances where their work 'with new *forms* of dance led to new *uses* of dance'.[17] Halprin's material placed her in the avant-garde, in turning to the everyday, in moving performance out of the proscenium stage, and drawing in and from the community in the creation of dance. City streets became the performance venue, motivated in part by financial practicalities that turned political in disputes with city authorities. In 1967, Halprin challenged city ordinances requiring a permit for gatherings of 25 or more people. Groups of 24 people carried blank placards, walking a block apart from the other group, and literally taking art to the streets and to new audiences who were free to imagine their own protest slogans on the placards.[18]

Halprin's dances encapsulated issues at the centre of social debates in the headlines. *Ceremony of Us* (1969) confronted racial prejudices by bringing together black and white dancers. Racial and sexual tensions were worked out through movement, transformed into performance material. Initially segregated by race, the lines of colour crossed physically in a 'snake dance' which drew in the audience. One writer described it as 'A ceremony of coming together, of forming as a group, performing together, of discovering each other and beginning to work as a group... [leading to] the discovery of difference, of separation and conflict, of racial competition, identity, strength, [and] soul'.[19]

A fundamental shift was manifest in the perception of dance as a transformative practice, one which would create change in the individual, and thus society. Halprin emphasised a collective creativity while recognising the potential power of the audience in theatre dances such as *Five-Legged Stool* (1962) and *Parades and Changes* (1965) which responded to the cultural circumstances and castings of the individual performance situations. The critic and historian Janice Ross labels the events as 'urban rituals,' distinguished from the ritualised theatre spectacles of modern dancers such as Martha Graham. Halprin's practice involves 'rewriting the role of the spectator, making her a witness: an individual who is present at the performance to support it with her attention rather than to look to it for diversion or entertainment,' in order to 'initiate an experience of perpetual awakening'.[20] She remains a major presence, restaging the influential

---

17 Anna Halprin (1995) Rachel Kaplan, ed, *Moving Towards Life: Five Decades of Transformational Dance*, p. xi (emphasis in the original).
18 Ibid. p. 11.
19 James T. Burns [orig. pub. 1969] 'Microcosm in Movement,' ibid, p. 166.
20 Janice Ross (2004) 'Anna Haprin's Urban Rituals'. *The Drama Review*, pp. 49 and 51. Also see Janice Ross (2007) *Anna Halprin: Experience as Dance*.

Parades and Changes in the Berkeley Museum in February 2013, its nudity and task-based choreographic processes ground-breaking when it premiered in 1965. As Halprin explains, the transformation of everyday movement into a dance separated her work from that of Judson which retained the actions as 'realistic tasks'.[21] Out of the early radical innovations, others continued to work in collectives to forge different performative paths.

In 1973 the all-female collective Tumbleweed was co-founded by Theresa Dickinson, Terry Sendgraff, and Rhodessa Jones, with Jon Raskin as musical director. Engaging with the local community, their works were staged in city spaces, clubs and places such as San Quentin Federal Prison. Interspersed with technically grounded dance phrases, Sendgraff's innovative acrobatics on the motivity trapeze, a single point aerial apparatus, expanded the spatial possibilities for dance. Tumbleweed members sang, danced, and acted in their challenges to the ideological mainstream. *Bare Soles* (1979), directed by Nora Burnett highlighted issues of poverty and sexism in the troubled low-income Tenderloin district where the performance was set.[22] Confrontational strategies contrasted to the ritual aura of Halprin's work, as Jones recalled: 'We were very powerful ... very *macha*, we were like gunslingers, we'd be very politically incorrect.'[23] Although Tumbleweed's collective ended in 1980, its members continued to influence the local arts community through their teaching, performing and activism.

The use of contact improvisation and collective creation not as process but as artistic product was advanced in the all-male group Mangrove. Founded in 1975 by James Tyler (1940-1989), Byron Brown, John LeFan and Curt Siddall, the group embodied a countercultural philosophy. Brown explained: 'We broke out of categories that everybody assumed you needed to be in; that we were a group of men, that we were very physically affectionate but it wasn't about sex; that we were talking onstage, that we were obviously improvising, that we had no plan, that we were using music but playing it ourselves. There were so many ways that we weren't normal.'[24] Ross compared Mangrove's autobiographical content to 'a dance version of a sit-com in a very positive way,' with each performer personalised and individualised through narrative as well as movement.[25] Eastern and Western philosophical and movement forms (akido, yoga and gymnastics), and non-dance theatrical practices shaped works which had a pre-determined beginning, but were unstructured beyond that, a

21 Ann Murphy (2013) 'Parades and Changes over the past 43 Years, an Interview with Anna Halprin', *Writing Dance*, 14 February 2013.
22 Janice Ross (1980) 'Bay Ways: A Climate for Free Spirits,' *Dance Magazine*,
23 Interview in Austin Forbord and Shelly Trott (2000) *Artists in Exile: A Story of Modern Dance in San Francisco*.
24 Bryan Brown, ibid.
25 Janice Ross, ibid.

contrast to Tumbleweed's political focus. One critic argued, 'The free flow of energy and movement is seen as an end in itself. There is no content, no meaning, nothing is communicated beyond affability and commitment'.[26] Entertaining the audience remained a priority for Mangrove, although the integration of emotional content allowed the dramatic and comedic elements inherent in relationships between dancing bodies to flourish.[27] As with other groups explored here, individual members of the collective had creative relationships with a wider network of artists. The non-profit Mixed Bag Productions was created by members of Mangrove and Sara Shelton Mann in 1977, establishing alternative production and support systems for project based activities.[28]

Ed Mock is another pioneer whose influence has been felt long beyond his years of teaching and inspiring local dancers. During the 1970s he was a teacher, performer, and mentor who worked with improvisation in his own company and in his classes. A leader of the experimental arts scene who died of AIDS related illnesses in 1986, he is described as a highly charismatic gay African-American performer. Mock's legacy continues in the work of students and collaborators who have become Bay Area stalwarts, including some performers discussed here – Mann, Wayne Hazzard, Joanna Haigood and Pearl Ubungen.[29]

Margaret Jenkins and the professionalisation of modern dance

A dance boom in the 1970s ushered in a new kind of professionalism, initiated in part by the return of Margaret Jenkins, who Felciano credits with helping to shape today's dance scene.[30] As a fifth generation San Francisco native, Jenkins draws together east and west coast artistic impulses. Art and politics were interlinked in her youth, as the child of a labour organiser and poet mother. Jenkins began her dance training with Bay Area pioneers, Lenore and Judy Job at the Peters Wright School of Dance, also studying with Lathrop and Unti.[31] Further training at the Julliard School in New York and at the University of California, Los Angeles, ensued before Jenkins spent

---

26 James Armstrong (1977) 'In Contact with Mangrove,' *Dance Magazine*, December, p. 43.

27 Cynthia Novack (1990) *Sharing the Dance*, p. 187.

28 Email communications from Keith Hennessy and Jess Curtis, 2 & 3 April 2013.

29 Rita Felciano (2013) 'In his footsteps: A new site specific work pays tribute to local legend Ed Mock', *SF Guardian*, http://www.sfbg.com/2013/06/12/his-footsteps?page=0,0, accessed July 28, 2013.

30 Rita Felciano (2003) 'A Rich Diversity,' *Dance View Times*, www.danceviewtimes.com/dvw/features/2003/bayareasurvey.html, accessed 29 December 2006.

31 Gloria Unti (b. 1924), daughter of Italian immigrants, co-founded the Performing Arts Workshop in 1965 which took dance into the more economically deprived areas of the city and has continued in its mission engage young people in the arts, see documentary video, http://www.youtube.com/watch?v=PWY8XVn_sYQ

twelve years as a special assistant to Merce Cunningham and performed with postmodern luminaries such as Twyla Tharp and Viola Farber, among others. Returning to the Bay Area in 1970, Jenkins began choreographing and significantly, teaching professional level modern dance classes. As Ross notes, Jenkins' roles as teacher and choreographic mentor are as crucial as her choreographic legacy, out of which former company members have become significant and distinctive choreographers in their own right.[32]

Jenkins perceives her artistic collaborations as a 'social activity,' evolving out of interactive creative relationships, with each artist able to comment on the work of the others.[33] Text takes on a significance with collaborative contributions from poet Michael Palmer. He explained that:

My role is not limited to that of writer nor hers strictly to that of choreographer. Rather, we evolve a work's structure together, its narrative (or non-narrative) structure, its image structure, and its movement structure. There may be more or less language, or none. There may be a 'silent' language that runs beneath the surface of the piece as a guide to choreographic decisions. There may be language interwoven with music, live language mixed with recorded, and so on.[34]

Other frequent collaborators are set and lighting designer Alexander V. Nichols, the composers Rinde Eckert and Paul Dresher, and the costume designer Sandra Woodall. Dense layers of information require a particular attentiveness by the viewer, with movement so rigorous that critic Deborah Jowitt claimed the dances 'make your brain ache'.[35]

Jenkins cites San Francisco's physical and artistic isolation as influential: 'You make art to find out where you are... The isolation of the west throws you back in profound ways. It demands you find your own concerns.'[36] Armed with a technically rigorous dance vocabulary and the experimental spirit of late 1960s New York City, Jenkins established an intellectually challenging format which defied easy access. The original Margaret Jenkins Dance Company (MJDC) premiered as a repertory company in 1974, gradually garnering critical acclaim and a broad audience base. Dancers are given tasks to explore in rehearsal, contributing movement and enabling them to maintain some stylistic individuality. Jenkins sustained a repertory company for twenty years, creating over sixty dances, and began crediting her dancers as co-choreographers. After working on a

32 Janice Ross (1984) 'Living on the Edge with Margaret Jenkins,' *Dance Magazine*, May, pp. 136-139; Janice Ross (1994) 'The End of the Beginning: The Margaret Jenkins Company at Twenty,' *Dance Magazine*, June, pp. 34-39.
33 Ross, ibid., p. 34.
34 Michael Palmer (no date) 'Crossroads/Collaboration Part 2,' *The Poetry Society Journal*,.
35 Quoted in Ross (1984), op.cit. p. 136.
36 Margaret Jenkins, quoted in Ross (1994) op.cit. p. 34.

project basis for ten years, she re-established the Margaret Jenkins Dance Company in 2004.

Themes range from the mundane to the esoteric in 'works that smother the viewer with overlapping patterns, steady streams of entrances and exits, articulate footwork and a breezy, springy attack'.[37] Although solid narrative threads are sometimes evident, there is an ambiguity through which multiple meanings extend beyond the concrete themes they reference. *Breathe Normally* (1999), about the tragic consequences of a car crash and based on an actual event, utilised performers ranged in age from 32 to 72. Her treatment allowed 'a specific event to resonate into a more universal meditation on life and death and on memory's coloring of the past'.[38] Ellie Klopp, a company member starting in 1985 and then associate assistant director of MJDC was credited as the overall director, defying traditional hierarchies of dance companies named after their founder.

The exquisite *Fault* (1996) was inspired by the unstable landmass upon which the state rests and arose out of a three-year residency at the University of California at Berkeley. The creative process involved contact with geologists, their study of earthquakes and other scholarly and metaphorical engagements with the word. According to Felciano, *Fault* proves that chaos theory is true, presented through unsentimental and non-literal explorations of walking and standing: the dance is 'about cause and effect... A dancer shakes a wrist and the energy shoots through space and changes all it touches.'[39] The MJDC's international presence is increasing, travelling to India and expanding intimate gestural foundations to accompany the expansive technical phrases. This is seen in *A Slipping Glimpse* (2006) where Nichols transformed the performance space with red platforms: 'One by one the dancers find individual ways to lower themselves onto the equally red floor. In a traditional greeting gesture, they fold their hands in front of their faces, then open them as if peering into a mirror or book. Then off they go, on communal, loping runs that move forward and also recoil back. Picking up gestures from each other, they pull and they yield.'[40] The company was joined by four classical Indian dancers from the Tanusree Shankar Dance Company while residencies in China also generated a trilogy of dances in 2009, working in Guangzhou with the Guangong Modern Dance Company and its deputy artistic director, Liu Qi.

37 Ross (1984) op.cit. p. 136.

38 Anna Kisselgoff (1999) 'When Fate is in the Driver's Seat,' *New York Times*, 1 April , http://www.nytimes.com, accessed December 27, 2006.

39 Rita Felciano (1996-1997) 'San Francisco Report: Floods, Faults and Loneliness,' *Dance View*, 14:1, p. 26.

40 Rita Felciano (2006) 'Multi-angle magic: Margaret Jenkins Dance Company gets Kaleidoscopic with 'A Slipping Glimpse',' *San Francisco Bay Guardian*, 23 May, http://www.sfbg.com, accessed 28 December 2006.

Despite the topical connotations in the title *Danger Orange*, which premiered just prior to the 2004 American presidential election, an overtly political dance retained a subtle approach to its theme. *Danger Orange* refers to the colour coded terror alerts instituted by the Department of Homeland Security (DHS), created after the 9/11 attacks. Perceived threats to the nation (or 'homeland') frequently announced Level Orange (indicating a high risk of terrorist attacks), the fourth highest level on the scale of five. The alerts were met with increasing scepticism when it was revealed that level changes were pushed through by politicians despite the DHS's own assessments.[41] The company's site-specific work was set at Justin Herman Plaza, an iconic public space located alongside the bayfront in downtown San Francisco. Framed by the Ferry Building and palm trees, the Vaillancourt Fountain is the plaza's centrepiece where water flows over an asymmetrical industrial-looking structure of concrete blocks into a basin around which tourists and office workers gather. The designer, Nichols, covered the fountain with orange netting, creating two large platforms for the dance action. Smaller boxes function both as pathways and cavernous spaces into which dancers are swallowed up. *Fractured Fictions* (2003) formed one section, danced to Patrick Grant's score, while Jay Cloidt added industrial sounds to those of modern warfare. Solos are interspersed between fleeting group sections and duets shift between intimate and tender relationships to aggressively virtuosic ones. Critic Rachel Howard proclaimed that that *Danger Orange* is not 'political art', but rather a work of 'visceral impact' shaped by intimacy of expression and complex spatial compositions. The connotations of the title were obvious, but the focus was on emotional resonances, Jenkins achieving a symbolically rich formalism, communicating the aftermath of events rather than dictating their causes in a subtle yet powerful treatment of social relationships.

Joe Goode Performance Group

Once labelled as the 'bad boy of modern dance',[42] Joe Goode has moved firmly into the cultural mainstream. During the 1970s in New York, he studied with Merce Cunningham, performed with Twyla Tharp, in Sophie Maslow's choreography at the Yiddish Theatre and in Off-Broadway theatre productions. Frustrated by the trend towards formalism which demanded

41 Department of Homeland Security, http://www.dhs.gov/xinfoshare/programs/Copy_ of_press_release_0046.shtm, accessed 28 December 2006. According to the chronology, the level has shifted between yellow (elevated risk) and orange with one exception when it has been raised to red, indicating a severe risk. http://www.dhs.gov/xabout/history/ editorial_0844.shtm.
42 Janice Ross (1989) 'San Francisco's Joe Goode: Working hard to be the bad boy of modern dance,' *Dance Magazine*, January, pp. 46-50.

suppression of his identity, Goode left the dance and theatre world: 'I was always being asked not to be gay ... the most abstract modern dance erased all vestiges of your actual identity. We don't want to see any soft hips or limp wrists.'[43] In 1979 Goode moved to San Francisco and began performing in Jenkins' company where he was encouraged to develop as a choreographer.

Early on, Goode turned to the personal for choreographic material. An eclectic background – a BFA in drama from Virginia Commonwealth University, childhood dance classes which included baton twirling, and a strong foundation in what were then mainstream dance techniques – contributed to the development of his content-driven style. Text is integral to Goode's dance theatre in ways distinctive from his mentor Jenkins, as characters are set in specific situations, their introspective musings externalised. Founded in 1986, the Joe Goode Performance Group has retained a core of dancers whose vocal and acting abilities match their strong physical talents, with upcoming generations of performers infusing some early works with a new presence. Goode developed a virtuosic physicality combined with a weighty, languid quality, the dancers indulging in suspended leans to either catch themselves at the last moment or take the impulse to the floor in fluid acrobatic falls. Dance phrases shift between those which expand upon the narrative to ones where roles are abandoned briefly, the movement responding to the musical accompaniment or conveying overall mood. In partnering work, the dancers manipulate each others' weight, taking a contact improvisation-based impulse and infusing it with stretched limbs in suspended counterbalances and controlled lifts. Goode's extensive university lecturing and choreographic workshops encourages the creation of pools of material drawn from 'felt experience' utilising diverse creative strategies drawn from drama and dance pedagogies.[44] He describes his dances as being 'human scale':

> By 'human scale' I mean placing the emphasis on the unglamorized body, the body in more intimate moments, when it is fallible or agitated or inept. My intent is not to create merely pedestrian movement, but to make dynamic movement that is a combination of gesture and partnering. The challenge is to find the velocity and force in the movement and yet still retain its intimate, conversational quality.[45]

Central to the communicative act is the use of voice in relationship to movement: 'I want each dance to be a "telling"; telling with the body (where have I been? where does my longing reside?), and telling with the voice (this

---

43 Joe Goode, telephone interview with author, 18 October 2005.

44 Maria Maria Junco (1998) 'Choreography Through Inner Mapping,' *Dance Teacher Now*, October, pp. 53-59.

45 Joe Goode, Our Process, (no date) Joe Goode Performance Group website, http://joegoode.org/about/our-process, accessed 1 June 2013.

is how I see the world).' Steeped in autobiographical references, Goode's creations move beyond personal introspection although identity issues and personal loss infused many dances during the 1980s and 1990s. In the oft-performed *29 Effeminate Gestures* (1986), the embodiment of masculinity is challenged in a gender-bending solo and a celebration of a camp aesthetic.[46] Discussing *Remembering the Pool at the Best Western* (1990), created after a good friend died of AIDS, critic and historian David Gere highlights how Goode confronts homophobic oppression and fear of AIDS through metaphysical musings and ghostly dances. Elizabeth Burritt is dressed as a camp gothic spirit guide who leads Goode through his journey. Significantly, Gere recounts how *Remembering the Pool* conveys a spirit of optimism and resistance rather than victimisation.[47]

Goode views humour as cathartic and empowering, offering the possibility to shift perceptions, where laughter can allow things to slip in, 'new ways of thinking, a new perspective, new ways of being tolerant about somebody else's issue'.[48] Myths of the American dream are central to the narratives, contrasting to the reality of Goode's childhood in a military town in southern Virginia. There 'the sense of security and prosperity and stability that we all associated with America, being American, were out of reach. It wasn't how I grew up, it wasn't what I saw around me. I saw illiteracy and racism and spousal abuse.'[49] As a tenured professor in dance and performance studies at the University of California at Berkeley, Goode reaches a wide audience and subversively crosses boundaries to pave the way for transformation, rather than making overt political statements.

Personal reflections transcend their specificity by evoking the familiar and popular. The eternal quest for romantic love is metaphorically linked to natural disasters in *The Disaster Series* (1989, partially restaged in 2004). Chaos reigns in the vignettes, the result of failed relationships or the loss of traditional values. In *Doris in a Dustbowl*, Burritt appears in a short 1950s style wedding dress, pondering her lifelong expectations for romance. Proclaiming Doris Day as her role model, she is joined by Goode as a debonair suitor á la Rock Hudson. They evoke the idealised cinematic couple, undermined by Hudson's sexual orientation. Goode's characteristic lifts flow into expansive off-centre turns, contrasted by Burritt's tantrums

46   A filmed version was broadcast c. 1989, *Alive From Off-Center* Series, program #510, KTCA/TV, Minneapolis. See Stacey Prickett (1996) 'Subversive Others: Humor and Gender-Bending in the Joe Goode Performance Group' and (1995) Blurring Edges of Difference in Performance and Society. See also David Gere (2001) '*29 Effeminate Gestures*: Choreographer Joe Goode and the Heroism of Effeminacy,' in Jane Desmond, ed., *Dancing Desires*.

47   Gere, ibid.; See also David Gere (2004) *How to Make Dances in an Epidemic*, pp. 206-227.

48   Joe Goode interview with author, 18 October 2005.

49   Ibid.

of frustration at unfulfilled expectations, the outbursts taken out on a chair which she both hurls and vaults herself over. The dustbowl of the title appears when Goode scatters flour over Burritt and in front of a fan, recalling the disasters of the 1930s prairies where drought and winds blew away arable land. Fictional and other-worldly characters populate productions about the search for acceptance, belonging, and happiness. In *Take/Place/This is Where I am Now* (1995), fantastic characters (a Mermaid and a lost Princess) recite and dance out their desires as Goode plays an overgrown Pinocchio, whose paper nose increases in length throughout the show.

The award-winning *Deeply There (stories of a neighborhood)* (1998) interweaved earlier themes, juxtaposing grief with the absurd through text, song and movement. The stories in the title allude to the high death count from AIDS in the Castro District: 'As you walk this day, someone isn't here.' Eulogies pay tribute to the dead as a seated chorus performs a gestural mourning dance. A spotlight illuminates Wayne Hazzard shovelling a mound of dirt at the side of the auditorium, as if digging a grave, its pungent earthly scent wafting through the house. With inhibitions loosened by swigs from a whisky bottle, a dialogue opens between Goode as Frank, whose lover is dying from AIDS, and Burritt as Joyce, his homophobic sister. Preconceptions of each other dissolve as they careen around and over a sofa, their ideological and emotional battles embodied in a drunken duet. Iconic imagery mixes the tragic and the humorous as Goode leads a mixed gender group of 'Jackie Os,' wearing suits in the style made infamous by the First Lady on 23 November 1963 when President John F. Kennedy was assassinated. Neighbourhood loss morphs into a more universal sense of grief, but the journey is transcendental one, ending in a note of optimism.

Critics refer to Goode's cinematic values, noting his title of 'director' of *The Maverick Strain*, a combination installation piece and 'theatrical collage'.[50] The spectacle embodies the mythology of the American West, interspersed with popular film and television references. Others marginalised by career, sexuality, or life circumstance, are also central characters, such as the anonymous store clerk in *Convenience Boy* (1993). In *Gender Heroes* (1999), an American folk was portrayed, starting Goode on a quest for 'a kind of "folk" art that can be expertly crafted, yet feels unsophisticated, naïve, credulous' through which to explore 'inappropriate' people, those who are outside the mainstream,' in order to humanise them.[51] In a trilogy beginning with *Folk* (2003), diverse perspectives on the everyday, the unspectacular, the quest for home and belonging are developed. In *Hometown* (2005), a suburban couple (Burritt and Felipe Barrueto-Cabello) talk and dance about

---

50 Janice Ross (1996) 'Joe Goode Performance Group', *Dance Magazine*, October, p. 103.
51 Joe Goode Performance Group website, http://www.joegoode.org, accessed 17 January 2007.

contrasting desires. Hers are middle-class yearnings for the familiar, the house to be made into a home, with a grass yard marked off by a white picket fence, while he is content with the small patch of grass with a bench, tree and lamppost which slides onto the stage, its proportions decreasing in size each time it reappears. Projected images of freeway traffic, birds and houses were created by participants in the Teaching Intermedia Literacy Tools training programme. The composer and clarinettist Beth Custer created the original score for *Folk* and *Hometown*.

The second of the trilogy, *grace* (2004), explores the search for love, for relationships that work, for clarity in life, often found in the unexpected. Goode's onstage role is limited to storyteller and songster, followed by six dancers who echo his narrative. Local critics perceived a transcendence in *grace*, in the expansive movement qualities and economic reliance on the text.[52] A blend of humour, rhythmic vocals, characterisations and movement continue to present challenges at a subversive level, while engaging with broader existential themes.

Zaccho Dance Theatre and Site Dances

San Francisco is the home for a number of dance innovators in site dances, a term which encompasses a range of practices – not always site-specific as some productions are performed in multiple locations.[53] Joanna Haigood takes her solid technical foundation into unusual realms through the integration of aerial dance. A charismatic solo performer, Haigood also directs Zaccho Dance Theatre (Zaccho is the term used for the base anchoring a classical Greek column to the ground), which she co-founded in 1980. Some works have celebrated the natural environment, although Zaccho increasingly reinforces hooks' argument that class matters in historical and contemporary circumstances – underemployment and marginalisation, social injustices faced by African Americans and the legacy of slavery such as disproportional incarceration. Large interdisciplinary productions take as their starting points historical aspects of a specific site, turning it from a mere location into a meaningful sense of place. Haigood begins the creative process by asking: 'How do we define a place? Is it people, is it demographics, is it architecture, philosophy or cultural trends? What is the physical and psychic evidence of history left behind?'[54]

52   Rachel Howard (2005) 'Joe Goode finds a safe place to end trio in *Hometown*,' *San Francisco Chronicle*; Rita Felciano (2005) 'The Home Inside,' *Dance View Times*. Additional analysis is drawn from recordings of *Hometown, Folk* and *grace* provided by the company.

53   Kloetzel, Melanie and Carolyn Pavlik, eds. (2009) *Site Dance: Choreographers and the Lure of Alternative Spaces*. The introduction explores multiple interpretations of the terminology.

54   Joanna Haigood, Picture Powderhorn Project, Director's Notes, http://www.zaccho. org accessed 8 October 2005.

A graduate of Bard College in New York, Haigood also undertook Graham-based conservatory training at the London Contemporary Dance School in England. She focuses on the minutia of everyday life, transforming mundane tasks into movement motifs endowed with intent and poetic meaning. To this is added the expansive and weightless qualities of aerial dance techniques, which result in alterations to perceptions of space and time. Unique spatial dimensions of bodies and buildings are brought into focus, overlooked aspects of the location come into the viewer's awareness. *Invisible Wings* (1998) was inspired by the Jacob's Pillow Dance Festival in Lee, Massachusetts, which is located on the site of an Underground Railroad station, before the Civil War a stopping point for escaped slaves. Haigood set out to challenge understandings of the past, 'to draw lines to the current social and political trends as they related to race, class and international relations'.[55] Over a three year period, she collaborated with ethnomusicologist Linda Tillery and storyteller Diane Ferlatte. They drew on African American vocal music, oral histories and archival sources, trips to visit Gullah and other African American communities with links to slave traditions in the South. Choreographic processes involved a re-embodying of the past, presenting the inequities of power relations through theatrical tableaux.

The premiere of *Invisible Wings* was at San Francisco's Fort Point, where the sound of foghorns competed with Ferlatte's stories, featuring Haigood as the escaped slave Mary on her path to freedom via the Underground Railroad. A physical engagement is required to observe the dance, as viewers traverse the fort to witness scenes that emulate the physical brutality and psychological oppression of the auction block and incidents of abuse, accompanied by the distinctive crack of a bullwhip whipping through the air. My memories of viewing are bound up in recollections of my physical responses, how narrative was enhanced by the extremes of weather, body tensed against a cold chill and damp fog; the hardness of concrete; negotiating uneven ground outside the fort; craning to catch a glimpse of Robert Henry Johnson as he moved with speed and attempted stealth in a journey of escape; the sound of the bells from his slave collar getting louder.

The transformation of African cultural practices by slaves evoked a spirit of resilience and the power of resistance. Alongside contemporary dance and musical components, the traditional dances of Master Juba is mimicked by the blackface Jim Crow, minstrel stereotypes from the 19th century.[56] Ending with a literal and metaphorical escape to the song *I'll Fly Away*, Haigood leads others to freedom. They climb up the walls and reappear overhead, harnessed to aerial rigging to float high above the courtyard and

---

55 *Invisible Wings* programme notes, 1988.
56 See Thomas DeFrantz (1996) 'Simmering Passivity: The Black Male Body in Concert Dance', in Gay Morris, ed., *Moving Words: Re-writing Dance*.

over the walls of the fort. Human scale is brought into focus, with flying bodies framed against the Golden Gate Bridge looming in the night sky. Jennifer Dunning wrote of the Jacob's Pillow performance that 'much is suggested ... It is a marvellous distillation of material. It is also an unpreachy vivid history lesson.'[57]

Cultural geographer Doreen Massey's analysis of the politics of space highlights how locations are endowed with social interactions which can be disrupted temporally and spatially through artistic interventions. Massey proposes different conceptualisations of a 'postmodern nostalgia', a look to the past often arising from responses to globalisation in the search for communal identities. Heritage sites exemplify one approach where particular versions of their social history are re-presented beyond the physical history of the buildings. Specific moments from the past offered through written guides or the recreation of daily life, present particular visions that limit the possible interpretations associated with a location: 'Instead of questioning memory and pre-given understandings of the past, the classic heritage site will provide them ready-made. Instead of de-familiarizing the supposedly familiar, it is meant as an aid to further familiarization.'[58] New perceptions of history were revealed through Zaccho's productions. Although not directly linked to the Underground Railroad, construction of Fort Point began prior to the Civil War and played a role in the local Union-Secessionist struggle while Jacob's Pillow had a historical resonance as an Underground Railroad refuge.

Educational components for *Invisible Wings* included community-based activities (such as a family quilt project), and programme notes which detailed the history of slavery, the Underground Railroad and the relevance of the performance sites. Slaves are named and given voice in published excerpts of their stories. An extensive schools project culminated in 'All Hid', a dance involving 150 students from the Bayview-Hunters Point district—an area where race, class and environmental issues have set it apart from the tourist havens and business centres nearby. The area is a site of environmental racism due to the extensive toxic waste which remained after the Hunter's Point Naval Shipyard was decommissioned in 1974.[59] The dance project helped challenge the day-to-day experience of disproportional high black unemployment and crime rates experienced by local children. Zaccho's studios in a former mattress factory have established a place for young people to develop creatively and transcend the marginalisation of their neighbourhood.

In an interview, Haigood explained how she felt that she was looking

57 Jennifer Dunning (1998) 'Hope and Sanctuary on a Tortuous Journey,' *New York Times*, 27 August.
58 Doreen Massey (2000) 'Space-time and the politics of location', in Alan Read, ed., *Architecturally Speaking*, p. 55.
59 Ahimsa Sumchai (2004) 'Put Your Head in it!' in Carlsson, op.cit.

into her own past, into her father's African American roots. With three *Picture Projects* (2000-2002), Zaccho ventured into new territory by interacting directly with the people living in a neighbourhood, rather than dealing with historical subjects. Haigood wanted to avoid being an outsider, 'not just artists thinking about a community', and imposing their interpretations.[60] The *Picture Projects* are interdisciplinary performances set in blighted neighbourhoods whose identities and livelihoods have come under threat: Bayview-Hunters Point in San Francisco, the Minneapolis Powderhorn district and the Red Hook area of Brooklyn, New York. The vital worker communities underwent industrial decline and periods of high unemployment, with rampant drug and crime related issues that bring class issues to the forefront. In each site, grain silos stand as testaments to their shipping legacies, providing a common focal point and a poetic function. To Haigood they represented 'a metaphor for the sustenance, growth and aspirations of people for the future. I also chose them for their prominence as architectural and historical monuments in the American landscape.'[61] At intensive workshops in the Red Hook community, local teenagers learned audio-visual documentary techniques, their observations of the neighbourhood explored in choreography workshops and integrated into the media collage compiled by Mary Ellen Strom and Lauren Weigner. Images were projected onto the silos, 100 feet high, intercut with film of the area during its earlier heyday, and internal workings of a functioning grain silo and live video feed of the dancers. Weigner's sound score combined music, children's songs, and sounds of a working terminal, and was the aural backdrop against which seven performers were picked out by spotlight. Movement derived from harvesting actions evoking agricultural labour, unison somersaults against the sides of the silos echoed the buildings' curvature. The spectacle also drew on the expertise of collaborators Wayne Campbell, who designed special rigging, and lighting designer Jack Carpenter.

Other Zaccho projects focus on San Francisco's industrial past and the impact of urban regeneration. For *In Steel's Shadow* (1994), Haigood drew on Walter Listor's experience as a worker in the American Can Company, which was transformed into Theatre Artaud after the factory's closure in 1968.[62] The installation *Ghost Architecture* (2004), reflected upon the San Francisco Redevelopment Agency's transformation of the area south of Market Street. To make room for high rise hotels, a conference centre, the

60 Joanna Haigood, interview with author, 14 October 2005.
61 Joanna Haigood, Picture Powderhorn Project, Director's Notes, http://www.zaccho. org, accessed 8 October 2005. Joanna Haigood provided video excerpts of *Picture Powderhorn* performances. Unless otherwise indicated, descriptions of the *Picture Projects* are drawn from video analysis.
62 Ann Murphy (1994) 'Joanna Haigood', *Dance Theatre Journal*, 11, no. 2, 18-20.

San Francisco Museum of Modern Art and an arts centre, a wide swath of city blocks housing SROs (single room occupancy residency hotels) and local amenities was demolished in 1970. The majority of the area's inhabitants were financially marginalised, including transients, retired seamen and dock workers on low pensions. In researching what was absent, Campbell identified the original site of the SRO West Hotel and the Peerless Theatre, a segregated cinema for blacks which later became an adult film cinema. A physical 'footprint' of the hotel and theatre was created using architectural plans, photographs and computer software to forensically situate facsimiles of the walls, floors, ceilings and a stairway of the West Hotel. A camera obscura that brought the street activities into the set, repeated movement scores utilising precise quotidian actions contributed to a fragmented ghostly atmosphere.[63] Other installations explored the South of Market redevelopment, seen in *The Shifting Cornerstone* (2008) which took place around a street corner and site of the Yerba Buena Arts Center, and also invoked the absence of buildings and people.

In *Sailing Away* (2010) on Market Street, the stories of eight prominent African Americans were evoked as they led a mass exodus from San Francisco in 1858, when the rights of 'free Negroes' who had successfully built up a middle class presence were jeopardised.[64] As with *Invisible Wings*, newspapers fleshed out the historical detail of discrimination and the journey to Canada by those looking for racial equality. Social injustices, incidents of racial profiling, discrimination, high rates of ethnic minority incarceration, have fed into some smaller productions. *Dying while black and brown* (2011) was commissioned by the Equal Justice Society. The organisation champions anti-discrimination legislation that was signed into law after the Civil War to establish citizen rights of former slaves. Haigood worked with composer Marcus Shelby for a benefit performance at the prestigious Yoshi's Jazz Club, working with a frame of a small house that became a cell for the African-American male performers. Both Shelby and Haigood are opposed to the death penalty and the choreography set out to convey a 'picture that resonated with humanity', to explore how people reconcile their relationship to the idea of home in a prison environment. Haigood asked 'where does redemption fit in this?', particularly poignant when the percentage of blacks in the prison population is eight times higher than the percentage of white people.[65] *Between Me and the Other World* (2012) explores W.E.B. DuBois's notion of double consciousness, while *The Monkey and the Devil* (2011) took its title from ethnic slurs. The audience could wander

63   Rita Felciano (2005) 'Ghost Architecture,' *Dance Magazine*; also see the Ghost Architecture Project page, http://www.zaccho.org, accessed 7 January 2007.
64   Rachel Howard (2008) 'Zaccho Dancers Slip Through Time in Yerba Buena Show', *San Francisco Chronicle*, 19 August.
65   See project page on Zaccho website: Eric Foner (2009) *Give me Liberty*, p. 1024.

through the performance installation to see two couples, one Caucasian, the other African American, in a physically unstable room that was cut in half – it tipped to whichever side the balance of weight was on. With an explicit text, physical and psychic tension became manifest, described as 'devastating in the way it lays bare the festering wounds of racism'.[66]

The impact of Bay Area activist choreographers can alter perceptions of place in the memories of viewers while some of Flyaway Productions' site-specific and aerial productions leave a physical impact long after the performances themselves. Calling herself a 'citizen artist', artistic director Jo Kreiter defined *Sparrow's End* (1997)as her signature work. It is set in an alley frequented by transients, drug users and prostitutes but also a home to children and those struggling to get by. The work claims value in those disregarded by the mainstream. The productions reveal the communities to themselves as well as the outsiders who travel to witness the productions. Images of some of dancers were added to an existing mural on which the *Mission Wall Dances* (2002) was performed. The work drew attention to a site that used to house those living on the edges financially and socially but was transformed into a tourist hotel after a fire.[67] Kreiter danced for years with Zaccho, developing a focus on women's issues in her own company that has evolved a distinctive aesthetic and ethos.

Other choreographer-performers challenge official histories that inform activist artistry. Filipina American Pearl Ubungen's productions in the 1990s drew on documentary representations and residents' memories of migration and social inequalities to give voice to marginalised San Franciscans. Pearl Ubungen Dancers and Musicians created *Refugee* (1995) combining ritual and meditative action with contrasting edgy dance phrases set on and around the fountain at the United Nations Plaza near the Civic Centre. *Take me to the Tenderloin Now!* (1997), created with photographer Ken Miller and performers drawn from the community's young people, used the recreational dancers' movements as a foundation in the work which told their stories.[68] A new dance cycle draws on her Buddhist meditative practice and years at the Naropa Institute in Boulder, Colorado. Kim Epifano, a Contraband collaborator, has curated an annual 'Trolley Dances' event for a decade, the public art accessible for the cost of a Muni trolley ticket. As long-time resident, dancer and scholar Joanna Harris recalled, she became conscious of the out-of-way spaces of the city, the areas affected by the lack of transport when they ended up at the end of the trolley line.[69]

66 See individual project pages on the Zaccho website, www.zaccho.org; Rita Felciano (2011) 'Zaccho Dance Theatre Review', *Dance Magazine*, April.
67 Jo Kreiter (2012) in Kloetzer and Palvik, op.cit.; Rita Felciano (2012) 'Fly, on the wall: Niagara Falling' takes to the air to take on the recession', *SF Guardian*, 26 September.
68 Michael Blanding (1997) 'Coming of Age in the Tenderloin', *San Francisco Chronicle*, 1 April.
69 Joanna Harris, interview with author, 23 August 2013.

Contraband's rituals and myths

During its project-based incarnations from 1985-1994, the group Contraband created evening-length works described as 'equal parts Greek tragedy, New Age confessional, Fellini-esque carnival and punk forum on public policy'.[70] Labelled a 'movement matriarch' and the 'inspirational center of San Francisco's radical arts scene',[71] Sara Shelton Mann was the group's founding force. Originally from rural Tennessee, Mann relocated to San Francisco in 1979, with a dance pedigree from Alwin Nikolais, Murray Louis, Erick Hawkins and Merce Cunningham. While Contraband traces its beginnings to 1979, the focus here is on a period of creativity starting in the mid-1980s when Mann was joined by Canadian Keith Hennessy and California-born Jess Curtis who helped manage and publicise the group's productions and were key collaborators. Mann moved increasingly into contact improvisation and embraced an eclectic mix of music, theatre and text created by a core of multi-talented dancer-performers, musicians and designers. The archival record leaves an incomplete picture, however, as a number of performers made significant creative contributions not fully credited in contemporaneous reviews and programme notes. Norman Rutherford perceived his musical direction and Mann's choreographic direction as 'a kind of collage artist' relationship where a working process would be established, and everyone would bring ideas that were worked through spontaneously in rehearsals and then were edited and put together.[72] The list of early contributors includes Nina Hart, Brenda Munnell, Brook Klem and A. Dibz while later productions bear the imprint of Kim Epifano, Julie Kane, Elaine Buckholtz, Peter Overton and Kathleen Hermesdorf, among others.[73] Mann was the overall director of Contraband, explaining that: 'there's not enough time for everyone to be equally powerful in everything. We try to learn from the mistakes of communes in the '60s.'[74]

At times there was little separation between artistic and personal lives, as living space at Project Artaud overlapped with the rehearsal studio. Tensions between the sexes, with *Evol* (1985) – love spelled backwards – were played out onstage, the duet work between Mann and Curtis inspired by their offstage relationship as lovers. *The (Invisible) War* (1987) pitted the sexes

---

70 Apollinaire Scherr (2000) 'Dancers Run Away to a Home in the Circus', *Dance Magazine*, August, p. 50.

71 Dennis Harvey (1990) 'Movement Matriarch,' *SF Weekly*, 26 December, p. E-25.

72 Norman Rutherford, personal email correspondence, 2 April 2013.

73 I am grateful to Keith Hennessy and Jess Curtis for providing corrections to my 2007 article, helping establish a more accurate history of Contraband.

74 Kate Regan (1988) 'Contraband Dancers Show a Subtle Side,' *SF Chronicle-Examiner*, 6 March, pp. 33-34.

against each other with a raw physicality, pushing limits of risk and trust, emotional confrontation offset by absurd humour. Curtis nailed vegetables to a table while announcing that he has the right to treat them the way he wants.[75] Collaborations with the composers Rinde Eckert and Rutherford, the designers Lauren Elder and Julian Neff, and the lighting designer Jack Carpenter resulted in theatrical landscapes, other-worldly environments that juxtaposed elements from nature (earth and water) with manufactured 'found' discards from urban life. Props had multiple functions of design and practicality, integrated into the movement language and the creation of a vibrant visual and aural spectacle.

Contraband's events took different forms, from the site-specific *Religare* (1986 and 1989), to the transformations of theatre space seen in the *Mira* trilogy (1991, 1992 and 1995). *Religare* was performed in and around a large pit at the corner of 16th and Valencia Streets, a site made derelict by an arson fire that destroyed an apartment block and killed a number of residents of the SRO (single room occupancy dwelling). The space served as a shelter for the homeless, evidenced by the detritus of drug and alcohol addiction which littered the place. Communal energies made *Religare* possible as volunteers pitched in to clean up the space and install lighting rigs. A ritual and literal cleansing occurred as debris was cleared and ghosts of the dead were exorcised.

The critic Paul Parish described the event as a healing ritual, evoking the power of Allen Ginsberg's poetry:

> [Contraband] used shamanistic practices to give forms to very dark impulses in the community soul: they wore black; they tore their clothes; they covered themselves with dirt; they ranted; they impersonated holy fools, winos and sluts; they rattled the foundation walls; they danced in the collective grave of some twenty bums who died in a flophouse fire. . . . It reminded me of *Howl*'.[76]

Rutherford, Gwen Jones and Richard Klein collaborated on a score that borrowed from other cultures (the Indonesian *kecak* trance chant and gamelan), played by about 15 musicians while Eckert's recorded section was played on a boombox. Episodic scenes shifted the centre of activity around the space. Mann described the first section as a carnival where people could wander around and watch solos, individual vignettes that took place in decorated rooms.[77]

For Curtis, the *Religare* site was symbolic of the long standing struggle

75 Kate Regan (1987) 'Contraband: It's the Animal in Them,' *San Francisco Chronicle*, 9 November.

76 Paul Parish (1987) 'San Francisco Season,' *Ballet Review*, 15, no. 2, Summer, p. 92.

77 Norman Rutherford, email communication with the author, 2 April 2013; Sara Shelton Mann, interview with author, 19 October 2005.

between San Francisco's renters and owners, which left 'a gaping wound in the Mission' District and they set out 'with an intention about changing something about the energy' of the space.[78] Locals happened upon the performance by chance, and it broke down spectator-performer barriers as some repeat viewers learned the songs and script and joined in the action. Two years later, a similar journey into the territory of San Francisco's disenfranchised took place in an abandoned apartment building. Once again, Contraband members cleaned up excrement, spent needles and the remnants of squatters' daily lives. Delicate negotiations and direct engagement with squatters and a range of institutions were required, such as the Mission Housing Development Corporation, which later rebuilt housing on the site. Despite their alternative political ideologies, they also negotiated the intricacies of planning commission politics, acquired portable toilets and liability insurance to legalise the events.

Photographs show dishevelled-looking dancers hunched over in the centre of the performance space, demarcated by a white circle on the ground, with spectators standing both at ground level and peering down on the action from the remnants of the building a floor above. In others, bodies are captured mid-flight as dancers hurl through the air, their pointed feet and taunt limbs attest to a strong dance technique which underpinned the integration of forms yet to enter into mainstream dance vocabularies: capoeira, contact improvisation and martial arts. Although pushing the limits of bodily control with a high impact virtuosity, the movement phrases are tightly structured with a strong rhythmic unity.

The political impetus in Mann's work comes from a recognition that something 'is wrong in the world and it hurts. So you want to create something to address that, either by doing it directly or through beauty, looking at contrasts or bringing people somehow into the conversation'.[79] Both approaches are evident in the *Mira* trilogy, which evolved over a five year period of intensive research. Critics perceived an aesthetic shift with *Mira I* (1990-91), generating a hitherto unseen elegance, and a refinement of movement ideas from previous works: 'Initially Contraband was a defiantly outlaw operation; it wore the sobriquet 'rowdy' with pride, its costumes were thrift-store finery, its movement vocabulary a rough-and-tumble variant of contact improv, and its message a tireless cry against social injustice.'[80]

Here mythical and autobiographical narrative threads link the struggles of two women: Mirabai (a 16th century Indian poet, saint and social reformer) and Mann, during her own troubled adolescence. Mirabai's story

---

78 Jess Curtis, telephone interview with author, 23 February 2006.
79 Mann, op.cit.
80 Janice Ross (1991) 'Contraband review,' *Dance Magazine,*October, p. 85.

is told through her poetic declarations of faith and love, sung or spoken by the cast. An all-consuming devotion to the Hindu deity Krishna led her to abandon powerful ties of caste, family and tradition to ultimately embrace an ascetic and nomadic existence. Her *bhakti* (devotion) was channelled into prayer and poetry, her interactions with lower castes ensured her mythical status as a social reformer and instigator of a spiritual revival in India.

The *Mira* trilogy celebrated empowered women rejecting the stranglehold of tradition, alongside a critique of sexual oppression and violence. *Mira I* was inspired by traditional upbringing and a move towards spiritual commitment to Krishna. *Mira Cycle II: The Fall* examines Mirabai's rejection of conventions, defiance of expectations of caste and family, trusting instead in her spiritual journey. In 1994, *Mira III: Return to Ordinary Life* turned to nature and Mirabai's search for the sublime in ordinary life. The stage version evolved out of creative workshops at various beaches in San Francisco, utilising objects found in the debris which covered Tire Beach and importing four tons of gravel into the theatre.

Mira I opens with a Mann in a seated solo, harmonica clenched in her mouth as her long limbs explode outwards only to contract back in again, described as 'a capsulization of the violence in her life, her wide-spread legs whispering of desire and coercion, her sharp feet fending off oppressors, her coquettish expression disarming them, and us'.[81] Mira's poems are interspersed by dance phrases with ecstatic turns initiated by twirling heads. The dancers' trances mesmerise the audience, and are interrupted by rhythmic footwork sections that build in speed. Bodily movement enhances the aural pulse of instrumental and vocal accompaniment and episodic segments critique topical issues such as nuclear testing. Musical director Rutherford was joined by composer/performer Jules Beckman to co-direct and create the score using non-western rhythms and instruments to transform props such as a clay pot from stage dressing into percussion and wind instruments, evoking a folk or tribal atmosphere. Elaine Burkholtz's lighting revealed Elder's haunting landscape in which branches frozen in hanging blocks of ice gradually defrosted above piles of earth. Thus, nature and its processes are present onstage alongside human constructions. Unsettling memories are recounted by Mann: religious fundamentalism in tent revivals, the screams of a woman being raped, her father taking her to have her first abortion. Dressed in a floaty silk dress, a delicate femininity is offset by the Doc Marten-style boots she laces up – a woman negating the violence of her past, claiming a power of her own. Brutality to the psyche is manifest in bodily extremes of acrobatic strength and risk. Dancers repeatedly hurl over each other, smash to the

81 David Gere, 'Contraband premieres elegant 'Mira' excerpts,' *The Oakland Tribune*, 2 April 1990, (no page, clippings file, SF PALM). Unless otherwise noted, all other analysis derives from viewing the dances in performance or from watching videos held at San Francisco Performing Arts Library and Museum.

UNIVERSITY OF WINCHESTER
LIBRARY

floor in flying rolls and bounce back up. Disparate episodes include a body-building section led by Epifano, with highly toned bodies placed on display.

A climactic whirlwind of sexual energy built up at the end, with the men (Hennessy, Curtis and Beckman) chanting in an almost animalistic mating dance. Eric Hellman labelled the finale as a 'cathartic, sexy sort of romp... very good-natured and almost vaudevillian; [where] sex is restored to its proper place as a creative, happy play'.[82] Violent resonances fade against the celebration of physicality and power. The strong personalities of Contraband's performers familiar to viewers of the alternative dance scene were increasingly developed into characters. As Ross noted, there was 'a widening gap between the performers' true selves and constructed stage personae'.[83]

Gender issues came to the fore in Contraband's *Mandala* (1988-1990) when Beckman, Hennessy and Curtis offered up male performative voices through their personal stories while confronting gender stereotypes. The programme notes describe 'the ecstatic journey of three young Euro-American men, seeking an initiation into the world of their fathers at the same time that they must reject the world their fathers have created'.[84] Clyde Smith's analysis traces *Mandala*'s impetus from the mythopoetic men's movement which gathered strength in the early 1980s, but was also shaped by a strong feminist impulse.[85] As Hennessy explained, his biggest area of study and practice is in the field of experimental and postmodern dance and improvisation: 'I have always picked up on the political aspects of this work (the feminism in non-gendered movement of either [Merce] Cunningham or contact improvisation, the anarchism and feminism of non-hierarchical and collaborative processes, the challenges to the spectacle and virtuosity, the democratization of dance gesture and performance sites...).'[86] Some performances of *Mandala* included a pre-show spectacle which involved contact improvisation, a driverless car crash and setting it on fire. Once inside the theatre, an exploration of the men's relationships with their fathers took us on a journey through tales of familial conflict, abandonment and love, told through text, song, movement and music. In an autobiographical section, we learn the men's full names, dates of birth, and about their emotional extremes of paternal relationships. The roller coaster of laughter and empathy for their displays of loss, despair, anger, teach us not only of their past but show us how the body holds these emotions.

---

82 Hellman, op.cit.
83 Ross (1991), op.cit.
84 Unless otherwise noted, the analysis of *Mandala* is based on the author's attendance at performances and later viewing of the video at San Francisco Performing Arts Library and Museum, October, 2005.
85 Clyde Smith (1999) 'Mandala and the Men's Movement(s)'.
86 Keith Hennessy, email correspondence with author, 15 February 2006.

Hennessy, Beckman and Curtis continued their collaborative relationship in highly innovative and at times, dangerous events. *Ice, Car, Cage,* commissioned for the Lesbian and Gay Dance Festival in 1997, was advertised as 'live action urban poem whose images are made from 3 guys, a driverless car, a steel dog cage, a 300# block of ice, and the city'. The Contraband dancers often invoked multiple identities with a single performance which would dissipate during the danced sections but in *Ice, Car, Cage* characters stood as an archetypal trio, developed into an exploration of their interrelationships.[87]

Gathered in a parking lot surrounded by low industrial buildings, the audience formed a circle around an old car, a block of ice and a cage. The soothing strands of a Chopin nocturne emanating from a boom box drew attention to Curtis working on a garage door nearby, dressed as a carpenter, his hammer beating time with the piano. Breaking from his tasks, Curtis indulges in a languid solo, full of long lunges, flowing arm circles, expansive arabesques and lyrical musicality. In the main arena, Hennessy sits in a large dog cage, while Beckman nonchalantly eats an apple before they move off to examine the car engine. Once started, the car assumes a life of its own as the steering wheel and accelerator are anchored in place, so the driverless vehicle can maintain a consistent circular path. Open car doors double as hurdles; its trunk, roof and hood a lounging spot and gymnastic pommel horse. A series of dare-devil physical tricks evoke gasps and a sense of voyeurism due to the potential danger. From a headstand on top of the circling car, Beckman drops prone on the ground perilously close to the wheels' relentless path, his body rolls picking up the turning action of the back wheel. Grabbing the rear bumper, he is dragged across the asphalt. Other virtuosic feats flow fluidly into the next – running up and over the length of the car, riding it like a surfboard, cartwheels off the trunk – slapstick vaudevillian clowning, requiring impeccable timing to avoid injury. To the sounds of Beckman's electronic score Curtis curls up on top of the ice block and Hennessy manipulates him around by the legs. As Curtis chips away at the ice block, Beckman drives off with Hennessy back in the cage on top of the car.

The collaborative relationship pushed physical and psychological boundaries with the new group CORE when the three men were joined by Stephanie Maher, a former dancer with Margaret Jenkins and Contraband, and Stanya Khan, now an established video artist. Absurd juxtapositions, with edgy and manipulative contact work offset by the sight of rubber ducks, *Entertainment for the Apocalypse* offered 'intense meditations on being alive'.[88] Although it

---

87 Curtis (2006) op.cit.

88 Publicity material on *entertainment for the apocalypse* (1997), San Francisco Performing Arts Library and Museum clippings file on CORE.

was CORE's only production, sections of the work toured internationally, its provocative intensity memorable decades later. In 1998 Hennessy, Beckman and Curtis left the Bay Area to join a contemporary French circus group, Cahin-Caha, a *cirque bâtard* (bastard circus). When he returned to San Francisco, Hennessy co-founded the contemporary circus group Circo Zero, which premiered in 2002.

Politicised rituals: Keith Hennessy and the Community

Since 1985, Hennessy's work bears the impact of AIDS, either through overt reference to the disease or in direct challenges to social taboos and fears about the body, highlighting its political symbolism. In *Saliva* (1988 and restaged in 2009), performed in the shadow of a street overpass, Hennessy begins by evoking his suit-wearing father, then donned a dress like his mother while six dancers portray him and his siblings as he lectures his audience on anarchy, AIDS, and desire. In stripping away clothes, his body becomes a ritual site. Viewers join together through the metaphoric mingling of their saliva in a bowl, which Hennessy spreads on his body (after adding non-oxynol-9). David Gere's and Rachel Kaplan's readings of *Saliva* catalogue the challenges to conventions: through nudity; narration of explicit sexual acts; confrontation of gender assumptions; and most significantly, by his manipulation of symbolically loaded bodily fluids, his own and those of the community. In confronting taboos – particularly the association of homosexuality, bodily fluids and dance with AIDS – Hennessy seeks to transcend fears, to transform negative associations into positive ones.[89]

Bodily fluids and physical extremes are recurring motifs in Hennessy's solo and later group works. In *Chosen* (2004), which begins outside the Dance Mission Theatre, Hennessy, clad in a wedding dress modified with fetish detail (black lacing up the back revealing a bare back and a spiked dog collar around his neck) climbs onto a fire escape ladder. Taking sips of apple cider vinegar through a straw, he leans forward to stop the dribble of spit soiling the dress before launching into the text of *Illegal Bride*, 'A piss and vinegar letter in honour of the dead world citizens since 11 September 2001'. The poetic rant is addressed to architects of the 2003 Iraq war, corporate members of the military-industrial complex and the common people. Hennessy riles against the government's foreign policies, the creation of a culture of fear, the physical and psychological torture at the Guantanamo Bay prison, and the human cost of the Iraq wars. Bizarre juxtapositions are introduced into the act of protest: clothing (recycled wedding gown), the

---

89 Gere, *How to Make Dances*, op.cit., pp. 51-63; Rachel Kaplan (1990) 'Spit your way to the Holy Land,' *Contact Quarterly*, 15:1, pp. 36-39. Additional detail provided in email correspondence from Hennessy, 2 April 2013.

visceral self-induced gagging, and the catalogue of death and destruction. Rather than retching to *épater la bourgeoisie*, however, the metaphors of bodily fluids parallel those in *Saliva*: both the apple cider vinegar and the retching action have cleansing functions linked to natural remedies. He explains, 'it's this conflict between healing and being sick, trying to purge myself of all the negativity and hurt and hate by saying it in a ritual space, by gagging and spitting it with sacred witness, by demonstrating that we don't have to keep this poison inside us'.[90]

Inside the theatre, *Chosen* moves into cabaret format, as Hennessy shifts between lecture mode, dance and song segments. His thesis expanded from the Middle East situation into a critique of broader socio-political institutions of imperialism, post-colonial struggles, class and race imbalances and gender oppression. Eloquent references pepper his monologue, with a bibliography in the programme notes. Self-deprecating quips lighten the tone when Hennessy improvises before establishing the body as an overtly political site. Appearing from behind a US flag hanging vertically centre-stage, Hennessy introduces Mark Twain's *War Prayer*, written in response to the policy of Benevolent Assimilation between 1899-1901 in which hundreds of thousands of Philippine citizens were killed. Critical of unquestioning patriotism, the *War Prayer* was widely circulated on the internet after 11 September 2001.

On his knees, clad in stars and stripes boxing shorts with flag-embossed boxing gloves, Hennessy raises his arms and closes his eyes in supplication to recite Twain's biting critique. Back on his feet, he proceeds to box with himself, the sound of fists hitting various body parts – head, chest, stomach, legs, groin – attest to the intensity of contact. Occasionally falling to the floor in an apparent daze, Hennessy struggles back to standing. Physically spent, he removes the gloves and shorts. Clad only in protective jock strap, two laser lights trace across his body as he stretches up and bends forward in slow motion. As red tape around his hands falls away, he strips down completely, as if metaphorically removing the defence of the flag that both protected him and embellished the gloves that pummelled him. A pale light washes over his vulnerable body. The interior of his mouth illuminated by the lasers' eerie red light, Hennessy breaks into a cappella rendition of the Christmas carol 'O little town of Bethlehem'. Iconic images are rendered – the Silvester Stallone character in the *Rocky* films, the prayerful pose juxtaposed with Twain's images of death and destruction, and the Christmas carol issuing forth from a glowing mouth. Turning to face the flag, Hennessy pulls on two strings and the last vestiges of the Stars and Stripes fall to the floor.

While sections of *Chosen* are blatantly political with a didactic tone, the

---

90 Keith Hennessy email correspondence with author, 25 July 2006.

audience is also entertained. Hennessy sings of the middle-age artist's blues (hair loss, crooked teeth, lack of health insurance and death of his parents), strumming the same guitar chord over and over. Gospel, hymn, and folk music forms feature in Hennessy's work with Circo Zero, the contemporary circus comprised of multi-talented performers – contortionists (such as Jade Blue Eclipse), acrobats and singers. Their CD *A Cabaret of Danger and Compassion*, offers contemporary versions of traditional folk and gospel songs, a miners' strike song, and the *Star Spangled Banner*, causing one to listen to old messages with a new consciousness. Hennessy explained that the musical choices stem from recognition of America's mongrel character, its mixture of blood lines, evident in the Celtic and West African spiritual music of Southeastern United States which is influenced by struggle and successes of survival.[91]

Hennessy expands upon theatrical precedents of the Living Theatre, which he cites as a strong influence. Established in 1947 in New York City, its co-founders, Julian Beck and Judith Malina, were influenced by Antonin Artaud, Erwin Piscator, and Bertolt Brecht. Their unwavering commitments to anarchy and non-violence resulted in imprisonment for participating in demonstrations and for tax evasion, leading to a period of exile in Europe. In highly experimental and increasingly political productions, the Living Theatre sparked controversy by blurring boundaries between theatrical illusion and reality. Improvisatory components endowed actors with power conventionally held by the director; they broke through the 'fourth wall' and communicated directly with the audience. Connections between politics, art and the personal were increasingly drawn together, inspired by a belief in the power of theatre to awaken the audience to direct action and affect change in society.[92]

Krissy Keefer and Dance Brigade

Krissy Keefer, artistic director of the Dance Brigade, also lists the Living Theatre as an inspiration. From its roots in the 1970s women's movement, the Dance Brigade is the oldest and, some might argue, the most politically vociferous dance company extant in the Bay Area. Co-founders Keefer and Nina Fichter (1954-2003) honed their choreographic and management skills in the Wallflower Order, an all-female dance company established in 1975 in Eugene, where Keefer majored in dance at the University of Oregon. The women's collective was 'just making pieces about our lives', resonating with wider artistic trends of the period and drew on a feminist

---

91 Keith Hennessy, email correspondence with author, 5 March 2006. Circo Zero's cd, *Circle: The Songs of Circo Zero*, 2003, is available from CounterPULSE, www.counterpulse.org.

92 Aronson Arnold (2000) *American Avant-theatre: A History*, pp. 54-55.

network.[93] Keefer notes that their artistic isolation and distance from New York meant that they developed on their own rather than responding to east coast trends. When the Wallflower Order split in 1984, the San Francisco-based Dance Brigade was established with Fichter as co-director until 1997 when she was debilitated by ill health. The Wallflower Order's search for a women's spirituality and its strong links to the community continued with the Dance Brigade.

With Keefer's strong background in ballet and a childhood watching the 'Fractured Fairytale' cartoons on television,[94] the ballet classics were a natural choice for Dance Brigade's big projects. *Cinderella: A Tale of Survival* (2002) altered the fairytale into an indictment of domestic abuse and celebration of female strength and love, with allusions to *Giselle*. A ten year run of the *Revolutionary Nutcracker Sweetie* began in 1986, the reworking of E.T.A. Hoffmann's tale offered audiences an escape from the traditional holiday fare. According to the Dance Brigade website, it reached a cumulative audience of 40,000. Tchaikovsky's score formed the basis for a commissioned jazz score by Marty Watson, played by a live band, with additional non-western musical sections. Like the cartoons, quirky narrative twists are subversive and overtly political in places. The Stahlbaums are replaced by the McGreedy family, with irritable and selfish Mrs McGreedy (danced by Keefer) and a bespectacled Paul Parish as Mr McGreedy.[95] Epifano played Drosselmeyer, their long-absent daughter, who entered on the back of a motorcycle in the 1992 version, declaring her lesbian sexuality (although arriving on a skateboard another year), reminiscent of the Dykes on Bikes group who lead San Francisco's Gay Pride Parade.

Life is injected into the usually staid party scene, peopled by a range of over-the-top characters (blonde bombshell tap dancers, aerobic fitness buffs, Madonna impersonators, and masked ninjas). The first 'doll' to dance is a Native American woman. A ritual chant evokes her ancestral spirits, recalling their oppression, offset by prayers that all men, women and children walk in peace and beauty. An African-American youth group performs a cross between a step-dance and hip-hop, their song a tribute to an African motherland. The mice king's seven heads are caricatures of

93 Other members of the Wallflower Order were Suchi Branfman, Lyn Neeley and Pamela Gray. Anna Kisselgoff (1982) 'Dance: Wallflower Order's Politics,' *The New York Times*, 24 September.

94 The *Fractured Fairy Tales* cartoons by Jay Ward premiered in 1959 on the *Rocky and His Friends* cartoon show, renamed *The Bullwinkle Show* when it moved from ABC to NBC in 1961. Subtle changes to some of the titles (Sweeping Beauty, and The Prince and his Popper) hint at the satirical social commentary in the twisted tales. See http://bullwinkle. toonzone.net.htm, accessed 8 November 2006.

95 Analysis of the *Revolutionary Nutcracker Sweetie* is taken from a video of the 1992 production.

presidents and world leaders, and his minions in dark suits and sunglasses battle with freedom fighters.

Maria is transformed into three Claras, undocumented domestic workers forced from their Central American homelands by political events. Hope arrives in the shape of a black female Nutcracker, danced by Shakiri. A narrator provides linking threads to support the mimed actions, her words translated into American sign language for the hearing impaired. Keefer reappears as the Sugar Plum Fairy, reading from Mao's Little Red Book to declare that 'the people united will never be defeated', a bomber jacket atop her tutu enhances a fighting spirit. To Tchaikovsky's pas de deux music, an Angel of Resistance descends to the stage to join her in a duet. The Mouse King is undone by a broom over the head, distracted during a tango with the Angel. The waltz of the snowflakes section is set in a lake, with aerial work emulating weightlessness of water, danced by seahorses, jellyfish and an array of colourful water creatures. The narration alludes to humanity's disregard for nature as the exotic creatures face extinction.

Dance phrases are tightly constructed, blending balletic legs with sweeping torsos and arms that carry through the expansive impulses to celebrate the hope of freedom in unity. Long flowing skirts worn in the all-female waltz of the flowers enhance the circularity of their turns. In Act II, dances celebrate diversity in various forms: the indigenous population of the Americas (Aztecs), disability with the integrated Axis Dance Company, the Hawaiian *hula kahiko* with spiritual roots rather than the tourist version. For ten years, the inclusive spectacle was accessible across a broad spectatorship, transforming the celebration of the season into a call for freedom and equality.

A dance trilogy that confronts female stereotypes also tracks the company's development over a ten year period, starting with *Ballet of the Banshees* (1996), created with Kim Epifano. In the solo *Queen of Sheba* (1999), Keefer portrayed a variety of characters. For *Cave Women* (2002), Keefer turned to archaeological research into yogini, sorceresses who lived 1,000 years ago in caves between Afghanistan and Pakistan. Sima Belmar characterised the movement as 'aggressive ballet phrases inflected with African and acrobatic movement. What makes this broad pastiche successful is Keefer's tone: She honours the cultures from which she borrows by never crossing the line into exoticising or fetishizing. Even the explicitly sensual portions of the dance averted objectification.'[96]

In recent years, critics have noted a change in the volume of Keefer's polemic. Reviewing *Cave Women*, Ann Murphy warned:

> Men in the audience may want to take cover. The women onstage reclaim their libidos, but their sexuality has a carnivorous edge – reclaiming the

96 Sima Belmar (2002) 'Dance Brigade review', *Dance Magazine*, April.

'primal feminine' apparently doesn't mean the end of fury. Fortunately, the fury isn't lethal; it's just so deeply felt and radically in-your-face that it gives a whole new meaning to the word 'torrid'.[97]

Limiting her performances to acting roles since 2002, Keefer describes a new-look Dance Brigade as a multi-generational group that offers a glamour absent in its past incarnations. The addition of taiko drumming, a Japanese form of percussion using large stationary drums, coincided with blockbuster films that took martial arts to new heights (such as *Crouching Tiger, Hidden Dragon*). In another shift, over half the reservations for *Cave Women* were from men: 'We used to have a feminist core ...[but] this wasn't just Krissy and her friends.'[98] Although a strong focus on women's issues remains, those of class, race and sexuality are inseparable, the links drawn in bold strokes. Themes include environmental threats (*Dry/Ice*, 2005), and remnants of the cold war ideology towards Cuba (*Dear Fidel*, with additional choreography by José Navarette, 2005). Dance Brigade collaborated with Iraq Vets against the War in a production of Aaron Loeb's play *The Proud* (2012) about war-related post-traumatic stress syndrome and women's experiences of rape in the military, providing a Greek chorus to support the main action. Their theatre spectacles have high production values, drawing on the area's rich musical talents with commissioned scores. A long-time collaborator, Joe Williams' lighting designs shape the stage into dramatic environments with minimal sets, at times augmented by video projections.

Politically inspired collectivity

A strong camaraderie and porous company membership has characterised the dance community and collaborative events often cross company lines. With the 2004 presidential election looming, Hennessy and Circo Zero joined Keefer and the Dance Brigade to create a performance ritual titled *13 Spells for World Peace*. Here, pagan rites and audience participation were integrated into a site-specific spectacle generated in response to anti-Bush feelings. The original title, *13 Spells for Regime Change*, played on President Bush's sound bite repeatedly invoked as justification for the second Iraq war. Advised that the title made a political statement, potentially endangering the company's non-profit, tax-free status due to the 2004 election, Keefer changed the spells, although 'regime change' was later reinstated.

Performed at Somarts (South of Market Arts) space, Hennessy and Circo Zero performers began *13 Spells* outside. An opening prayer welcomed the 'Citizens of Possibility' together, with viewers invited to prove that people can still work together. Hanging upside down from a tree, Hennessy questioned

---

97 Ann Murphy (2002) 'Wise Bird,' *SF Weekly*, 16 January.
98 Quoted in Allan Ulrich (2003) 'Dissent and the Dance Brigade,' *Dance Magazine*, June.

the disappearance of faith by calling on the 'Citizens of the Dead' to remind them of the power of collective action. To vocal accompaniment by the trio Copper Wimmin, the performers represented natural elements using 'movement imagery [that] was simple, highly controlled, and appropriate to their characters'.[99] In the second part, Keefer appeared as Hecate, Queen of the Witches. As Ann Murphy recounts, 'she presented a scenario of a world rotting in order to be renewed. And just before things got too lugubrious or portentous she would with her deft timing quip: "Where's Martha Stewart when we need her?"'[100] Six 'witches' join Keefer in a series of possession dances and a pagan ritual power was enacted: 'We had people write spells down before they came in, and we nailed them to a board and we'd light it on fire.'[101] The 'spells' on the pieces of paper were not broadly legible, yet provided for individual inclusion while engaging in communal protest. Critics commented on the ritual element and the strength of communal feeling achieved – the audience drawn together in an ecstatic release of frustration at political processes. Yet amidst the praise, some remained distanced from the 'healing circle' which closed the event. Felciano explained that it was 'too much Sunday-night-at-church' for her.[102]

Undeterred by descriptions of her work as agit-prop and dogmatic, Keefer stresses the integrity and commitment of Dance Brigade's audiences: 'It's really easy to get caught up in the darkness of the world right now, but Dance Brigade shows are exhilarating. They don't come because the shows are dark and heavy, they come because they are funny: it's enormously powerful to watch women playing drums; the dancers are stunningly beautiful, the costumes, the sets – everything has got so much magic that it is gripping and transforming, it changes the audience at a molecular level.'[103]

Keefer has also been influential as a producer, organising events such as the Lesbian and Gay Dance Festival from 1997 to 2000, co-founded with Anne Bluenthal and Dancers. Other dance festivals are created on political themes, in 2005 these included Women on the Way, the Cuba Caribe Festival, the International Arts Festival and the Manifesti-val for Social Change. At Dance Mission, the Dance Brigade sponsors their own community outreach with scholarships offered to students from the local middle school, providing a safe place to expel adolescent energies. Four hundred children aged two to seventeen participate in their youth programme. The 'Grrl' Brigade was created in 2004, offering performance opportunities which

99 Keith Hennessy, email correspondence with author, 5 March 2006; Rita Felciano (2004) 'Best Wishes – and curses,' SF Bay Guardian, 20-26 October.
100 Murphy (2004) op.cit.
101 Krissy Keefer, interview with author, 10 October 2005.
102 Ibid.
103 Quoted in Debbie Lemmam (no date) 'Art, Activism & Magic: Krissy Keefer in her Own Words', Gilded Serpent, http://www.gildedserpent.com, accessed 20 May 2006.

combine technique, taiko drumming and social issues for girls aged twelve to seventeen. Recreational classes range from Salsa and Afro-Cuban modern dance to tap and hip-hop, drawing in the community beyond the stage.

Performance and Community Spaces

San Francisco's wealth of alternative dance and theatre venues contribute to the innovative breadth of the performance community. A level of artistic freedom is enhanced by the ability to self-produce without constraints of curatorial oversight.[104] Jenkins opened one of the first studio-performance spaces in 1974, marking a rich period of artistic creation as other spaces soon followed. Joining forces with ODC (formerly the Oberlin Dance Collective, led by Brenda Way) in 1983 they purchased an old stable in the industrial area of the Mission District, transformed into the New Performance Gallery, a studio and 250 seat theatre. A real estate boom devastated the arts community in the late 1990s, when soaring rents combined with shifts in the funding environment jeopardised many dance companies and independent choreographers. Jenkins took drastic measures in 1993, selling her share of the company home and disbanding her permanent company to work on a project basis in rented rehearsal space. In 2004, Jenkins opted for a return to stability and opened the Margaret Jenkins Dance Lab. The following year the ODC Dance Commons opened – home to the dance company, a training and performance space – the building serving even more of the dance community since it opened in 2005.

A survey in 2000 of artists and non-profit organisations indicated that 'at risk' arts spaces with average rents of $12.70 per square foot per year had soared to $55 per square foot.[105] In 2000, the Brady Street Dance Center (directed by Keefer) closed after twenty years, and the Dancers' Group Footwork Studio, home to the Joe Goode Performance Group, was forced out in 1999 when their rent increased over 400%, from $3,100 per month to $15,000. For eighteen years the dance space had served approximately 2,500 dancers, students and audience members per month. Hazzard of Dancers' Group, mused that the need to rent a theatre could result in artistic constraints in order to get 'bums on seats', a change from the freedoms inherent in performing in their own space.[106] The community responded vociferously, with dancer-activists gathering forces under the acronym AARGG! (All Against Ruthless Greedy Gentrification). A five-hour performance at Dancers' Group culminated in a three-day occupation of the space in which ten were

---

104 Apollinaire Scherr (2000) 'Space: The Final Frontier,' *Dance Magazine*, April, pp.60-63.

105 Levy Chonin and Dan Levy (2000) 'No Room for the Arts,' *San Francisco Chronicle*, 17 October.

106 Steve Winn (2000) 'Survival Stories,' *San Francisco Chronicle*, 18 October, C-1.

arrested.[107] The Art Strikes Back coalition took their protests to the streets in a site-specific performance series and an occupation of City Hall.

The history of another alternative performance venue exemplifies problems and possibilities inherent in the freedom to self-produce. In 1992, the 848 Community Space opened in a spacious storefront that housed a jazz club at one point, located on Divisadero Street in the Western Addition district. Volunteer activists started the space – Hennessy, saxophonist Michael Whitson (aka 'Med-O') and sculptor Todd Eugene – although Eugene was replaced by Jess Curtis six months after they opened. With living space upstairs occupied by those who made it run, the ethos was informed by an anarchic spirit, functioning as a multi-disciplinary site for diverse communities. They had a policy of 'no one turned away for lack of funds', initially operating independent of external grants and offering a unique gathering spot, gallery and performance space. Hennessy described it as 'an intentionally cultivated space for investigating community as a social support network, healing context, and as an organizing tool'.[108] Curtis and Hennessy co-directed the space until their departure from the city in 1998, while Curtis and then wife Maher rented an apartment in the mid-1990s which they made into an auxiliary space.[109]

A sign on the door read 'An urban site for Art, Spirit, Sex & Justice' and the quarterly calendar described it as: 'a community access, do-it-yourself space available to artists, activists, and community experimenters for meetings, performances, public discussions, rituals, art exhibits, and safer sex events'.[110] Workshops and art exhibitions were scheduled alongside Buddhist meditation classes. Contact jams became a weekly event, established by Maher and ongoing at their new location, CounterPULSE. Entering and leaving the stage space through the kitchen, established artists (including Lucas Hoving, Halprin and Charlip) and young choreographers adapted to the spatial quirks in their performances. Donated technological accoutrements transformed the studio space into a theatre and utility bills were 'auctioned' to help defray running costs.

The inclusion of sex events marked the site's difference to other alternative performance venues and generated substantial controversy. In the wake of the AIDS epidemic Hennessy felt that a space for positive sex education and celebration was needed. Despite liberal attitudes in San Francisco, tensions arose due to what some perceived as an overt sexual emphasis to the

107 Sam Whiting (2000) 'Groups that Keep the Heat On,' *San Francisco Chronicle*, 18 October.
108 Keith Hennessy email correspondence with author 5 March 2006.
109 Hennessy and Curtis personal correspondence, 2013, op.cit.
110 Keith Hennessy (1995) 'Hype or Revolution or What?', Hennessy, Keith and Rachel Kaplan, eds. *More Out Than In: Notes on Sex, Art and Community*, p. 3.

detriment of programming which commented upon class and race issues. Some dancers boycotted events and widespread gossip prompted Hennessy to call for essays on the issues. Published in *More Out Than In*, the contributions provide contrasting perspectives about issues of sexuality and performance, raising questions about self and institutional censorship.[111]

Despite the departure of Hennessy and Curtis, 848 remained open until it merged with the Bay Area Center for Art and Technology in 2005. The new organisation, CounterPULSE, moved to a larger space, exemplifying changing fortunes for arts in the Bay Area, away from a period when young artists could realistically earn enough to survive on and have sufficient time to devote to their artistic endeavours. In an interview, Jessica Robinson Love, director of CounterPULSE, pondered how the political tone has changed alongside economic shifts: '848 was very much in this DIY, do it yourself aesthetic of the early nineties that relied on people being able to not work so much and have a lot of free time to put into that sort of anarchic endeavours'. A professionalisation of the dance community has occurred at some levels, as dancers are required to function within more formalised structures, whereas the volunteer and fringe aspects that flourished in earlier decades are diminished. Love spoke of the need to rise to new challenges of a larger budget, and achieving the organisational shifts required for survival in the current climate, 'how to look good to funders and keep that community participation element'.[112] The dance component shares space with other cultural activists and is engrained in the ethos of some of the groups that use the space, such as the prison reform group Critical Resistance. Post-performance discussions and opportunities to actively engage audience members through letter campaigns to political representatives encourages individual agency. The cosmopolitan zeitgeist of performers who split their time between countries is evident in the programming, which has become increasingly international in scope. The Dance Discourse series of panel discussions opens the way for developing independent intellectual inquiry, for artists to connect with academics, exploring debates over representation (such as Judith Butler in a session on gender and performativity), class, funding and practicalities of producing work. CounterPULSE has become a home to the multiple diasporic groups since 2009, co-sponsoring the Performing Diaspora series with a diverse collective of community and cultural groups.

In shifts away from identity politics as a focus of dance seen in the 1980s and early 1990s, Love perceives a divide between artists from an activist background making work about their issues and 'people coming from an art background who may decide to make a piece about war and the next

---

111 Hennessy and Kaplan, eds., ibid.
112 Jessica Robinson Love, interview with the author, 14 October 2005.

time decide to make a piece about the role of women. It's not *their* issue.'[113] But for those profiled here, there is no divide. In a 1977 *Dance Magazine* article, Eleanor Rachel Luger highlights the collaborative character of the Bay Area dance community, one which arose out of necessity due to the lack of an institutional framework to support professional dance practice and performance.[114] In the ensuing decades, the situation has changed, with numerous institutions providing a foundation on which a professional dance community thrives, despite the economic upheavals of the 1990s and the financial crash of 2008 and its slow recovery. The ongoing struggle for funding requires ingenuity, perseverance and grant-writing expertise.

After the closure of dance spaces, resolve and determination to maintain the vibrancy of their artistic impulses has seen the opening of Dance Mission, Dance Brigade's current home, which houses a 150-seat theatre and three studios. Jenkins' energies have continued to support the wider dance community through diverse projects. The National Dance Lab offered subsidised rehearsal space for choreographers and their collaborators at the University of California at Berkeley's Extension campus in San Francisco. In 2004, she was instrumental in establishing CHIME (Choreographers in Mentorship Exchange), a formal mentoring programme where young creators are partnered with more experienced choreographers, and are supported through stipends and free studio space. CHIME's mission includes the alleviation of the choreographer's sense of isolation, and to encourage the sharing of experience among independent choreographers. The project also expands critical frameworks in the creative process through the one-to-one relationships and in forums, panel discussions and informal performances and has garnered sufficient funding to support out-of-state choreographers.[115]

Other institutions have been resurrected since the devastation caused by the real estate boom. Dancers' Group's new home opened in 2007 near CounterPULSE in the SoMa area and collaborate on projects with their neighbour. Dancers' Group also sponsors *In Dance*, offering a publication outlet for artists to explore historical and current issues and practices, moving the discourse forward for themselves, scholars and interested afficiandos. The San Francisco Dance Center, home to Alonzo King's Lines Ballet, reopened in a new location. ODC's years of work raised the $9.5 million needed to open their new home in which the various strands of the company's work have expanded. Although not discussed in depth within this article, the longevity and diversity of the ODC's community

---

113 Ibid.
114 Luger op.cit.
115 CHIME Pilot Final Report, http://www.mjdc.org (accessed 17 March 2007). The multiple manifestations of the mentoring programme are detailed on the CHIME website, http://www.mjdc.org/CHIME/chime.html, accessed 23 July 2013.

ventures and educational outreach have been an integral part of the dance ecology, providing performing, training and creative space to independent choreographers and dance teachers.

Moving Forward

Rachel Howard's 2006 article, 'Dancing in the Bay Area: Dance Guide A-Z,' attests to a rich aesthetic diversity among more than 100 companies, venues and festivals.[116] As she acknowledges, the guide details only a portion of the area's vibrant dance community as does this article. I am conscious of omitting numerous choreographers, teachers and performers and am reassured by the number of MA dissertations and PhD theses that have multiple Bay Area dance activities as their subject. In particular, more research is needed into those who pioneered African and African-American dance and its collectives. The Black Choreographers Festival: Here and Now came into being in 2005, ten years after the demise of the annual Black Choreographers Moving into the 21st Century festival. The Ethnic Dance Festival has continued since 1978, its open auditions as much an audience draw as its three week run every summer. The ground-breaking work of the integrated Axis Dance Company continues to challenge perceptions of disability. Others whose work intersects with social issues focus on diverse Asian identities and the history of oppression, and Sean Dorsey's Fresh Meat Productions brings transgender and queer issues to the forefront. Howard's guide reveals the extent to which a new alternative dance community has emerged, integrating a wide range of movement techniques (from butoh to hip-hop).

Those chosen for in-depth investigation here remain significant for their longevity, their influence on younger choreographers and for the reach of their impact beyond the local area and increasingly, internationally. Many discussed here have served as CHIME mentors. Haigood's commissions span the country and Europe, she is a regular in New York's Dance in the Streets Festival, and continues to reveal social histories of racism and hope. Goode has taught technique and choreography locally and in universities across the country. Jenkins' residencies have taken her company to India and China and the mentoring programme is expanding. After touring internationally with performance artists Guillermo Gómez-Peña and Roberto Sifuentes, Mann continues to explore a range of contemporary social themes with diverse collaborators.

A significant presence in Europe and in universities has been established by the Contraband and CORE collaborators. Hennessy performs extensively in New York and Europe where he spends three to four months a year and he remains engaged in San Francisco's dance, performance, queer and activist

---

116 Howard, Rachel (2006) 'Dancing in the Bay Area: Dance Guide A-Z,' *San Francisco Chronicle*, 29 January, pp. PK-14.

scenes. The University of California Davis Performance Studies programme includes Hennessy and Curtis in their postgraduate alumni. Curtis is based in Berlin half the year, his company Gravity tour internationally to critical acclaim, and Curtis has choreographed for the integrated dance company, Blue-Eyed Soul, based in Shropshire, England. Maher settled in Berlin in 1998 and co-founded Ponderosa in Stolzenhagen, Germany, a performance and living collective created on ecologically sustainable principles, and set in a rural village. Collaborative, community, and non-hierarchical ideologies shape the ethos of training sessions that bring practitioners together to live as well as dance, think, discuss and explore their surroundings. Working with Kathleen Hermesdorf and other San Francisco artists, residency courses and intensive summer training sessions build on the somatic and improvisation practices evident in productions that push performance and physical boundaries in multiple ways. The intellectual discourses about the relationships between art, life and political embodiment have been furthered by opportunities to engage in debates and exploration on multiple continents.

Keefer's Dance Brigade shows continuously sell out to an increasingly diverse audience and they have begun working with theatre groups in Columbia. Dance Mission offers a vital resource for established and new choreographers, many of whom work at grassroots levels within diverse communities, either with stand-alone projects or sessions linked to productions. The belief in the transformative power of dance is evident in Epifano's educational group, Mudd Butt International, co-directed with Sally Davies, which takes young Americans to remote locations such as India and Tibet to move them out of their comfort zones and work cross-culturally with dance.[117]

The choreographic drive of those who call San Francisco home is augmented by the wealth of talented musicians, visual and media artists and musicians who help shape the theatrical messages of diverse performers. Even the 'mainstream' choreographers are required to engage in the never-ending search for funding, although university teaching offers some respite from financial struggles, providing the stability and resources for further explorations into the intersection between art and politics. Those investigated here exemplify the tip of the creative iceberg, the performer-choreographers express a generalised recognition of the power of community, the belief in art as a healing tool at a multiple levels. Keefer, Hennessy and Mann all speak of alternative spiritual or pagan sources which inform their work and their perception of art's power. Although these revelations may reinforce stereotypes of San Francisco dance as the embodiment of 'new age' philosophies, the performances are rigorously researched, well crafted, and entertaining while the political voice remains vociferous and vibrantly

---

117 Kim Epifano (2008) 'A Red Thread', *In Dance*, September.

engaging. Intense and at times deeply personal, San Francisco's postmodern dance theatre offers confrontations and entertainment which challenge viewers on physical, emotional, intellectual, social, and for some, highly spiritual levels.

Chapter 4

Encountering the South Asian Diaspora: Dance Education, Heritage and Public Performance in London

Denigrated as dance is in the national curriculum, underfunded by the government, hugely at risk in the current Arts Council reorganisation, the dance community has no option but to fight back to nourish and win the public in its own way on its own terms. The alternative is oblivion.'[1]
Peter Brinson, 1991

'13 years on from its inception as part of the ISTD [Imperial Society of Teachers of Dancing], the new Classical Indian Dance Faculty recognises the success of both Bharatanatyam and Kathak in the UK and, with its new name, states Faculty Chair, Sujata Banerjee, 'Anyone can call them-selves a Classical Indian Dancer no matter where he or she comes from'.[2]
Ann R. David, 2013

In 1991 dance advocate and scholar Peter Brinson challenged Britain's dance community to work together to engage the public. Twenty-one years later, one might assume the fight has been won. In 2012 dance took a central place in the public celebrations of royal longevity (the Diamond Jubilee marking 60 years of Queen Elizabeth's reign) and international sporting events of the Olympic Games and Paralympic Games in London. Mass choreographic spectacles, community and social dance activities, and dance theatre performances populate a vibrant cultural landscape where non-western styles such as South Asian dance are prevalent. New objectives, new audiences and new forms have emerged, challenging and changing perceptions of multicultural Britain. This has occurred alongside continual struggle for funding as different sectors strive to establish and retain a place in the dance ecology. A wealth of accomplishments rests on the foundations of an institution-building process involving networking and lobbying, advances in dance education at all levels, and performances in public arenas, conventional theatres and alternative spaces. According to the national dance organisation Dance UK, approximately 200 dance companies exist in Britain (encompassing England, Scotland, Wales and Northern Ireland)

---

1 Peter Brinson (1991) *Dance as Education*, p. 44
2 Ann R. David (2013) 'Change of an era': http://www.istd.org/news/istd-news/change-of-an-era/, 18 June..

and government funding has been central to the development of the field.[3] Situated within physical education, dance is compulsory in primary schools (ages 5-11) and optional in secondary schools (ages 11-16) where it can be studied as a specialist subject separately from physical education. A vibrant community dance profession has evolved, offering myriad opportunities for engagement with multiple dance styles. The South Asian dance field – encompassing forms from India, Pakistan, Bangladesh, Sri Lanka and practised by diasporic communities around the world – is a highly successful sector, creating opportunities for people to engage with diverse styles as spectators and practitioners, from recreational to professional levels.

Since the 1980s, an increased presence of South Asian dance can be linked to shifts in the nation's demographics, as documented extensively in scholarship and reports that situate activities in relation to wider society, dance and performance fields. As early as 1986, research on interculturalism in the arts in Britain brought together scholars from different disciplines to work with a performance group (musicians, dancers, singers, writers and filmmakers) from Africa and Asia, exploring their traditional practices within contemporary Britain. The Pan Project helped establish a model of cultural interchange between performers and scholars, analysed through anthropological and sociological methodologies that interrogated performance as a mode of enhancing cross-cultural understanding. Still functioning as the Pan Intercultural Arts, the mission to use arts for social change is seen to reinforce cultural diversity and empower those in marginalised circumstances.[4] In 1997, Alessandra Iyer's edited anthology of articles by scholars and dancers continued the exchange and reflection from within the field while the comprehensive South Asian Dance in Britain Report (SADiB), by Andrée Grau, was published in 2002. Commissioned by the Leverhulme Trust, it summarises conclusions from a two-year investigation of South Asian dance within the British dance ecology at the turn of the 21st century. Case studies that interrogate identity politics (gender, nationality, religion) and aesthetic discourse are explored by Grau, Ann R. David, Avanthi Meduri, Alessandra Lopez y Royo and Janet O'Shea among others.[5]

---

3 'Things you should know about dance', Dance UK, http://www.danceuk.org/resources/dance-facts/ accessed 8 June 2013.

4   Andrée Grau (1992) 'Intercultural Research in the Performing Arts'. The Pan Intercultural Arts website documents the group's history, http://www.pan-arts.net/pages/about.html, accessed 15 September 2013.

5 Alessandra Iyer (now Lopez y Royo), ed. (1997) *South Asian Dance: The British Experience*; Andrée Grau (2002) *South Asian Dance in Britain*, with research by Alessandra Lopez y Royo and Magdeline Gorringe. The list of significant scholarship grows every year, however, some key resources include Ann R. David (2005) *Performing Faith: Dance, Identity and Religion in Hindu Communities in Leicester and London*; Avanthi Meduri (2008) 'Labels, Histories, Politics: South Asian Dance on the Global Stage'; Avanthi Meduri (2008) 'The

The discussion which follows draws on this foundation to contexualise an overview of where the diasporic dance is situated in the early 21st century. Demographic changes recorded in the 2011 census generated sensationalist headlines announcing the decline of white British population in London. Despite assumptions about increased migration generating this flight, the departures can be seen as evidence of rising affluence and class mobility.[6] The multicultural mix that makes London such a vibrant place is cause for celebration or anxiety, depending on one's outlook. Britain's imperial past, its leadership of a commonwealth of now independent nations, perpetuates relations of postcolonial power that raise questions of inclusion where diasporic forms such as African People's dance (with roots in the African diaspora) and South Asian dance are prominent in festivals and public events. The tagline 'world in one city' perpetuated an image of harmony among diversity within the capital city in publicity campaigns for the 2012 Olympic Games.

In this chapter, South Asian dance is explored within education and public arts frameworks, influenced by debates about multiculturalism that have shaped the arts establishment. Practitioners and advocates have helped construct and circulate a dance heritage that situates current practices as valid and valued aspects of social life – individually and collectively. Issues of training and hierarchies of style are investigated in the context of a complex and changing socio-political environment that undergoes radical swings in policies according to the ideologies of each government that holds power. Dance is embedded within the education system at formal and informal levels, with a distinct South Asian dance presence in secondary and further education qualifications. To what extent is a broad awareness and appreciation of the styles influenced by dance training and education? How have practitioners been instrumental in shaping the discourse of the field which has had a phenomenal growth in a few decades? What role does the contemporary choreography of artists such as Shobana Jeyasingh and Akram Khan play in the understanding and appreciation of diasporic dance practices? Close scrutiny reveals a mixed picture about what is taught and how it shapes perceptions of both classical and popular styles – from bharatanatyam (historically situated in the south of India and linked to India's nationalist movement prior to independence in 1947) and kathak (associated predominantly with North India, with Muslim and Hindu influences) to Bollywood (a popular film genre) and bhangra (Punjabi folk dance form). Crucially, the field has developed upon the advocacy of grassroots organisations such as Akademi, Kadam, Sampad and Milapfest, among others.

Transfiguration of Indian/Asian Dance: Janet O'Shea (2003) 'At Home in the World'.
6 Mark Easton (2013) 'Why have the white British left London'. BBC News online, http://bbc.co.uk/news/uk-21511904.

A proliferation of performances in the nation's capital also interact with cultural and architectural locations, generating layers of meaning in events that celebrate the city's cosmopolitan diversity and its transformation from what sociologist John Eade describes as postimperial capital into a global city, when the might of colonial power diminished after World War II and a new service economy emerged by the 1980s and 1990s.[7] Framed by rich histories of monarchy, military and economic might, dance is visible in spaces that range from the naval and royal history that abounds in Greenwich to the monumental square honouring the battle of Trafalgar at the heart of tourist London. The city has supported production of theatrical spectacles that integrate classical as well as cutting edge South Asian choreography, a number of which have been toured to other locations, as I go on to discuss. These include exotic and nostalgic visions (*Waterscapes*, in Somerset House, 2004), explorations of meditative rituals (*Sufi:Zen*, Greenwich Park, 2010) and a celebration of the place of South Asian women in British society, including its labouring women (*Awaz/Voice*, 2006). Some productions are situated in historical landmarks where power relations between colonised and coloniser can come to the fore, richly evident in Traflagar Square events.

Explicit and implicit political readings of productions are facilitated by analysis of how they alternately complement and critique the heritage of city and nation. Cultural geographer Doreen Massey's analysis of the politics of space highlights how locations are endowed with social interactions which can be disrupted temporally and spatially through artistic interventions. Particular qualities are shared between dance and conceptualisations of space, with space always in construction and always 'social' because it deals with relationships. The construction of space, is 'active and dynamic *in itself* and not merely as a changing response to our moulding of it or through our (human) perception of it'. Of the qualities embedded in space, the most significant is power.[8] As detailed later in the chapter, concepts of power and space take on multiple manifestations, as choreographer Shobana Jeyasingh hinted at in discussing *Counterpoint*, commissioned in 2010 for London's Somerset House. She referred to the character and historical resonance of the courtyard, surrounded by neo-classical symmetry and formal lines, and the need for twenty dancers to create an appropriate presence.[9]

Larger questions of labelling and multiculturalism in themselves easily occupy days of discussion and reams of paper. This chapter utilises existing discourse to explore the professionalisation of the field, the institution-building processes and drive to make South Asian dance an integral part

---

7 John Eade (2000) *Placing London: From Imperial Capital to Global City*.
8 Doreen Massey (2011) 'For Space: Reflections on an Engagement with Dance', p. 36; see also Doreen Massey (2005) *For Space*.
9 Shobana Jeyasingh, panellist at Akademi's *Looking for the Invisible Symposium*, The Place, London, 25 February 2012.

of the dance ecology of Britain. Values and notions of heritage inform community activities and pedagogic developments at all levels, providing additional links between the profession and new generations of dance students, aficionados and the accidental viewer. The relevance of the forms' development in Britain extends beyond its localities as the global exchange of labour and culture circulates artistic innovations back to places of origin and on to other diasporic communities. An overview of significant performances in 2012 provides a starting point to consider where the dance resides within and shapes the cultural landscape.

London 2012 and the Cultural Olympiad

The wealth and range of performance associated with London's role as host to the Olympic and Paralympic Games of 2012 were unprecedented. As a national arts festival, a multi-year Cultural Olympiad presented music, theatre and dance events drawn from a broad spectrum, encompassing Britain's diversity and postcolonial relations. These were seen in *Manchester Meets Africa* (2012) and the South Asian dance and music 3D architectural project *Mandala* (2012) in Nottingham and Birmingham, among other performances. In London, two Arts in Parliament programmes brought the South Asian dance styles of bharatanatyam, kathak and odissi into the hallowed halls of government. Viewers negotiated airport-like security screening to enter Westminster Hall's cavernous room, its high stone walls dating back to the 11th century. The aura of power, of English, national and imperial heritage, were combined with the spectacle of traditional South Asian dance forms. Classical dancers have featured at other official events, such as Sonia Sabri Company's kathak performance at the Conservative Party Conference in Birmingham in October 2010. Sabri was joined by two women in a traditional danced evocation, opening the political gathering with a Hindu prayer and an appeal for arts funding to be sustained by the incoming government.[10] An interplay of forms also occurred, as boundaries between classical, popular and western dance styles cross in events such as the Queen's Coronation Festival performances. Choreographer Jeanefer Jean-Charles mixed rhythms from India with street dance from East London, using 75 dancers supported by 30 *dhol* drummers.[11] All genres were accessible in public spaces and while London activities tend to dominate national publicity and critical scrutiny, other cities such as Manchester,

10 http://www.parliament.uk/about/living-heritage/building/palace/westminster hall/. For example, on 5 July, *Maaya* was created by Gauri Sharma Tripathi, together with Nathaniel Parchment and Shivani Sethia, with a finale performed by Indian bharatanatyam dancer Priyadarsini Govind.
11 Carmel Smith (2013) 'Jeanefer Jean-Charles on dance at the Palace', www.londondance.com.

Birmingham and Liverpool have lively cultural calendars.

In a more casual yet symbol-laden environment and circumstances, a nation-wide week-long campaign 'Big Dance' culminated in a mass performance in Trafalgar Square, having grown from its small roots into a UK wide network of 21 Hubs. Established in 2006, the bi-annual calendar of activities encompasses more than 3,500 events in locations such as swimming pools, schools, high streets and shopping centres, parks and palaces. In Luton, for example, a town with a history of manufacturing and home to an important international airport, one could see Bollywood and bharatanatyam alongside capoeira, salsa and hip hop performers.

Led by professional choreographers, recreational and community groups were brought together in the final Big Dance event on 5th July as part of the London 2012 Festival to mark the end of the Cultural Olympiad. In Trafalgar Square 1,000 performers moved to contemporary choreography by Wayne MacGregor, artistic director of Random Dance Company and Associate Choreographer of the Royal Ballet. Sponsors included a range of organisations: international (the British Council); national (Arts Council England); local government (the Mayor of London); a fund-raising institution with potential monetary payouts to its supporters (the Lottery); and a national dance organisation (the Foundation for Community Dance). Estimates of up to five million participated in or viewed the Big Dance activities[12] – reaching the masses in numeric as well as ideological terms. Diverse identities and styles were embodied in the activities, traditional and classical; popular and social dance; young people and the elderly; and participants with disabilities. A cosmopolitan mix of nationalities and ethnicities was enhanced by interactive dance sessions with schools in India, Sri Lanka, Germany and Lebanon, part of a 5-a-day Fitness campaign.[13] Schools in Britain were linked to students overseas to perform simultaneous on-screen dance routines, the events helping to create a virtual international community.

Dance's association with youth and vitality offers a natural match for elite sporting events, the form emerging as an anti-obesity weapon with the appointment of Arlene Phillips as government 'dance tsar' in 2009. As television and stage choreographer and judge on talent competitions Strictly Come Dancing and So you think you can dance, Phillips and her team of dance ambassadors encouraged people to take up dance to improve fitness. There is an element of irony in Phillips' appointment, having come under fire in the 1970s from a campaign led by Mary Whitehouse to clean up broadcasts for family viewing. Phillips' television dance group Hot Gossip was seen by some to challenge standards of decency with 'raunchy' choreography, while

12 See Big Dance, About us, http://www.bigdance.org.uk/ and http://www.bigdance legacy.co.uk/; also Donald Hutera (2012) 'London 2012 Olympic Games'.
13 Jeanette Siddall (2013) 'Youth Dance Contexts (Part 2)', Lorna Sanders, ed., Dance Teaching and Learning.

others found the dances innovative and exciting.[14] Activities and branding perpetuate particular images and values, evident in the logo for the Olympic Games and the much newer Paralympic Games which have only been held alongside the established Olympics since 1960. The Paralympic competitions celebrated a homecoming, originating as the Stoke Mandeville Games in 1948 created for wheelchair athletes, many of whom had been injured in World War II.[15] The Games' off-kilter graffiti style logo '2012' – in pink, blue, green and orange was inspired by the 'energetic, spirited, bright and youthful' worlds of media, communication and fashion.[16] Inclusion and celebration were echoed in the city's welcome, with multiple sound bites reinforcing the cultural diversity of the Games and the city. Politicians proclaimed that 'every athlete will have a home crowd'; London offered 'a home for every nation' and 'a passion for sport'. In the years after 2005 when London was awarded the Games, tourists were reminded by the then-mayor Ken Livingstone that 'London welcomes the world with open arms and an open mind', with 200 communities that speak 300 languages, which became part of the zeitgeist of the summer of 2012.[17]

The opening ceremony of the Olympic Games included a tongue-in-cheek image of a nation conceived and directed by the film director Danny Boyle. William Shakespeare's *The Tempest* inspired the whirlwind trip through the *Isle of Wonder*, a half hour spectacle of music, dance, text and special effects that opened the larger ceremony. Televised to millions around the world on July 27, 2012, the show presented a nostalgic Britain of the past and 'cool' Britannia of the present. They brought to life the rhetoric of London's Olympic bid, emphasising the city's cultural diversity, juxtaposing vibrant popular cultural practices against a construction of heritage and tradition. Akram Khan's choreography to the singer Emeli Sandé's performance of the hymn *Abide with Me* occupied a central moment. Khan was given the brief of 'mortality' resulting in a dance performed by fifty professional dancers, a nine-year-old boy and Khan.[18] Introduced by a montage of photographs memorialising the 55 people killed in terrorist attacks on 7 July 2005 (referred to as 7/7), the day after London was awarded the Olympic Games, it was a marked contrast to the celebratory party scene and tour of

---

14 Emine Saner (2009) 'Let's Dance: We will if Arlene Phillips has her way'; Katie Gregory (2008) 'West End Girl, interview with Arlene Phillips'.
15 'History of the Movement', International Paralympic Committee, http://www.paralympic.org/TheIPC/HWA/HistoryoftheMovement, accessed 28 August 2013.
16 'About us' page, Cultural Olympiad website, http://www.london2012.com/about-us/cultural-olympiad/, accessed 4 August 2013.
17 Jon Lansman (2012) 'A Big Thank you to Ken for the Multicultural Olympics'.
18 Anon. (2012) 'Akram Khan in London 2012 Olympic Games Opening Ceremony', Akram Khan Company website http://www.akramkhancompany.net/html/akram_news.php?newsid=173&year=2012, accessed 4 August 2013.

social dance across the decades that preceded it. Crouched low in front of a golden orb of light at the start, the darkly clothed group built up a sense of community, moving in and out of disruption and unity. Rippling arms evoked flight, countered by rounded torsos and an inward focus, with cause and effect actions linking them together as undulating movement passed down the line of dancers. Reaches up and out in long lunges contrasted with sliding steps and jumps in place which conveyed a weighty quality. The atmosphere lightened when the focus shifted to Khan and the boy, both dressed in white, playing a game with an imaginary ball. The dance ends on a note of hope, as the boy hugs Khan before being carried and lifted high above the anonymous crowd. Some arm gestures and a rhythmic pulse link the choreography to kathak for those familiar with the style, but a contemporary dance vocabulary dominated the work.

Popular and social dance styles or a popular treatment of ballet featured in the four ceremonies – opening and closing events for the Olympic Games and the Paralympic Games. In the first closing ceremony, Virsa Punjab, a group of British bhangra (Punjabi-style) folk dancers, joined former Monty Python member Eric Idle in a South Asian-infused rendition of the song 'Always look on the bright side of life' from the film *Monty Python's Life of Brian* (1979). The parody struck a chord with some, with online forum comments of both approval and dismay at the choice of bhangra as the sole representative of South Asian dance in the ceremonies. Although Khan is often classified as South Asian in style, as British Asian by birth, many perceive him as a contemporary choreographer rather than representative of the wider diasporic community.[19] Indeed, his publicity – press releases, previews and interviews – constantly reiterate his work as 'a confusion of forms' rather than a fusion of east and west. There had been appeals broadcast on the BBC to include Bollywood in the Opening Ceremony, generating a mixed response that echoed sentiments about the bhangra group.[20]

A multicultural mix was evident in the spectacles of the ceremonies, one where the relations of power and representation sat easily beside each other. The hybridity, mixture of west and the rest, has taken decades to achieve, with government policies instituted in reaction to social unrest arising from racial discrimination and inequities which reached a boiling point in the 1980s. Multiculturalism continues to have its detractors, with polarisation between those who advocate for assimilation, deeming it a failure and those

---

19 See for example, the blog forum for the South Asian Dance and Music journal *Pulse*, http://www.pulseconnects.com/content/BollywoodOlympics, accessed online 23 June 2013.

20 Sita Thomas (2011) 'London 2012: Call to include Bollywood in Opening Ceremony', BBC News online, 27 October 2011, http://www.bbc.co.uk/news/uk-england-london-15480254; Pulseconnects forum, http://www.pulseconnects.com/content/BollywoodOlympics, accessed 4 August 2013.

who continue to assert its relevance for cross-cultural understanding.[21] The history of South Asian dance and its inclusion in prestigious activities are connected to its rising status within wider dance ecology.

South Asian Dance Performance

British-based South Asian dance practitioners stand at the international vanguard in part because of artistic innovation that builds on or diverges from aesthetics of the classical forms and the construction of traditions. A history of Indian presence in European theatres dates back to 1833 with performances of a version of *La Bayadère*, while Indian dancers appeared on London stages as early as 1847. The grand exhibitions and displays of the British colonial world put more Indian dance on display into the late 19th century which was overtaken by impressionistic performance by non-Asian women.[22] As Ann R. David notes, the western performers evoked orientalist perceptions of the 'other'. Uday Shankar and Ram Gopal disrupted these conventions, touring an amalgamation of styles in the 1930s and 1940s, helping establish perceptions of dance forms as high art.[23]

In the intervening decades, the art forms from the Indian sub-continent have become an integral part of mainstream British culture, as marked by the recognition of government honours. In 2013, Nilima Devi was awarded an MBE (Member of the British Empire) in the Queen's New Year's honours list, having celebrated the 30th anniversary of the Centre for Indian Classical Dance in Leicester which she established. She joins other practitioners and advocates in being acknowledged with MBEs, OBEs (Order of the British Empire), and the like for their artistic work: choreographer-dancers Jeyasingh and Khan; Mira Kaushik of Akademi and consultant, writer and artist Naseem Khan.[24] While the awardees represent diverse styles and activities, some also share a common time of arrival. Both Devi and Jeyasingh arrived in Britain in the early 1980s, when kathak exponent Pratap Pawar, bharatanatyam dancer and Carnatic musician Pushkala Gopal, and kathakali dancer Unnikrishnan were among those establishing schools and performing careers in Britain. Since then, grassroots efforts to enhance awareness of South Asian dance forms have coincided with advances in dance education at all levels and wider audience development. The non-western forms have global prominence, their British-based practitioners tour internationally, with summer schools and venues

21 For a comprehensive historical and theoretical summary of multiculturalism in the UK, see Andrée Grau (2008) 'Dance and the Shifting Sands of Multiculturalism'.
22 Grau (1992) op.cit.; p. 12.
23 David (2005) op.cit.
24 Avanthi Meduri (2008) 'Labels, Histories, Politics' analyses the significance of labels in Mira Kaushik's speech after receiving her MBE.

attracting performers and teachers of renown from around the world. The development of dance in general and South Asian dance specifically, has occurred through a range of strategic, efforts and lobbying activities to identify avenues of funding.

As the complex history has been detailed elsewhere, I touch only briefly on some key moments here to situate later discussion. In 1976, Naseem Khan's report *The Arts that Britain Ignores: The Arts of Ethnic Minorities in Britain* chronicled the decades-long but limited presence of what was then labelled Indian dance. Recreational practices in local community halls, temples and specialist cultural centres such as London's Bharatiya Vidya Bhavan persevered despite the lack of a supportive infrastructure through which to disseminate the classical forms. Established in 1972, the Bhavan Centre offers classes in language, dance and music as well as sponsoring summer schools and performances that attract international luminaries from teachers and performers of Indian classical dance and music. Bringing the diasporic dances out of the community group spaces and temples, and into proscenium arch theatres coincided with a broader support and recognition of minority ethnic arts in Britain. In the decade following publication of Khan's report, arts policies began to shift in response to extensive unrest and protests about social injustices and racial inequalities. In particular, London's coffers provided a rich resource for black and minority ethnic artists and those marginalised by their sexuality. Asian artists were classified as 'black', a label that encompassed not just race but political status, including a range of nationalities, ethnicities and religions across Asia, Africa and the former British colonies. The label South Asian dance began to replace 'Indian' dance in administrative, political and institutional frameworks – taking account of the transnational roots of practices which spread beyond national borders, while its community of practitioners continue to use 'Indian'.[25]

In the decade following *The Arts that Britain Ignores*, South Asian dance's place in Britain's theatre spaces was celebrated by an event which in retrospect highlighted the trajectory of the field. Naseem Khan recalled the official launch of the national dance organisation ADiTi in 1991. On an overcast summer's day in Bradford's city centre bharatanatyam, kathak, odissi, kathakali and raas garba (a folk form) dancers in costume gathered near the Alhambra Theatre.

At a given signal, the dancers flocked across the street to the pounding insistent thump of the Punjabi *dhol* [drum]. At the theatre, wave upon

25 Naseem Khan (1976) *The Arts That Britain Ignores: the arts of the ethnic minorities in Britain*, London: The Arts Council of Great Britain. The history of arts funding in relation to South Asian dance is detailed by numerous scholars, Grau (1992, 2008) op.cit. while Christy Adair (2007) summarises the history of funding and the political implications of the label 'black' dance in *Dancing the Black Question*. See also Meduri (2008) 'Labels' op.cit.

wave ran in unison to the large glass doors and symbolically beat on them. After the last wave, the Lord Mayor and his wife, grinning from ear to ear, flung open the doors, tossed flower petals under the advancing dancers' feet and welcomed them in.[26]

The community of dancers at the Alhambra included folk and classical styles, a diversity feeding into years of discussion about representation and aesthetics. Projects were supported by philanthropic organisations while government also funded research that established connections between academics and practitioners. Large projects are exemplified by the Arts and Humanities Research Council (AHRC) Cross-Cultural Research Project in Music and Dance Performance, a five year joint project between University of Surrey, SOAS (the School of African and Oriental Studies) and University of Roehampton, while ResCen is another intercultural research centre based at the University of Middlesex. New PhD research expanded debates about identity and representation, heritage and tradition, and the function of dance as marker of diverse identities – national, religious, gender, class and race. While attracting the interest of scholars from outside the community, debate was also coming from within the field. Jeyasingh's seminal essay 'Imaginary Homelands', published in a 1998 dance studies anthology, signalled the centrality of themes of belonging and diaspora as she explored her cosmopolitan roots in specialist dance journals as well.[27] There was an emphasis on the fluidity of identity and cosmopolitan sources of its construction in the writing and on the stages. As cultural theorist Avtar Brah argues, 'the concept of diaspora offers a critique of discourses of fixed origins, while taking account of a homing desire which is not the same thing as a desire for a 'homeland'.[28] Generational distinctions and expectations of arrival in a new home emerge in choreography discussed later in the chapter.

The wealth of research and dance development led to a level of acceptance within mainstream venues, seen in performance platforms such as Daredevas, where young dancers also develop choreographically. After the 6 October 2006 show at a prestigious central London venue, Naseem Khan declared that South Asian dancers were able to 'take a bow along with the other proper dancers, accepting the warm applause of the South Bank audience as if they were not interlopers and imposters – as if they were really entitled to it!'[29] A sense of heritage was established in the discourse that is recognisable beyond its diasporic origins. Khan noted that

---

26 Naseem Khan (1997) 'South Asian Dance in Britain', in Alessandra Iyer, ed., op.cit. p. 28.
27 Shobana Jeyasingh (1998) 'Imaginary Homelands', *Routledge Dance Studies Reader.*
28 Avtar Brah (1996) *Cartographies of Diaspora*, p. 177.
29 Naseem Khan (2008) 'Dance Heritage: Stone or Water?', *Pulse*, Summer, p. 7.

although there were only 100 Indians in Birmingham in 1939, 'they had no shops, no community centre, mosque, gurdwara [Sikh temple] or temple but they did hold onto their roots'. This connection to origins emerges as a recurring theme while questions of identity, of Britishness that occupy press and political debates, construct links to the past and often to a nostalgic version of culture. Khan notes 'In a sense, the South Asian dance world is in a privileged position because it has been dealing with questions that arise around the place of heritage and tradition for a very long time.' [30]

The expansion of British South Asian dance practices is linked to the influx of immigration from East Africa, from Sri Lanka and new locations in India, generating demands for folk or community-based recreational groups. Other practitioners were inspired 'to take "heritage" arts beyond the immediate community and make artistic spaces for Indian dance in the mainstream', however, Khan reinforced how the lack of a sufficiently large pool of professional dancers required them to go beyond their own 'cultural support team', in order to acquire public funding and attract mainstream audiences. [31] A period of phenomenal growth occurred as a result of strategic decisions, achieved through the work of support organisations in multiple cities. They have come together in the organisation SADA (South Asian Dance Alliance), encompassing a geographical and stylistic diversity: Akademi (London, formerly the National Academy of Indian Dance, est. 1979), Bharatiya Vidya Bhavan (est. 1972, London), Chaturangan (est. 2002, Liverpool), Centre for Indian Classical Dance (CICD est. 1981, Leicester), Kadam (Luton est. 1991), Kala Sangam (Bradford est. 1993), Milapfest (Liverpool est. 1985) and Sampad (Birmingham est. 1990).

The place of women within the dance community conforms in many ways to their dominant numbers as dancers, teachers and students in western dance styles. Extensive scholarship has conceptualised how notions of heritage and nation, perpetuating ideas around tradition, are conveyed through the female dancer. In an intriguing reversal of gender dominance, most of the South Asian dance organisations established in the 1980s and 1990s have women in managerial, administrative and creative positions. The proportions are remarkable, particularly in contrast to articles lamenting the absence of female choreographers in ballet and the dominance of men in positions of power in dance institutions. The predominance of women within dance organisations also challenges widespread perceptions of patriarchal power among the South Asian diaspora, where women are perceived as subordinate within their local communities despite living in a western society that claims a more equitable gender balance. [32] Whereas some

---

30 Ibid. pp. 7-8.
31 Naseem Khan, Chitra Sundaram, Ginnie Wollaston and Piali Ray (2001) 'Moving Margins', http://www.narthaki.com/info/articles/article13.html.
32 See for example, Susan Crow (2002) *Invisible Women* on women in ballet and

class, caste, religious and national groups do constrain female agency and independence, there are many women in the South Asian and British Asian community whose entrepreneurial and educational achievements defy such stereotypes. Two South Asian dancers have been acknowledged with Asian Women of Achievement Awards in the category of Arts & Culture: Anusha Subramanyam of Beeja Dance Company (2011) and Shalini Bhala (2013), founder of the *Just Jhoom!* exercise franchise, as discussed later in the chapter.

Creating institutions such as the ISTD

From ballroom to natural movement styles, ballet to high society balls, British dance institutions have paved the way for the codification and standardisation of dance training at international levels. Some examination systems were established as early as 1909, such as the ISTD, setting out a level of pedagogic uniformity, and a forum for the international dissemination of ideas about style, training and evaluation as explored in chapter two. The institutionalisation of contemporary dance education and training occurred alongside a professionalisation of the forms which had multiple strands. European modern dance and movement training and analysis systems, derived from the work of Rudolf Laban, helped establish dance education within teacher training. As in the USA, dance has long associations with physical education departments at university level while physical education teachers were early advocates of dance in British schools.[33]

Laban's philosophy was instrumental in spreading dance in the 1950s and 1960s, feeding into a more formal integration of dance into the English state education system in the 1970s. The activities which led to the inclusion of dance in schools sets out a model of advocacy comparable to the South Asian dance community's engagement as documented later in the chapter. This was facilitated through relationships between the profession and the mainstream education system which raised the status of dance as a serious subject of study. A new generation of dance practitioners emerged who were able to negotiate the administrative complexities of arts institutions.[34] Lecture-demonstration formats were fundamental to a growing awareness and appreciation of modern dance and spread of American training systems in the 1960s in conservatories such as the London Contemporary Dance School (est. 1966) and later at the Northern School of Contemporary

contemporary dance. Women in South Asian communities in Britain are discussed in Amrit Wilson (2006) *Dreams, Questions, Struggles: South Asian Women in Britain*. Discussion of the transmission of tradition and female dancers is found in Pallabi Chakravorty (1998) 'Dance Hegemony and Nation' and (2008) *Bells of Change*; within bharatanatyam in Meduri (2004) 'Bharatanatyam as a Global Dance'; and within Britain's dance community in Grau (2002), op.cit.
33 Nicholas (2007) *Dancing in Utopia*, pp. 136-142.
34 Bonnie Rowell (2000) 'An Expanding Map', in *Europe Dancing*.

Dance (1985). An innovative period of dance education also flourished at Dartington College of Art in Devon, an idyllic rural location where creative experimentation was supported and shaped in part by American postmodern dance innovators.[35] Over the years, a close adherence to Laban's principles was perceived by some as being too codified and standardised, excluding stylistic diversity and reinforcing a hierarchical perception of the art form also advocated by classical ballet exponents, ultimately constraining the concept of dance education.[36]

Despite the criticisms, the systemisation of dance teaching opened avenues for practitioners to develop professionally within the education system. A late-comer to dance, the educationalist and scholar Peter Brinson was one of the leading activists who helped argue the dance education platform. He initially challenged class-based perceptions of dance as the province of the elite, using lecture-demonstrations to attract new audiences to ballet. In 1964 he helped establish Ballet for All, which became a touring educational unit of the Royal Ballet, perpetuating a 'best for the rest' approach that broke through class and ideological preconceptions about the place of ballet in society and who could access it. Brinson reported on the overall state of dance education and training for the philanthropic Calouste Gulbenkian Foundation, worked with the Council for Dance Education and Training (CDET) as well as university lecturing and helping establish the first BA in Dance at the University of Surrey. Although just one of a number of advocates who have influenced the growth of British dance, Brinson leaves a rich account of ideologies behind the lobbying efforts that resulted in dance becoming part of the national curriculum within physical education in 1988. Brinson argued passionately for recognition of the form on its own merits as art, rather than its marginalised position within PE. The debates continue, with assessments at school level shaped in part by an emphasis on performance which fulfil aims and objectives of a PE rationale, while dance programmes in many universities today are located within an arts rather than a physical education context.[37]

At a fundamental level, Brinson argued for a politically informed British contemporary dance practice to develop, with an ability to discuss and critique a national dance culture and fulfil a social responsibility by creating works to 'seize the imagination and stir the mind'.[38] He noted a decline in dance theatre with an overt engagement with contemporary themes, calling for dance to challenge class-based traditions. A clear ideological imperative is visible in Brinson's writing and advocacy, urging dancers to develop

35 Nicholas (2007) op.cit.
36 Brinson, ibid. 66; see also Sanders, Lorna (2006) *Dance education renewed*, p. 57 for summary of the criticisms of Laban.
37 Sanders (2006), p. 97.
38 Brinson (1991) op.cit. p. 28.

deep connections in the arts – between aesthetics and politics, education and cultural understanding – in opposition to policies of Prime Minister Margaret Thatcher's government which had been in power since 1979, instituting educational reforms that emphasised 'consumerist values', alongside a broader commodification of the arts.[39]

Brinson was not alone in lamenting dance's decline, advocating that its increased marginalisation could be turned around through outreach work and making choreography more accessible to its audiences. *Stepping Forward: Some suggestions for the development of dance in England in the 1990s* was a 1989 report by Graham Devlin for the Arts Council of Great Britain's Dance Department which acknowledged that the dance boom of the 1970s and early 1980s was not matched by increased government funding. Venues were also wary of booking new dance companies which 'are often regarded as being arrogant, unapproachable and uninterested in their audiences'.[40] In contrast, African or African-Caribbean dance companies such as Adzido or Kokuma were praised for their stimulating and accessible work while an 'audience-centred approach' would help achieve a 'productive dance ecology'. The report argued for development to be undertaken by community practitioners in the South Asian and African and African Caribbean fields rather than prioritising dance companies.[41]

The inclusion of dance in the national curriculum in 1988 followed on significant developments in how the education system responded to shifting demographics which opened avenues for South Asian arts to be used to enhance cultural understanding. Tariq Madood and Stephen May summarised how a post-war influx surge of workers from African-Caribbean and Indians, Pakistanis and Bangladeshis in the 1960s to 1980s were followed by their families. Education policies slowly responded to Britain's increasingly multicultural student population starting in the 1960s.[42] Large groups of East Africans of South Asian heritage also arrived from former British colonies after being effectively expelled from Kenya in 1967-1968 and Uganda in 1971, resulting in restrictive immigration legislation. Under the leadership of Thatcher, a conservative cultural identity was promoted, one predicated on 'Victorian virtues' including 'patriotism, hard work, thrift and private charity'.[43] Research into the values of diversity was generally ignored, leading to a 'bipolar' perception where multicultural and antiracist education was perceived as 'deracialising' while ignoring the impact of racism. A complex and at times seemingly contradictory discourse of policies and platforms emerged. Key issues which impacted upon dance

---

39 Brinson, ibid. p. 56; Clive Gray (2000) *The Politics of the Arts in Britain*, p. 12.
40 Graham Devlin (1989) *Stepping Forward*, p. 36.
41 Ibid. pp. 29 and 39.
42 Tariq Madood and Stephen May (2001) 'Multiculturalism and Education in Britain'.
43 Robert Hewison (1995) *Culture and Consensus*, p. 218.

and education were the perpetuation of a black/white binary and lack of recognition of Asian voices and experiences as distinct to those with African-Caribbean roots.[44]

The collapsing of identities has shifted, however. The 2001 census data revealed that of the 9.1% of the population classified as black and minority ethnic groups, Asian or British-Asian residents comprised the largest group at 4.6%. The 2011 census reveals 7.5% Asian or British-Asian people in England and Wales, with the declared white population of greater London at 59.8%. A very high Indian population is seen in locations such as the city of Leicester at 28.3%.[45] Analysis of progression rates among immigrant groups reinforced disparities between ethnic minority groups that comprised overarching categories. According to Madood and May, African-Caribbeans are at greater disadvantage than South Asians, and within the latter category, those of Pakistani and Bangladeshi heritage were at a greater disadvantage than Indians while Asian Muslims were economically poorest.[46] Inequities documented by quantitative data are beyond the focus of this chapter, but they underpin the imperatives which inspired advocates to situate dance within the education system, arguing its transformational value on a personal level while contributing to cross-cultural understanding.

The growth of a grassroots dance culture was facilitated by the spread of a community dance movement. From its roots in the radical arts movement in the 1960s, there was a rapid institutionalisation of the field, with national organisations advocating on behalf of independent practitioners. The National Association of Dance and Mime Animateurs (NADMA) marked the increasing professionalisation of the field, followed by the Community Dance and Mime Foundation in 1989. Numerous scholars and dance activists have examined the myriad tensions between community arts and 'high' art aesthetics, creativity and quality in broader contexts, documenting the extent to which the arts agendas have been aligned to government arts policies. The community dance field is world-leading with a level of professionalism that matches professional dance companies.[47] As I delved into the history of the field, it appeared that some of those who are

44 Madood and May (2001), op.cit.. p. 309. They also consider the impact of the increased presence of Muslim communities in the UK, where gender issues are significant and tensions arise between advocates of secular and religious multiculturalism.

45 Ann Bridgwood, et al. (2003) *Focus on Cultural Diversity: the arts in England*, ACE Research Report 34, Summary, p. 4. See also 2011 Census data for England and Wales, http://www.ons.gov.uk/ons/rel/census/2011-census/key-statistics-for-local-authorities -in-england-and-wales/sty-enthnicity-in-england-and-wales.html. Census data relating to culture and sports was not available at the time of publication.

46 Madood and May (2011) op.cit.

47 Sara Houston (2002) *Quiet Revolutions?: Philosophical and other concepts of community dance*; Brinson (1991),op.cit. pp. 133-136.

leading South Asian dance organisations today were the ones hired to go to schools, teach workshops, and function as cultural ambassadors as well as dancers, as I discuss in more depth below.

Government funding came from multiple revenue sources, with a valuable monetary stream coming from the National Lottery, established in 1994. Overall, Arts Council support had increased from seven dance organisations in 1969-1970 to 74 by 1998-1999. During the 1980s Arts Council and regional funding expanded to specifically target marginalised groups that included youth groups and arts programmes aimed at the elderly and disabled. The decade heralded the rise of the New Dance movement with small companies and independent practitioners working collaboratively, challenging modern dance conventions in terms of what constitutes dance and where it is performed. Additional support for black and Asian dance was allocated alongside educational outreach programmes of dance company recipients. Select South Asian dancers-teachers-performers began receiving state funding at a time when the percentage of arts funding for dance declined from 25% in 1969-1970 to only 8% in 1989-1990.[48] The list of recipients included Shobana Jeyasingh, kathak exponent Nahid Saddiqui and the dance and music organisation Kadam.[49]

The inclusion of a dance policy for the 1992 Labour Party general election manifesto, with input from Brinson, signified a substantial difference between the two main political parties. When New Labour came to power in 1997, they modified the Thatcherite legacy rather than revert to the socialist platform of the party's predecessors who were aligned with the working class and industrial union base decimated by the Tory government.[50] However, some crucial linkages occurred, as dance scholar Sara Houston examines, where the aims and objectives of community dance coincided with New Labour rhetoric, particularly in relation to ideologies of 'social inclusion'. Houston summarises Prime Minister Tony Blair's central values as 'equal worth, opportunity for all, responsibility and community'.[51] The role of the state was reshaped to advance a platform of individual agency, but one embedded within communitarian concepts. The creation of the Department of Culture, Media and Sport in 1997 drew together separate departments to support the nation's 'culture industries'. DCMS has had a substantial impact, commissioning research that reinforced particular values: 'Our aim is to improve the quality of life for all through cultural and

48 For an overview of the New Dance movement, see Stephanie Jordan (1992) *Striding Out: aspects of contemporary and new dance in Britain*, London: Dance Books. Jeanette Siddall (2001) *21st Century Dance*, Appendix 2; Brinson (1991) op.cit.; *Glory of the Garden*, p. 15
49 David (2005) op.cit. pp. 35-36.
50 Hewison (1994) op. cit.; Andrew Marr (2007) *A History of Modern Britain*
51 Houston (2002) op.cit. p. 52; Sara Houston (2005) 'Participation in Community Dance: the Road to Empowerment and Transformation?' *New Theatre Quarterly*.

sporting activities, support the pursuit of excellence, and champion the tourism, creative and leisure industries.'[52]

The DCMS also organised the Cultural Olympiad and 2012 Games and established new awards to reinforce the place of art in schools and wider society.[53] Dance organisations increasingly lobbied politicians and funders on behalf of their diverse constituencies, commissioning work, asking questions and offering sites to debate aesthetic and practical issues which shaped a rich and broad dance discourse. A number of government-commissioned reports have examined the place of dance in Britain, endowing it with a formidable presence at official levels. For example, the DCMS *Arts Development – Dance* report was published in 2004 while Tony Hall of the Royal Opera House led the 2008 *Dance Review*, which generated a *Government Response to Tony Hall's Report* for the Department of Children, Sport and Families and the DCMS. In 2006 a high profile Dance Manifesto was launched in Parliament, setting out four key 'ambitions' that drew together representatives across a range of dance styles while an All Party Parliamentary Working Group emphasised social and physical benefits from dance.[54]

Dance and education

Any observer of the swings of fortune of Britain's main political parties would be familiar with common perceptions of arts policies and funding, simplified into 'the Labour Party is good for the arts; the Tory (or Conservative) Party, is bad'. Closer scrutiny reveals a complex history in which funding strategies may have had immediate negative effects while setting out frameworks for increased provision for the arts during more sympathetic periods. Arts funding was initially cut under the Conservative government (1979-1997), but dance was integrated into the national curriculum in 1988 as part of the physical education syllabus for primary students. The validation of dance as a subject for General Certificate of Secondary Education (GCSE students aged 14-16 years) and as an Advanced Subsidiary and Advanced Level subject (AS and A Levels, generally 16-18 years of age), has contributed to dance awareness at a broad level and provided avenues to learn more about non-western dance styles.

Although this discussion focuses predominantly on dance training and education for students aged 14 and above, political challenges to the place

---

52 Andrew Miles and Alice Sullivan (2010) *Understanding the relationship between taste and value in culture and sport*, p. 2.

53 Sanders (2006), op.cit. p. 269.

54 Dance UK website, Dance Manifesto page http://www.danceuk.org/metadot/index.pl?iid=22683&isa=Category; All Party Parliamentary Working Group page, http://www.danceuk.org/metadot/index.pl?id=24862&isa=Category&op=show, accessed 5 June 2012.

of dance in schools and further education may also affect the integration of South Asian dance as developed below. Throughout 2013 education policies have been in a state of upheaval with ideological disputes raging about the nature and scope of the national curriculum, the value of arts education, the responsibility of the state, and the need for inclusion and access for every student. The stability of dance within the curriculum is precarious under a coalition comprised of the dominant Conservative Party joined in government by Liberal Democrats. Dance was labelled as a 'soft' subject by the Education Minister Michael Gove who is advocating a narrowing down of the curriculum content perceived as exclusionary on multiple levels. Dance is a subject under threat due to proposals where physical education would prioritise competitive sports. Prime Minister David Cameron supported his minister's stand, with a comment that received substantial negative press coverage: 'I see it with my own children... the two hours that is laid down [for physical education] is often met through sort of Indian dancing classes. Now, I've got nothing against Indian dancing classes but that's not really sport.'[55] The outcry from dance professionals was immediate and vociferous, criticising the conflation of sport and dance as devaluing the art form while misunderstanding the nature of Indian dance. Thus, being situated with physical education rather than arts in the national curriculum has been a double-edged sword. Physical education studies scholar Tansin Benn argues that the fields of dance, professional sport and education have drawn closer together; however, many in dance dispute this as the long list of online detractors of Cameron's statement indicate.[56]

Despite the constant challenges to its place within the education system, multiple pathways have emerged that lead to dance qualifications, such as an award element of Big Dance. As an umbrella project, national qualifications are associated with performance outcomes, supported by the government's Learning & Skills Council and affiliated with the prominent 'dance house', Sadler's Wells Theatre in London. Alongside a focus on the creative abilities of its 14-19 year old participants, Big Dance enhanced skills associated with personal success and employability, identified as 'lateral thinking, problem solving, negotiation, communication and team working'. Participants were provided with individual learning plans and a visual record of the experience, which culminates in a performance and an arts award advertised as equivalent to a GCSE.[57]

Dance foundation and B-tech courses of study have a stronger vocational focus than the GCSE and A Levels. Although the diversity of dance styles

---

55 Anon. (2012) 'Dance celebrates its role in Olympic ceremonies whilst dance leaders respond to David Cameron's comments', *Dance UK News*, 23 August http://www.danceuk. org/news/article/dance-celebrates-its-role-olympics/ accessed 23 June 2013
56 Tansin Benn (2004) '"Race" and Physical Education, Sport and Dance'.
57 Big Dance, op.cit.

has been expanded in the B-tech curriculum, its examination body reported that 'teaching staff and students have a preference for working with contemporary dance as it is perceived as having greater potential for the development of students' creativity'.[58] The courses support both commercial dance sectors and feed into higher education dance degree programmes, shaped in part by the location of the institution and the priorities emphasised in guidance from teachers. The rise in dance student numbers has been rapid and high. GCSE candidates in dance numbered 6,192 in 1997; rising to 15,928 in 2005.[59] In 2007, 911 schools and colleges offered GCSE dance courses with AS and A Level courses available at over 500 institutions (although the one-year-long AS Level qualifications are being phased out).[60] With the instability caused by education policy proposals, the number of students sitting the Performing/expressive arts qualifications declined in 2012/2013. The downward trajectory reflects economic uncertainties, while restructured funding for higher education affects career decisions at early stages of education.

In addition to technique training in the GCSE, selected professional dances and subject areas (such as the Royal Ballet, the Alvin Ailey American Dance Theatre and Netherlands Dance Theatre) provide contextual case studies and are related to practical creative tasks, providing movement motifs or examples of choreographic structures for analysis. GCSE students focus study on one dance whilst AS and A Level students study two out of the three dances on offer. There is an expectation that students will view additional works across a range of styles, 'in order to compare, contrast and develop their understanding and interpretation of the context and form of different dances and dance styles'.[61] Examination results reveal that the most popular dances chosen for analysis, for the most part, have been restaged and toured for years. A good example is Christopher Bruce who combines ballet with folk and contemporary dance in the politically evocative works *Ghost Dances* (about political disappearances in Chile, 1981) and musical theatre vocabulary in *Swansong* (about a political prisoner and two guards, 1987). Matthew Bourne's *Nutcracker!* (1992) has played large theatres during Christmas seasons while David Bintley's *Still Life at the Penguin Café* (1988) has been staged by multiple ballet companies and filmed for broadcast by London Weekend Television. Recordings of the ballet and music by Simon Jeffes can be purchased – a family-friendly, bums-on-seat attraction with a message about the impact of global warming. Some students were praised by course evaluators for articulating ideas about the postmodern, more

58 Marie Hay (2010) *Changing Positions: Dance and the FE-HE transition in the UK*, p. 14.
59 Sanders (2006) ibid. p. 4.
60 Emma Gladstone (2007) *Dance, Film and the Curriculum*, p. 2; other statistics are accessible from the Dance UK website, http://www.danceuk.org/resources/dance-facts/
61 Gladstone (2007) op.cit. p. 3.

abstract character of Siobhan Davies Dance Company's *Bird Song* (2004) and *Rosas danst Rosas* (1983, film 1997) by Anna Teresa de Keersmaeker.[62] These posed different interpretive and choreographic challenges than the popular choices which had a stronger narrative or character component.

Dance educationalist and consultant Lorna Sanders highlights how the values and analytical frameworks remain consistent with those set into place in 1986 when the first version of the qualification was implemented, predicated on ideas about the universality of dance and fixing the language which is used to analyse choreographic styles that did not exist when the GCSE was established.[63] As Sanders argues, the content chosen for the theoretical component endows it with academic integrity, establishing artistic criteria, notions of heritage and organising principles of choreography, performance and appreciation. Despite the preference for contemporary and ballet case studies, the classification of styles relaxed, seen in the 2001-02 inclusion of Jeyasingh's *Romance...with footnotes* (1993) with phrases and rhythms drawn from the classical bharatanatyam vocabulary. The other options were Davies' *White Man Sleeps* (1988), Bourne's *Swan Lake* (1995) with its male swans, Kenneth MacMillan's *Winter Dreams* (1991) and Marius Petipa's *Sleeping Beauty* (dated as 1890).[64]

Jeyasingh's *Faultline* (2007) was among the 2012-2013 GCSE offerings. It is described as a combination of 'Bharatanatyam, contemporary dance and pedestrian gestures', based on the novel *Londonstani* by Gutam Malkani (2006). The theme responds to perceptions and the reality of Asian Muslim young men's lives in Britain, viewed with suspicion in a post 9/11 world (and post 7/7). The choreographic style is classified as 'narrative and cinematic, combines the everyday with classical Indian mythology'. A strong political focus is spelled out in the fact file detailing the production's emphasis on 'youth culture, gender stereotypes, gangs, city life'.[65] The resource pack identifies two *hasta mudras* (hand gestures) that are integrated for the way 'they give tension to the body, energising the arm and spine. These shapes contain the shapes within the body'. The *Alapadma* (open) and *Kathakamukha* (closed) hand gestures are distanced from any 'intent or meaning'.[66]

For older students, A Level set works offer a diverse slice of British choreography which has included African dance, ballet, modern and contemporary dance, and physical theatre. Dances are chosen for study

---

62 *AQA General Certificate of Secondary Education (year), Dance, Report on the Examination,* (Specification 4230), Unit 1: Critical appreciation of dance; version 1.0., Manchester: AQA.

63 Sanders (2006) op.cit. p. 228.

64 Ibid. pp. 74 and 272.

65 *AQA Teacher Resource Bank (2011) GCSE Dance Prescribed Work, Fact File,* Manchester: AQA, p. 7

66 *Faultline* Resource Pack, March 2012, Shobana Jeyasingh Dance Company

based in part on practical considerations such as the availability of appropriate recordings and adequate copyright clearance. Demands for workshops by those involved in the chosen performance expand performers' interactions with the education system.[67] Overt political themes include Bruce's choreography which overlaps with the GCSE options while Lea Anderson's *Cross Channel* (1991) and Bourne's *Swan Lake* cited earlier, have been analysed for their gender representation. Counter-hegemonic themes such as the exploration of homosexual identity and critique of religion in DV8 Physical Theatre's early productions have gained acceptance over the years, achieved in part through their inclusion as case studies (such as *Cost of Living* created in 2000 and *Enter Achilles* from 1995).

In 1992 South Asian dance and African dance were added as set study options. Cultural diversity was integrated from the start with input from Biskha Sarker who trained in creative dance with Amala Shankar (wife and dancing partner of Uday Shankar) and Manjusri Chaki-Sircar who called the form *navanritya* (meaning 'new dance'). She was joined by bharatanatyam exponent Pushkala Gopal, although the syllabus prioritised classical ballet or contemporary dance styles.[68] Sanders was critical of the lack of accommodation for diversity of approach in the assessments: 'This incorporation of cross cultural practice did not seem to occasion any concern that the subject content, terminology or assessment criteria might be challenged by the different artistic codes and their associated aesthetic values, the structure and underpinning was felt to be universal and therefore deemed unproblematic.'[69] There was potential for confusion arising from a lack of specificity in choreography based on classical forms and few candidates took up the South Asian or African performance options. Categories were collapsed into an 'overarching genre' while Sanders points out that 'Pratap Pawar is a Kathak choreographer and not merely a South East Asian choreographer'.[70] Changes were implemented in 2009, focusing assessments in modern (or contemporary) dance, ballet and jazz.[71]

On one level the significant milestone of inclusion broadens appreciation and access to the work of two prominent choreographers – Jeyasingh and Khan – who cross between classical dance styles (bharatanatyam and kathak respectively) and contemporary dance. On the other hand, there

---

67 Gladstone (2007) op.cit.
68 Alessandra Lopez y Royo (2003) 'Classicism, Post-classicism in Ranjabati Sricar's work. For biographical information on Bishaka Sarker see http://www.chezfred.org.uk/chat/BisakhaFootprints.htm; for detail of Pushkala Gopal's career see http://sanskritiuk.net/index.php/team/pushkala-gopal/
69 Sanders (2006) op.cit.. p. 71.
70 Ibid. p. 164: fn. 29.
71 *AQA GCE Dance AS and A Level Specification AS exams 2009 onwards and A2 exams 2010 onwards (version 1.5)*, Manchester: AQA.

are constraints on how the material is presented and to the types of student engagement within the structure of the assessments and qualifications. As author of study guides and teacher resource packs, Sanders' micro-analysis of changes to A Level specifications raised concerns about the restrictive character of the relationship between assessment and knowledge and in one instance, interpretive processes. In particular, the guidelines dictated analytical frameworks that she found problematic for articulating crucial aspects of Khan's aesthetic qualities evident in *Rush* (2000). She described polar opposites 'that might be interacting to produce multiple and ambiguous meanings',[72] with assessment mechanisms that reveal hierarchies rooted in past conventions. Any dance style can be used in the solos students create, however, some choreographic approaches place the student at a disadvantage due to their treatment of space, gestural vocabulary or dynamic range. Weighting may be unbalanced and not acknowledge technical skills: 'Only five marks are awarded for rhythmic control (in a category that also includes dynamics) for example, yet this very quality is a significant feature of Kathak. A candidate attempting to answer a choreographic question with a Kathak-based technique would be disadvantaged even if the action content was deemed appropriate for the intention of the dance.'[73] Assessments based on Khan's trio *Rush* were criticised because of the limited use of space, while a rebounding quality and specific pathways were highlighted in the resource material as distinctive.

Concerns about gaps between western pedagogic practices and South Asian dance styles are reinforced by practitioners' experiences. Birmingham-based Sabri encountered perceptions of kathak as 'old-fashioned, not relevant and doesn't fit with contemporary styles'. The absence of narrative context in much contemporary choreography leads students to believe that the expressive aspect isn't relevant, that it 'conforms more to ballet'. Once dancers participate in a kathak workshop, however, Sabri found that barriers broke down as they 'discover how can the body be used in an expressive sense rather than with architectural focus'. Responses to creative tasks that prioritise rhythmic emphasis were challenging, as many contemporary dance students lack levels of musical sensitivity seen in kathak training which isolates movement in relation to beats or to musically translate the intonation of syllables. In some situations, Sabri emphasises mathematical structures or cycles as metaphors for life, depending on whether participants seem open to discussion of cultural or spiritual roots of the form.[74]

The impact of stylistic hierarchies and aesthetic clashes within the education system are not limited to non-Western forms, however.

---

72 Lorna Sanders (2008) 'Power in Operation', fn.22, p. 237.
73 Ibid. p. 232.
74 Sonia Sabri, interview with author, 24 June 2009.

Assessments that drew on popular dance were received with negative evaluations in the 2007 report by the examining body AQA (Assessment and Qualifications Alliance): 'It was pleasing to note that there were fewer instances of "pop" or street dance styles being offered for assessment this year, as it has been noted in previous years that dances in these styles rarely allow for dynamic change, spatial interest or interaction between dancers.'[75] As universities increasingly integrate elements of hip-hop, urban and/or street dance styles into their BA undergraduate courses, it remains to be seen whether the GCSE and A Level curriculum will change to reflect this diversity.

Grau's analysis of dance in education in 1997 and later in the SADiB Report in 2002 warned of the danger of 'tokenism' with the inclusion of Jeyasingh's work in the GCSE and A-Level content, however, there has been an almost unbroken inclusion of South Asian dance from the first examinations. So has the situation moved beyond tokenism? The A Level set dances for 2013-2015 are *Prodigal Son* (George Balanchine, 1923), *Zero Degrees* (Akram Khan and Sidi Larbi Cherkaoui, 2005), and *West Side Story* (1961). Analysis of set dances over the years reveals that South Asian and British Asian artists produced some of the most contemporary productions, integrating rich multi-disciplinary design and international casts of performers, with commissioned scores, at the avant-garde of the dance field. Resource materials offer some analysis of the classical styles, providing exposure at various levels to notions of heritage and tradition, whether it is fully comprehended or marginalised by assessment criteria and constraints as Sanders sets out.

Dance Training and Professionalisation

Recreational dance activities can also be structured around formal assessments with the Imperial Society of Teachers of Dancing (ISTD) examination system. The move for inclusion in the codified training systems portfolio came from within the field and involved standardisation processes that established bharatanatyam and kathak on a level of training with other recreational dance forms with potential for advancement to more professional level study. For example, at Morley College, Sushma Mehta's once a week adult education kathak classes follow the ISTD syllabus although those who want to pursue the examinations need to add another class to achieve an appropriate level of proficiency.[76] There is discussion of adding classical styles of odissi and kuchipudi in light of the success of

---

75 *Performing Arts: Dance - AQA GCSE Report on the Examination* 2007 June series, AQA, p. 4.
76 Sushma Mehta, personal email communication, 8 August 2013. For discussion of the ISTD South Asian Dance Faculty see Stacey Prickett (2004) 'Techniques and Institutions'.

bharatanatyam and kathak. Accredited teaching qualifications support the transformation of practical dance experience into skills validated for moving into careers in further and higher education.[77]

Part of the validation of South Asian dance's wider significance is seen in government funded Centres for Advanced Training (CATs) for gifted students ages 10-18. The 15 national pre-vocational training centres support approximately 2,000 English and music and dance students, described on its website as 'the pinnacle of the Government's support for performing arts training in residential and non-residential conservatoires' with sessions held during the school breaks. Means-tested funding also supports training with local teachers and associated costs (such as physiotherapists, travel and 'bespoke expenses for individual students').[78] DanceXchange in Birmingham facilitates bharatanatyam training led by Anusha Subramanyam and Sujata Banerjee, who also chairs the ISTD Classical Indian Dance Faculty, leads kathak.[79] South Asian dance students follow the ISTD syllabus with their local dance teachers or 'home tutors'. Crucially, a reading and writing component contributes to an assessed portfolio of work in both syllabi to support a wider understanding of the forms, their cultural foundations and current manifestations. Requirements to attend live performance depend on availability and encouragement by teachers.[80]

It is telling that South Asian dance is in a unique position from other genres where the CATs website documents its graduates' progress onto shows, into dance companies and other vocational courses. A disclaimer for kathak and bharatanatyam graduates explains:

> Currently the South Asian graduates do not have a vocational training option or a university based degree course in a classical dance form for them to progress on to after graduating from the CAT. Many students turn to [other] academic courses and continue their dance training with a private tutor. Their passion and commitment to dance does not disappear at graduation but their choices are limited and the opportunity for mentoring and apprentice roles within established companies are available but also limited.[81]

This absence of courses is not without lack of trying – there have been a

77 ISTD Faculty news, http://www.istd.org/classical-indian-dance/faculty-news/, June 2011, accessed 26 August 2013.
78 Erin N. Sanchez, Imogen J. Aujla and Sanna Nordin-Bates (2012) 'Cultural background variables in dance talent development', Research in Dance Education, p. 10.
79 CAT/DanceXchange website, http://www.dancexchange.org.uk/participate/cat; http://www.dancexchange.org.uk/participate/cat/south-asian-kathak-and-bharatanatyam
80 Sujata Banerjee, personal email correspondence, 8 August 2013.
81 CATS Graduates page, http://www.nationaldancecats.co.uk/graduates/, accessed 31 July 2013.

number of BA courses in South Asian dance which were not sustainable, starting as early as 1992 at De Montfort University.[82] Different dance techniques have been offered, however, within contemporary dance dominant departments, and postgraduate study options are attracting South Asian dance practitioners from outside Britain, reinforcing a two- way exchange as they resume careers at home that are influenced by western dance scholarship and choreographic approaches.

Multiple issues impact on professional training in South Asian dance by those with diasporic heritage. Research and anecdotal evidence reveals cultural opposition among some to studying dance at university level and pursuing it as a career.[83] Putting ethnicity aside, however, while none of her students have expressed interest in a BA dance degree, Banerjee recommends options that can be seen as a 'parallel' degree to dance, such as sports, dance science, physiotherapy or English literature. She explained that they have high standards brought on by years of training in the classical forms, and 'they are still hungry for the classical dance – so the course has to be attractive enough for them to take further challenge – or a combined degree where the family can be assured that their children are still getting other qualifications or skills'.[84] An emphasis on employability, the practicality of a dance degree, is a common theme in all university course marketing.

The dance community in Britain is fed by higher education in multiple ways, with 470 courses across 78 universities which include dance components performance studies subjects as well as dance as a single subject.[85] In 2012, 7,865 people applied to study dance, out of which 1,336 were accepted onto courses. In 2011/2012, 1,375 people achieved a BA undergraduate degree in dance.[86] This represents a substantial increase in university acceptance rates from 2007, up from 946 (out of 7,013 applications).[87] Like the secondary school qualifications, a decrease in numbers has been recorded, arising from potential changes to the education system. If dance ceases to be a required subject on the national curriculum, career options will be undoubtedly affected.

82   Andrée Grau (1997) 'Dance, South Asian Dance, and Higher Education', in Alessandra Iyer, ed., op.cit.; Stacey Prickett (2003), 'Degrees of Change'; Ann R. David (2003) 'Where have all the courses gone...?' *Pulse.*
83   Sanchez and Nordin-Bates (2012) op.cit. p. 13. Research into an urban dance CATs cohort included an Asian/Indian British student.
84   Banerjee (2013) op.cit.
85   Siddall (2010) op.cit. p. 48.
86   Higher Education Statistics Agency, 2011/12 Qualifications by Subject, http://www. hesa.ac.uk/content/view/1897/239/
87   Applications (choices), acceptances and ratio by subject group (2012), http:// www.ucas.com/data-analysis/data-resources/data-tables/subject/2012; Applications (choices), acceptances and ratio by subject group (2007), http://www.ucas.com/data-analysis/data-resources/data-tables/subject/2007

UNIVERSITY OF CHESTER LIBRARY

During the short-lived South Asian dance specialism in the BA degree at the London Contemporary Dance School (2003-2008), kathak exponent and lecturer Gauri Sharma Tripathi reflected on different conceptualisations of the body and analytic processes. Students started 'looking at the combination of the heel, the flat foot, and the side, assessing the quality, the dynamism, the strength'. Such aspects are implicit, taken for granted in traditional teaching methods she experienced in India, but for Tripathi pedagogic practices in higher education provided another level of clarity.[88] She also became aware of distinctions concerning the impact of physical space upon the body, recalling how she would watch her mother practising in place for hours in a very small room. In India, the idea of choreography had a more internalised relationship to space, it was 'more about the way the body moves', whereas in Tripathi's choreography in Britain, a different relationship to space is prioritised: 'we're looking at the space outside... everything is a show piece'.[89]

Other pathways for professional development exist outside the academy. The Bhavan Centre is a stalwart and vital site for the perpetuation of classical forms as noted above. Akademi, on the other hand, made its focus the support of artists who wanted to push at the boundaries of their form.[90] As Grau indicates, the separation between the two is ideological as well as financial. Bahvan has received Arts Council England (ACE) funding but has been supported primarily through private sources and by those who frequent its classes. Akademi survived on project support until it became a Regularly Funded Organisation (RFO) by ACE. Kadam is another commissioning body funded through ACE and the National Lottery, sponsoring a summer Unlocking Creativity choreography course culminating in a work-in-progress performance, bringing together contemporary choreographers with diverse South Asian dance and music practitioners.

The ISTD's name change in 2013 from South Asian Dance to Classical Indian Dance Faculty reflects ongoing debates about the symbolic capital of categories and political issues around terminology, the action a recognition of dominant vernacular usage of labels.[91] Debates over the terminology are just part of an evolving field, where critical reflection takes place at symposia with contributions from international academics, practitioners and artists from other disciplines. These are open to the public, and multiple generations engage in debates about aesthetic practices and art's place within socio-political contexts, while British-based dancers are given rare performance opportunities in venues such as the Linbury Theatre at the Royal Opera House. As early as 1983, a three-day conference asked key questions about

---

88 Tripathi, interview with author 12 September 2006.
89 Ibid.
90 Grau (2002) op.cit. p. 61.
91 David (2013) op.cit.; Meduri (2008) 'Labels' op.cit.

The Place of Indian Dance in British Culture. Sampad sponsored *Navadisha 2000,* while *Talam on the Thames* was sponsored by the SADiB project at the South Bank Centre. Akademi commissioned reports documenting events such as: *Looking for the Invisible – The 'Abstract' in South Asian Arts* (2012) about concepts of abstraction in multiple disciplines. *Negotiating Natyam* (2005) explored the classical form bharatanatyam. *No Man's Land – Exploring South Asianness* (2004) engaged with identity issues in wider society as well as the arts, while *South Asian Aesthetics Unwrapped* (2002) had contributions from the visual artist and sculptor Anish Kapoor as well as Jeyasingh and Mavin Khoo, among others.[92] Outside London events such as the Nartan conference in Leicester in 2006 generated articles for a dedicated issue of the journal *South Asian Studies.* An integral connection exists between the events and the critical reflection they generate as each writer, dancer and scholar I spoke to mentioned a different event they found significant. On a more practical level, better communication between grant applicants, venues, and ACE evaluators and administrators emerged as a priority from *Moving On,* the National Symposium for South Asian Dance, sponsored by the CICD in Leicester. Networking is facilitated between generations of dancers, teachers and scholars while support systems emerge to guide artists through administrative, tax and grant application quagmires – helping them to survive as an independent, freelance artists.

What has remained constant since 1989 is a publication outlet for the field, one which resonates with the role played in the USA by *New Theatre* (1933-1937) and *Dance Observer* (first published in 1934) which disseminated aesthetic perspectives, institutional news and debate about 1930s modern dance. Providing a forum for reviews and feature articles on individual dancers, choreographers and their companies, analysis of musical and dance analysis, and letters to the editor gave voice to performers and creators as well as critics.[93] A South Asian dance infrastructure supported by publications shares listings, information, reviews and features and was generated with Arts Council support from 1989 to 2010. One of AdiTi's central activities from its inception until it closed in 2001 was the circulation of a newsletter, replaced for a brief period by the journal *Extradition.* The journal *Pulse* took over the remit in 2001 and continues to situate the British South Asian scene within an international context.

The publications function to unite a readership, much like Benedict Anderson's concept of an 'imagined community' where a population is drawn together by reading the national newspaper over breakfast.[94] *Pulse*

---

92 Reports are available on the Akademi web pages for each event. www.akademi.co.uk/ events

93 For an overview of the significance of the two American dance publications, see Gay Morris (2006) op.cit; Lynn Garafola (2005) op.cit.

94 Benedict Anderson (1991, 2nd ed.) *Imagined Communities.*

has documented and stimulated the level of debate, interrogating themes such as identity, classicism, tradition and their challenges, enhancing an understanding of the cultural contexts and aesthetics of the forms. Chitra Sundaram, who edited the journal from 2003 to 2007, spoke of responding to a high level of intellectual and critical reflection on questions of representation and aesthetics ongoing in Britain. The editorial team set out to put practitioners and academics 'on the same page', involving dancers in the debates rather than writing that 'treated dance as a specimen'. Sundaram explained: 'it is important for communities to know what the current thinking is about them in circles of current influence and history. It can be dangerous or foolish to ignore such powerful, privileged opinion. For example, if I had known about Orientalism in the 1970s I would have been a different person'.[95] *Pulse* came into being alongside a confluence of events, such as international conferences, where there was an interest in practice as research, facilitating artists' reflexive engagement. Things were led in part by what Jeyasingh was articulating about her own hybridity, informed by the work of theorists such as Homi Bhabha, questions which matched those interrogated in academic dance journals such as *Dance Research Journal* and other performance fields.

Sundaram recounts how *Pulse* content was determined in part by the fact that classical dance did not have a discourse. Classical dance summer schools organised by Kadam, now sponsored by Milapfest, provide opportunities for classical practitioners to learn about western choreographic structures outside formal courses. *Pulse* writers asked questions of prominent masters from India who shaped the canons of classical dance, such as kathak guru Birju Maharaj. Although questions such as 'what is choreography' are not a western preserve, there were differences in how processes were articulated. Themed issues of the journal provided multiple perspectives of topics such as the diasporic dance form in higher education, copyright issues, costuming, and the significance of texts such as the Natyashastra in shaping classical aesthetics. Advances in dance science and conceptualisations of the body in movement from western dance pedagogy were applied to actions such as the *ariamundi* position at the foundation of bharatnatyam, which functions like the demi-plié in ballet. Practitioners wrote about specific benefits of yoga and pilates for the South Asian dancer. Reflecting on the impact of the journal, Sundaram summarised: '*Pulse* helped move things to a different level, detailing technical understanding. It became important not just as a community but community with a force which was accepted at a high level and had a status within the wider world, and we were able to

---

95 Chitra Sundaram, interview with author, 21 August 2013, email correspondence, 27 August 2013.

request press passes.'[96] The 'Other shades of white' issue (Autumn, 2003) was important in shaping my research into identity issues at the time, investigating perspectives of race and representation with contributions from 25 international writers, scholars and dancers of various genres. A crucial connection between practice and research, the wider international discourse and academia was articulated in the journal pages. Topics were picked up in other dance journals, such as a dialogue between scholars (Andrée Grau and Uttara Coorlawala) about issues of multiculturalism, authenticity and scholarly authority which appeared in *Animated*, the journal for the Foundation for Community Dance in 2001 and 2002.[97]

A three-year Arts Council grant ran from 2007 to 2010 to support changes to the journal's editorial mission and design, prioritising a practical outlook that included music.[98] It is technologically coded so it can be scanned electronically, enabling readers to listen to music and rhythmic samples, accompanied by articles detailing the intricacies of Indian classical music such as *ragas*. The innovative technology advances a remarkable interactive learning tool. Whereas one can search out rhythms and artists on the internet, the inclusion of sound clips situated in relation to the detailed analysis in articles is unique. Audience education is a central objective alongside the dissemination of knowledge to practitioners, with features on dancers and choreographer profiles. The list of authors continues to attract an international elite of performers, teachers and scholars. Contributing to the construction of a heritage, a 'Young Pulse' section offers an outlet for young artists to write about their peers which sits alongside reviews of international performances, photographic essays and feature articles that document South Asian dance in Britain and its associated artistic practices.

Professional critics and journalists are regular contributors, including Donald Hutera (*The Times, Animated, Dance Europe*), Sanjoy Roy (*The Guardian, New Statesman*) and Kenneth Hunt (freelance music journalist, *The Independent*). ACE support was granted to develop critical writing sessions where activities where professional critics are brought together with students, practitioners and aspiring writers (Critical Writing sessions in 2012 and 2013). An innovative *Dance Audience Club* offers post-performance discussion sessions with the *Guardian* critic Roy which brings the knowledgeable together with the uninitiated but interested viewer. *Dance Dialogue* offers pre-performance discussion for 'effective viewing' while a substantial social networking and internet presence is developing. There is still space for academics to offer different perspectives on the issues although

---

96 Ibid.
97 Andrée Grau (2001) 'Dance and Cultural Identity'; Uttara Asha Coorlawala (2002) 'Response to Dr Andrée Grau's "Dance, Culture and Identity"'.
98 Sanjeevini Dutta, interview, 19 August 2013.

reflective development for practitioners and aficionados is prioritised.[99] The *Pulse* workshops help address the limitations of formal qualifications such as A Level and GCSE that Sanders identified.

Funding the Arts

The history of South Asian dance arts funding has been marked by a tension between concepts of tradition and innovation. Definitions of choreographic creativity are embedded within contemporary dance traditions – techniques evolved from the impetus of individuals to express themselves, whether an abstract concept or a narrative, music visualisation, particular emotion or atmosphere. In contrast, classical South Asian dance's conventional hierarchy of knowledge embedded within the teacher-disciple or *guru-shishya* tradition, choreography is passed down rather than dancers being trained in the choreographic craft and processes for the creation of individual works. The SADiB report highlighted the classical-contemporary tension in relation to government arts grants, while David documented the disparity in grant support Jeyasingh received for her classical and contemporary project as she began to break away.[100]

Analysis of ACE grant assessment criteria in 2006 exemplifies clear barriers faced by traditional dancers who were encouraged to move away from conventions: 'By taking artistic risks, artists often find ways to break new ground, reach new audiences or extend their own practice'.[101] The activity needs to 'serve a broad range of people – artists, participants or audiences'. Black and minority ethnic groups were identified as being at risk of social exclusion, so points were awarded for projects which 'benefit areas of the country and increase participation and attendance by communities which face social or economic problems'.[102] Slight changes in the ACE agenda for 2007-2011 detailed its priorities as funding for 'children and young people, the creative economy, vibrant communities, internationalism and celebrating diversity...'. There is a sense within the field that contradictory criteria exists, with evaluations predicated on ethnocentric parameters.

A number of choreographers have defied the categorisation of their diasporic or stylistic roots, often challenging labels of their work as fusion or hybrid as they move beyond the classical foundations on which they

99 Sanjeevini Dutta, personal email communication, 27 August 2013. See also http://www.pulseconnects.com/content/DanceAudienceClub.

100 Prickett (2007) *Guru or Teacher? Shisya or Student? South Asia Research*; Grau (2002) op.cit. p. 10; David (2005) op.cit. pp. 35-36.

101 Anon (2006) 'Grants for the arts – understanding the assessment criteria and our priorities', Arts Council of England Information Sheet, pp. 3, 9, and 11. The tensions were also highlighted in the SADiB report, Grau, op.cit. pp. 65-66.

102 Cristian Ceresoli (2004) 'A Complex Calculus', *Pulse*, Spring, p. 20; anon. (2006) *Arts Council England Dance Policy*.

built successful performing careers. There are perceptions that some British-based practitioners can 'strategically make use of their ethnicity to tap into the socio-economic grids of power that supports the arts'.[103] With classical dance foundations at the basis of their careers, Jeyasingh and Khan have garnered the most international prominence. Jeyasingh began by deconstructing components of the classical bharatanatyam in *Confluences* (1990). Rhythmically complex dance phrases evoke the gestural and percussive basis of the form, increasingly removed from its culturally specific symbolism, although new layers of meaning are perpetuated within innovative dance contexts.

Akram Khan's meteoric rise began with abstract approaches in works such as *Loose in Flight* (2000), integrating rhythms and gestures of kathak with contemporary dance. His work is coming under more in-depth scrutiny by a new generation of dance and performance studies scholars. For example, Royona Mitra argues that Khan's aesthetic has moved far from its roots in kathak and is a highly contemporary collaborative theatre genre. Evoking sociologist Pierre Bourdieu's construction of the field, Mitra identifies a 'relational dynamic' where Khan's voice developed in dialogue with those of senior artists, both within the South Asian dance community and his collaborators, many of whom are British Asian artists in other fields. Prarthana Purkayastha also analyses how Khan articulates a 'negotiated tradition'.[104] Significantly, Khan is one of a small group of dancers who have parallel practices, creating more contemporary creations alongside traditional kathak (Tripathi) or bharatanatyam (Khoo and Subramanyam).

Contemporary South Asian dancers are able to claim a classical heritage but also respond to funding imperatives that reward innovation, although individual cases would need to be made to determine how one constrains or frees the other. Nina Rajarani negotiated this balance with *Quick!* in 2006, which won the £25,000 Bloomberg-sponsored Place Prize, a bi-annual contemporary dance choreography competition. Rajarani used predominantly traditional bharatanatyam vocabulary for four male dancers. It opened with film footage of an electric kettle (the ubiquitous cup of tea), dramatic lighting and live musicians moving through the stage space to create a vibrant visual and rhythmic spectacle, the clarity of line, unison fast footwork emulating the urban energy of the filmed street scenes. Sabri's solo *Spill* (2006) also progressed to the semi-finals of the competition, using her version of traditional kathak vocabulary but set in unusual lighting and costume accompanied by layers of tabla *bols* (mnemonic syllables) and body percussion. Out of 204 applications, Rajarani and Sabri were among

---

103 Prarthana Purkayastha (2008), *Bodies Beyond Borders*, p. 264.
104 Royona Mitra (2011) *Akram Khan, Performing the Third Space*; Prarthana Purkayastha, (2010) 'Performing Identity Politics: South Asian Dance in Britain'.

20 semi-finalists, who each received £5,000 funding and studio rehearsal space, with the only constraint being to choreograph a 15-minute long production. Winners were chosen through an elimination process involving audience votes and a panel of dance professionals and critics.

There are ways around the contemporary/classical, innovative/traditional tensions, through 'finding a contemporary insight into their work' which fulfils the criteria of 'innovative work', as described by the funding bodies.'[105] Sonia Sabri Company's group dance *Red* (2005) exemplifies how funding issues can impact upon creativity. Sabri ventured away from a classical repertory – in costuming, choreographic structure and accompaniment, adding a saxophonist to the tabla and vocals. The three dancers' movement was drawn from the classical kathak, although modified in places. In the final section, *Red 6: Cheeky feet*, the focus was on footwork (*takar*) without arm movements. Inspired by the etymology of 'red' which Sabri linked with 'Rudra', 'the god Shiva in his aspect of anger', the publicity material set out diverse associations: marriage, blood, heat, religious ritual and passion. A departure from conventions occurred when the musicians moved centre stage, clapping out rhythms and vocalisations as the dancers moved around them. It was recommended by the ACE that Sabri work with a dramaturge, Rose English, to develop a stronger narrative thread overall. When the arts production company zeroculture funded a reworking of *Red*, however, its director Hardial Rai explained:

> A large part of South Asian dance has the ACE [Arts Council England] arts establishment imposition stamped on it – the influence of it in shaping new work (as part of the so-called 'audience strategies')... *Red*... attempted to place kathak into a modern sensibility, without any of the nonsense of collaborations with contemporary dance/performance devices. But *Red* was also muddled, ... in the instructed dramaturgy imposed by the ACE arts establishment. It reeked of interference from this imposition and in a very obvious way too. [106]

Rai felt the aesthetic of the imposed dramaturgy was 'very opposed to *Red*'s creative premise.' To correct this, Jatinder Verma, the founder and artistic director of South Asian theatre group Tara Arts, worked with the dancers, including the final interchange between dancers and musicians. Sabri explained that his ideas were to 'emphasise simplicity when working with rhythm ... and to explore characters'. [107] Athough Rai criticised the ACE recommendations, Sabri acknowledged she moved into new artistic paths as a result of the process. The Sonia Sabri Company has gone on to receive a three year ACE development grant.

105 Bithika Chatterjee (2002) 'The Spin Factor', *Pulse*, Autumn, p. 10.
106 Hardial Rai (2006) 'Why re-work Red?', *Pulse*, Spring, p. 32.
107 Sonia Sabri, interview with author, 13 September 2006.

Like the recommendations Brinson made in 1991, advocating audience development through accessible creations and education, strategic approaches have been implemented within the South Asian dance field. Sanjeevini Dutta, *Pulse* editor, advocated producing star quality dancers and making audiences literate in the dance forms. Funding bodies and venue booking managers unfamiliar with the forms consider classical dance styles such as kathak as being 'locked in tradition' and therefore inaccessible to a broad audience.[108] Ten years later, however, Sundaram noted that the British Dance Edition, a prestigious bi-annual festival for dance programmers, had shortlisted four classical dancers in 2012-2013. Overall, the level of scrutiny placed on practitioners has increased, emerging in part from scholarly and artistic debates. There is also increased competition within the field, and higher standards of professionalisation linked to advances in learning and teaching which sit alongside ACE criteria for 'moving the artform forward'. There is a sense now that classical dance has relevance, that dancers have more of a sense of control over how they shape their image.[109]

South Asian dance in alternative spaces

South Asian dance features prominently in public performances that contest and celebrate hegemonic narratives, utilising diverse theatrical devices to evoke meaning alongside those embodied in transnational dance vocabularies (such as classical bharatanatyam and kathak, contemporary dance and ballet). *Sufi:Zen* (2010) exemplifies location-specific shows that can be produced in multiple sites, as it premiered in Liverpool. The London premiere immersed the viewer in nature, the stage situated within a natural amphitheatre in the lush landscape of Greenwich Park overlooking the river. The night I attended, we traversed a candle-lit path, moving away from the riverside and the financial towers of Canary Wharf across the Thames. Set in the oldest royal park, birthplace of King Henry VIII, the location is rich in symbolic space. History can be unpacked beyond the obvious associations of imperial power manifest in the Royal Maritime Museum, the Royal Naval College and former hospital, and the royal history of Indigo Jones' elegant Queen's House. Glancing up the hill we could see Sir Christopher Wren's Royal Observatory, where one can stand on the median line from which international time zones are determined. It sits on a site of privilege, the only hill on London's eastern boundary. Depending on the journey there, one can also pass by the Cutty Sark's permanent home, a clipper ship launched in 1869, whose heritage evokes the significant trade with the east that shaped Britain's economic and colonial relations. Although this takes us away from the immediacy of the urban environment, the architecture of wealth

108 Sanjeevini Dutta in Ceresoli (2004), op.cit.; Chatterjee, op.cit. p. 9.
109 Sundaram (2013) op.cit.

from multiple centuries sits on the edge of our sightlines, evoking Massey's analysis of the relations of power that emanate from space. With music by Srikanth Sriram, Tripathi worked with contemporary choreographer Jonathan Lunn and bharatanatyam and ballet-trained Khoo. Trance-like turns and sculpted gestures featured in the exploration of the stage space, the dancers' pale costumes flowing out from their bodies in the mesmerising spins. The performance started at dusk to enhance the spectacular pyrotechnic displays from the group Red Earth, which illuminated the environment with torches and cauldrons of fire, rhythmic punctuations in movement were matched in places by bursts of flame against the night sky.

In general, the events complement and critique the heritage of city and nation, traversing a range of social and political spaces. Many events are co-produced by Akademi, which made a strategic decision to focus on large-scale events. *Coming of Age* in 2000 was a two day spectacle celebrating the organisation's 21st birthday, which filled the interior and exterior spaces of the South Bank Centre, built for the Festival of Britain in 1951. One hundred performers across three generations performed for 16,000 spectators. Like the symbolic entrance into the Alhambra Theatre in 1991, *Coming of Age* reinforced the presence of South Asian dancers and musicians within an iconic contemporary and classical performance venue. Assistant Artistic Director Pushkala Gopal described how the event 'celebrated individuality with collective identity'. For composer Srikanth Sriram, the event was 'poised at a moment where the term actually means something: it is the time where Asians in Britain are actually finding their own voice as British people in a number of fields...'[110] Sabri reflected on the significance of her work as a performer within the event with contemporary choreographer Filip Van Huffel which has helped her think differently about dance structures and shapes how she approaches her kathak choreography now.[111] Also at the South Bank Centre, the half-million pound production of *Escapade* (2003) celebrated South Asian popular culture – Bollywood and bhangra among other forms – with 134 dancers from community and youth dance groups supported by 60 technical staff. Akademi's director, Mira Kaushik, explained how site specific performances 'have transformed shows from South Asian events into London events'.[112]

The shows draw on multiple but dominant regional, religious and national imaginaries (Pakistani and Indian, Hindu and Muslim) rather than monolithic identity constructions, while contributing to a trend where location specific performances contest the 'narratives of space'.[113] Inspired

110 In Anbika Kucheria (2006) 'In your site: in your mind', *Pulse*, Summer, pp. 14-15.
111 Sonia Sabri with Shezad Kahlil (2010) 'Sonia Sabri: Intelligent Interpreter', *Pulse*, Summer, pp. 14-16.
112 Kucheria (2006) op.cit. p. 15.
113 Nicolas Whybrow (2011) *Art and the City*, p. 108.

by an Islamic Art exhibition, the Somerset House Trust commissioned *Waterscapes* (2004), an event that evoked Mughal Courts in North India through the classical style of kathak. The dancers moved in and through the courtyard of Somerset House as jets of water rose up from the flat fountain surface. The site of a former Tudor Palace, Somerset House has centuries of royal, military, political and commercial connections. The current building dates back to 1775 and housed the Royal Academy of Arts and Royal Academy of Sciences, and a number of government departments, including taxation up until 2011.[114]

Nicholas Whybrow analyses the relationship of public art to the cityscape, where work that revolves around the city and on city streets links public space with democratic space. Trafalgar Square exists as a site of both celebration and resistance, ceremony and anti-government protest:

> If London has a centre, and this is debateable, this is certainly a candidate with its conglomeration of key institutions, representing, inter alia, culture (The National Gallery), the colonialist Commonwealth (the high commissions of Canada and South Africa), the church (St Martins-in-the-fields), to say nothing of Whitehall's politics a few paces down one road and royal Buckingham Palace a few minutes down another.[115]

The 'fourth plinth' in the northwest corner of the square is an empty pedestal, the other three corners of the square are occupied by military monuments. Temporary exhibitions housed on the fourth plinth offer the potential to challenge hegemonic narratives, seen in a number of radical art works and performances. Mainstream productions in the wider space are supported by the Greater London Authority under the umbrella of the Trafalgar Square Festival, which celebrates cultural and religious markers for the city's communities, such as the Muslim festival of Eid, Hindu Diwali and Chinese (or lunar) New Year rituals.

Sapnay/Dreams (2005) was commissioned for the Trafalgar Square Festival, transforming all aspects of the site into performance platforms. Tripathi and Khoo combined dance styles to a remixed sound score of 'house' music by DJ Matt Ross and live *dhol* drumming. Tripathi spoke of the wonderful challenge of creating in response to various textures and levels of the location, of having to be aware of the three-dimensionality of an expressive body because audience was on all sides[116] *Sapnay* played the classical vocabularies of kathak and bharatanatyam against and with contemporary and balletic movement, performed by different groups distinguished by their costumes, in a celebration of 'hybridism' as described

---

114 For a history of the various institutions and buildings on the site, see the Somerset House Trust website, http://www.somersethouse.org.uk/history, accessed 23 May 2012.
115 Whybrow (2011) op.cit. pp. 106-107.
116 Tripathi (2006) op.cit.

in the programme notes. Tripathi led her group in traditional kathak phrases, believing there is a resilience and 'openings' in the form while remaining 'grounded in the tradition and constantly returning to it in order to keep true to it'.[117] Khoo crossed between bharatanatyam, ballet and contemporary dance, with a danced moment in the fountain, swirling fabric through and around the water, crossing gender conventions by emulating a Bollywood wet sari scene while transgressing boundaries of permissible access of the square's space. The kathak and bharatanatyam dancers wore relatively conventional costumes, the hues of reds, purples, and gold silks contrasting with the shades of grey worn by the contemporary dance/ballet performers. Phrases moved up and down the grand steps leading to the classical finale framed by the edifice of the National Gallery.

Other performances expand on creative processes and opportunities to push boundaries of the forms through their interaction with space. Mitra's analysis of *Weaving Paths* (2007) examines how the Sonia Sabri Company utilised the history of Bantock House, an Edwardian manor house in Wolverhampton, located in an industrial area in the West Midlands district. An engagement with heritage functioned on multiple levels, the diasporic dance activities 'interrogated the colonial power dynamics'.[118] Gaps exist between the classical traditions of the diaspora and the reality of their diasporic present, the latter in flux while the sense of connection to the past can reinforce conservative preservation of links to the 'homeland'. The performers' site specific interaction with space and place occurred through exploring the material objects, written history, architecture and atmosphere which facilitated their roles as 'interpretive agent'. Drawing on concepts developed around cultural outreach projects in museums, an interpretive agent arises from an active process of creativity in opposition to an 'objectified artefact'. Mitra explores how creative constraints in *Weaving Paths* arose from the inclusion of a group of community belly dancers in the finale set in the gardens of the house, resulted in the 'display of an essentialised and "Orientalist East"' in comparison to the collaborative and improvisatory creative process facilitated in other sections.[119]

In contrast to the references to heritage through classical dance seen in the *Sapnay* and *Sufi:Zen* where vibrant silks and stamped rhythms evoke an exotic elegance or meditative otherworldliness, *Awaz/Voice* (2006), embodied sweatshop labour that produces chic fashion. In Sundaram's choreography, representations of migrant women labouring at sewing machines were viewed against the imperial columns of the National Gallery. As part of the Trafalgar Square Festival, Sundaram was commissioned to create a work

117 Ibid., see also Bithika Chatterjee (2006) 'Boxes and Spaces, Elephants and Castles', *Pulse*, Summer, pp. 9-13.
118 Royona Mitra (2012) 'Performing Cultural heritage in *Weaving Paths*', p. 145.
119 Ibid. p. 155.

that celebrated South Asian women's achievements in Britain. While she took on the brief, she was concerned to have a wider acknowledgement of women's lives in the diaspora. Activist and writer Amrit Wilson's account of South Asian women garment worker riots gave Sundaram a starting point. *Awaz* was also the name of the first South Asian women's advocacy group in Britain, which functioned between 1977 and 1982 to challenge sexism and racism, and established refuges run for and by South Asian women. Initial plans to include two women's groups in the choreography proved difficult although two participants remained in the show, performing sewing actions from their factory days and joining in folk dance sections. Concerned to avoid tokenism with their inclusion, Sundaram recalled, 'when you take a story from someone, how do you do it right?'[120]

Awaz started with a procession, bringing dancer Magdeline Gorringe into the space dressed as a bride wearing flowing silks and a veil. A group of women wore long colourful skirts in red, vibrant turquoise and gold which covered their contemporary dance costumes. The eight female dancers removed the skirts, to show black or bright red tunics over sleek black trousers, and exposing Gorringe's advanced state of pregnancy which embodied an unusual vision of a female dancer, laden with her own symbolic power. Putting on sunglasses, scarves, red high heels and carrying a suitcase, the *Awaz* women transform from the traditional and exotic into the trendy and confident Londoner. They stride down the steps while the invisible worker is brought into focus, as migrant labourers wearing saris sit behind the main action working sewing machines. Bharatanatyam and kathak steps and gestures were interspersed with other material that moved into and out of the floor in moments of contact and pedestrian gesture.

Dancer Divya Kasturi had recently arrived from Chennai where she was trained in both bharatanatyam and kathak, and *Awaz* was her first professional performance in her new home. She recalled feeling strange performing in Trafalgar Square, wondering 'how would it appear?' feeling as though the dance was 'going back into the street'. Historically, the classical dance had moved from temples and outdoor, open spaces into proscenium stages that had 'elitist' associations. However, the strong classical foundations of other dancers involved in the project was reassuring. Kasturi also felt awkward about taking off layers of costume with the audience watching. Other practicalities were novel for her, such as health and safety issues dancing on the hard surface and levels of steps, concerns reflected in the movement choices. Kasturi's reflections reinforce the political resonance of the space as well – the juxtaposition of the traditional in the bridal procession with the contemporary business women stepping out; the richness of the fabrics versus the labour that produced them; some carefree

120 Sundaram (2013) op.cit.; Wilson (2006) op.cit.

folk dancing and the underlying social message; and power of expectations and the generational differences. The colonial versus the postcolonial was on display – the dancing bodies set against the symbols of empire. Trafalgar Square also presents a contrast between the conventional and contemporary, as Kasturi observed.[121] There is a constant sense of renewal, as a tourist location, with a flow of people, while the conventional is seen in the National Gallery alongside the postmodern architecture of the Sainsbury Wing. In an intriguing note of synchronicity, the performances occurred when there was another pregnant woman on display in the Square – Marc Quinn's nude sculpture of a pregnant Alison Lapper, a disabled artist, occupied the fourth plinth nearby.

Scholar Prarthana Purkayastha, another dancer in *Awaz*, explained the symbolism of a powerful finale where the dancers gather together at the sound of a plane overhead in Niraj Chag's score:

> I remember that the last image of dancers collecting and looking at the sky came out of a number of things... since the piece explored migration, in particular the lives of migrant women, the idea of hope, of starting something anew was something that we wanted to end with. Also, the glancing up towards the sky towards the flying aeroplanes – which brought migrant women from their home countries to a foreign one – was a symbol of both arrival and departure. It signalled at the journey that these women had been on, and at the sense of embarking on a new journey, tinged with a sense of loss.[122]

Awaz stands out among the other site works because of the narrative of diaspora, in contrasting expectations of different generations. The songs were those of farewell, about getting on a plane, love, getting beaten up, alongside ones in Urdu and Hindi which told of the expectations of a bride. Although Sundaram's social consciousness is apparent in some of her other choreography such as *Moham* (2002) she was concerned to avoid over-politicising the dance. The narrative context of *Awaz* was conveyed in a poetic introduction delivered by Sundaram, however, she worked to avoid ethnicising issues, or 'wearing your problem on your sleeve'. Unlike some political theatre, she explained, with dance, 'you can run through the emotions as well as entertain. While it is not mindless, or is even self-consciously mindful, it does not pose the threat of theatre in terms of confrontation – as there is room to interpret, if you want, that is. And there's music and movement and rhythm and costumes.... You may just watch, applaud and leave, happily.'[123] For this viewer, the social resonance has remained as well as a sense of community when the older women joined in the folk dance.

121 Divya Kasturi, interview with author, 29 August 2013.
122 Prarthana Purkayastha, personal email to author, 12 May 2012.
123 Sundaram (2013) op.cit.

Connecting to Communities

South Asian dance has grown alongside the constituency supported by the national Foundation for Community Dance (FCD), which has a broad lobbying remit and provides advice on practical matters to its practitioners. Creative Director Ken Bartlett discusses how both South Asian and community dance were placed into the 'boxes' by funding systems, the categorisation process stemming from confusion about the relationship between art and communities. Bartlett asserts this can be as liberating as it can be limiting, opening up the possibilities 'to make definitions that suit us, at any given moment for any given audience', and responding to 'the expressive needs and aspirations of individuals and groups'. By expanding the perceptions and definitions of what constitutes South Asian dance through community and education work, 'it has worked both within and against the traditions' of the field by engaging with diverse populations, so moving beyond identities.[124] The ACE's *Dance Mapping Report* also reveals how dance forms from the African and South Asian diaspora have appeal that crosses boundaries of social status. Unlike ballet and contemporary dance which attract audiences with higher social status, the non-western forms break through boundaries in terms of their ability to attract audiences.[125]

Many of Akademi's productions involve professional and semi-professional dancers, while community dance groups participated in the 2003 South Bank Centre festival, *Escapade*. This represents one extreme of the community dance spectrum – high visibility, vibrant and highly polished spectacle. At the other end of the spectrum are activities funded by a range of public bodies, with ideologically grounded objectives that move beyond but do not exclude artistic imperatives. A three year programme was established between London Councils and Akademi's education unit, to support arts and dance projects in 18 boroughs. Inter Action emphasises active health as a benefit of the workshops with older people while Creating Moves engaged 5 to 18 year olds deemed to be at risk. Some outreach activities integrate a broader cultural education linked back to the dance sources such as the three year Parallel Spaces project funded by the Department for International Development. It set out 'to enable primary and secondary school pupils to gain a greater understanding of the effects of poverty and global interdependence on young people in Britain and the Indian subcontinent.'[126] South Asian dance and storytelling offered the forms through which larger socio-political issues were addressed. An

---

124 Ken Bartlett (2006) 'Resisting the Box'. Akademi, http://www.akademi.co.uk/who weare/history-resisting-box.php, accessed 25 May 2012.

125 Susanne Burns and Sue Harrison (2009) *Dance Mapping Report*, p. 206.

126 Akademi, Parallel Spaces, http://www.akademi.co.uk/education/parallel-spaces.php, accessed 23 May 2013.

intergenerational project 'Who We Are' is 'about exploring heritage, identity and learning together'. Dance is just one component of the programme involving music and media workshops – there are dual aims of learning and having fun. A Learning Support Advisor liaised with the participants from across the 80 hours of their involvement, with participants predominantly black and ethnic minority and economically excluded families the children deemed to be underachievers, or 'at risk' of underachieving in schools.

To what extent do dance styles such as bharatanatyam and kathak offer different possibilities than those found in contemporary dance-based community and education projects? Other small company projects also utilise narrative strategies to connect to diverse groups within disparate communities. Sonia Sabri Company has worked with a number of diasporic women's groups, feeding into material for professional performances as well as helping women and marginalised groups explore new modes of expression. In working with Muslim women and young adult groups, culturally sensitive concerns about display of the body affect the project planning and the extent to which public performance is a component, so the extent of dance content differs according to the participants. Some of the movement motifs and emotional resonances in the show *JUGNI* (2013) were generated in workshops with women of different nationalities and ethnicities, drawn together through a call for participants. A significant aim of the SANGAM project is to offer new or alternative modes of expression to women unfamiliar with both performance and the reflexive and expressive creative processes. Sabri spoke of the intensity of the women's stories – from Somalia and Pakistan, for example. Another project involves oral histories and notions of heritage, documenting the role of women in communities along Birmingham's Ladypool Road, which is a main thoroughfare of the 'Balti belt', named because of the culinary innovations and traditions from the Indian sub-continent.[127] An example of work within schools is seen in Anusha Subramanyam's company. Beeja has collaborated with junior and primary school students in South Haringey on the creation of a dance theatre project with a non-violence and anti-bullying message. Beeja worked to ensure the project was integrated with other subject sessions and involved parents in the production, rather than offering it as an extra-curricular activity. In Liverpool, Sarker's Chaturangan Dance Company uses dance in arts and dementia workshops.[128]

---

127 Stacey Prickett (2012) 'Defying Britain's Tick-Box Culture'; Sabri, interview with author, 13 September 2013. Also see production pages at http://www.ssco.org.uk/productions/productions.html.
128 For descriptions of the project, see the Beeja website, http://www.beeja.com/beejainfo/projects.html, and Chatarangan Dance Company's website, http://www.chezfred.org.uk/chat/index.html. Both artists have been profiled in *Pulse*, see Donald Hutera (2012) 'Profile on Anusha Subramanyam', *Pulse*, Summer, pp. 10-12; and Gopa

Beyond these projects, South Asian dance is practised in multiple spaces and sites within the diaspora, for diverse purposes, seen in festivals, South Asian classical dance training in temples linked to ethnic and religious identities, performances by children and adolescents, and ritual such as a few hundred participants traversing the rhythmic circle of a *garba*, a group participatory dance. As David notes, there is a less generous funding environment for activities associated with community and religious groups. 'The fact that the Arts Council and the dominant culture in the UK has separated dance from religion contributes to a lack of interest and therefore a lack of funding for community dance practices within a religious context.'[129] Some ritual practices alter the city spaces in which they occur, organising and endowing them with sacred significance, while celebrating multiple identities in the diaspora.[130]

Popular forms may be last but not least for consideration – they capture the wider imagination and are increasingly accessible through other strands of practice. An innovative dance exercise franchise, *Just Jhoom!* combines Bollywood moves with fitness training science, offering an alternative to Zumba in the gyms. The folk form of bhangra has moved far from its roots in the Punjab area of North India and Pakistan, influencing and being influenced by British popular music and functioning on multiple levels within diasporic communities and beyond, with competitions being held at international levels, and formalisation and blending of styles along the way. Bhangra has attracted scholarly attention and documentation of its innovations, seen in how what was essentially a harvest dance performed by men has been reinvented in Britain, influencing Bollywood films and music in India.[131]

Conclusion

Returning to the public celebrations of monarchy and sport in the summer of 2012, South Asian dance has had a continuous presence. The classical dance forms gained status from their official designation from the state of India evoking the heritage of lineage, discipline and elite training. The visual spectacle conveyed an elegance and control, with bharatanatyam, kathak and odissi dancers costumed in in rich hues of silk performing in the spaces of government and tradition such as the Houses of Parliament

Roy with Bishaka Sarker, (2013) 'In search of a late style', *Pulse*, Autumn, p. 20.
129 David (2005) op.cit. p. 39.
130 Ann R. David (2010) 'Negotiating Identity: Dance and Religion in British Hindu Communities'; and (2012) 'Sacralising the City'.
131 For information about Just Jhoom! Bollywood style exercise franchise, see http://www.justjhoom.co.uk/; on bhangra in Britain see the Southall Story research project website, http://www.thesouthallstory.com/decades-of-music/.

Hall. The folk infused bhangra was seen in the tongue-in-cheek vision of cool Britannia in the Olympic Games opening ceremony show, accessible to billions around the world. In contrast, Akram Khan's meditation on loss struck a balance between grief and hope, the monumental theme allocated to a more contemporary dance form. The formal performances sit alongside street celebrations seen in Luton's Big Dance participatory dance activities.

The trajectory of Shobana Jeyasingh's career encapsulates and indeed, was integral to, the relations of power and community explored here. Starting from her classical bharatanatyam soloist practice in the 1980s, Jeyasingh began breaking down the dance structure. She was part of the cultural ambassador projects that took dance into schools to help advance cultural understanding. The process of breaking away from tradition began in her own practice and she published her reflections on identity and aesthetics, engaging with scholarship on the diaspora in the process. Initially she choreographed on a group of bharatanatyam trained dancers, and Jeyasingh's creations began a project of deconstructing the classical form. The Shobana Jeyasingh Dance Company was established in 1988 and has gone on to represent the nation abroad with British Council sponsorship. The extent to which Jeyasingh's creativity has transcended its cultural roots is brought to the fore in the company's 25th anniversary performances. Restaging an early departure from her bharatanatyam training and performing career, she developed the group dance *Configurations* from her solo *Miniatures* in 1988, performed to a commissioned score by Michael Nyman. She returned to the dance in 2012, a re-statement and deconstruction of bharatanatyam after moving away from the vocabulary in many productions in the intervening years. Jeyasingh also gave choreographic workshops for performers at the international celebration of hip hop culture, the Breakin' Convention, in 2012.

Some of Jeyasingh's dances fulfil the 'protest' imperative of this book's title – *Faultline* as discussed above in the GCSE syllabus and *Bruise Blood* (2009), created to Steve Reich's looped score of a black American who talks about being beaten by police in the USA. Others such as *Too Mortal* (2012) offered a haunting spiritual resonance that transcends cultural specificity. The site dance is set in English heritage churches with listed status, and is performed to small audiences standing in front of the altar. Six dancers arise up and over the high-backed pews, their limbs reaching out, then collapsing down as they use the gated pews as supports and hiding places. As a mediation on life and death, there are some recognisable strands of the classical form, but what one takes away from the performance goes beyond such considerations. As mentioned in the introduction, Jeyasingh's *Counterpoint* responded to the Somerset House space – the building as well as the white expanses of the courtyard which she described using terminology of 'imposing', 'grand', 'colonial' and 'masculine'.[132] Twenty female dancers wearing various shades of saffron orange costumes by Ursula Bombshell stood out in the summer light. Moving to a commissioned score by Cassiel, the choreography shifted between a contrast to the formality of the environment using intimate gestural interactions between dancers, to unison passages that emphasised a spatial linearity reinforced by jets of water that burst up from the ground. Associated community projects in West London helped reach new audiences and a mentoring element was established between the five more experienced performers and the 15 emerging performers. With other works in the education syllabi and associations with universities, Jeyasingh epitomises the complex network of institutions, artistry and politics of the South Asian dance field.

The rich documentation of the dance ecology sees South Asian dance as a consistent presence, its advocates and proponents setting out strategic pathways for professional and pedagogic development. Multiple organisations and a reflexive process have contributed to an ideological discourse where the heritage is established to classical forms while encouraging innovation. Identity politics ripple beneath the surface of debates but are fundamentally intertwined with aesthetic concerns which are further influenced by arts funding policies. The South Asian dance community has made such connections work to their advantage, identifying diverse sources of governmental support and performance opportunities. Strategic focus, institution building and advocacy sit alongside clarification of the forms for western audiences and a transnationalisation of the dance forms, broadening accessibility to viewer and participant to take it beyond a diasporic base. Its presence in dance education has moved beyond tokenism not because of the impact of multiculturalism but because of the artistry, the quality being created by world-leading British-based South Asian dance practitioners. A rising generation of performers includes Aakash Odedra, Amina Kayyham, Shane Shambu, Kali Chandrasegaram, Manuela Benini, and Katie Ryan, to name a few. Highly professional, they are able to move between classical and contemporary styles, performing traditional dances while developing as choreographers in their own right and advancing the forms through teaching in diverse situations. The multiple forums, publications and range of academic scrutiny have kept dialogues going, constantly interrogating aesthetic as well as political issues and themes of tradition, classicism, and contemporaneity. Relatively well-funded by government in various capacities – as public art, in social inclusion projects, in dance education, and as artistic expression in its own right – the field contributes to the British and global dance ecology.

---

132 See the project page and Jeyasingh in the *Counterpoint* trailer, http://www. shobanajeyasingh.co.uk/works/counterpoint/.

Conclusion

William Forsythe: *'it is just an act of citizenship'.*[1]

'Is it Dance? Maybe. Political? Sure.' is the title of a *New York Times* article by Diane Solway about William Forsythe Company's *Three Atmospheric Studies* (2006). For Forsythe, the indictment of the Iraq war arose out of a deeply-seeded imperative, an act of citizenship. In a similar vein, many of the dance activities explored here reveal a political impetus inextricably entwined with the dancers' sense of self, an embodied politics. In other examples, situating the works or practices in a socio-political context reveals broader resonances about class, race and/or gender representation which can be read as political. My findings demonstrate significant thematic continuities across the decades and continents, despite differences in social and institutional structures. Protest issues, narratives of oppression and oppositional stances are offset by positive celebrations of power and resistance, of solidarity and shared heritage.

A full circle is created with the opening and closing discussions of dances that portray female garment workers. I started with Edith Segal's work with the International Ladies Garment Workers Union (ILGWU), their Unity House summer camp in 1924 and the Needle Trades Dance Group. Their participatory dance activities functioned on multiple levels – as exercise, community cohesion and a mode for the expression of working-class identity and experiences. The last chapter focuses on *Awaz/Voice* (2006) by Chitra Sundaram, which placed South Asian female garment workers at the heart of her celebration of diasporic women's lives in Britain. Their stories inspired the theme and movement material while two of the retired workers joined in the dance on the steps leading to the National Gallery in London's Trafalgar Square. Narrative and socially conscious impulses are seen in both – telling about the lives of those who are often hidden – but diverse choreographic approaches and circumstances separate how the dances functioned artistically. In both instances the women were from marginalised positions, with similar struggles for equality, fair pay and safe working conditions as they laboured to produce goods for mass consumption.

On the pages between these two dances, further issues resonated across much of the choreography and recreational practices. Foremost is how construction of communities emerge at one level geographically – New York City, London and San Francisco – where networks were established and

---

1 Quoted in Diane Solway (2007) 'Is it Dance? Maybe. Political? Sure.' *The New York Times*, 18 February.

how dancers both engaged with and helped shape the social spaces of the urban environments while being part of an avant-garde zeitgeist. Influences expand beyond the immediate locales, however, with escapes to nature in the summer camps, dances in parks and transnational connections and exchanges. The significance of global flows between Europe and the early American modern dance is continually updated, seen in Susan Manning's work on American connections to German *Ausdruckstanz*.[2] New histories emerge here, revealing interactions between dancers in England and the USA, in trips to Berlin by Segal, the composer Alan Bush and decades later, San Francisco based artists. The South Asian dance community in Britain is also part of a larger artistic network, spanning multiple continents and which contributes to the transnational development of the dance forms.

Dance, protests and class

Themes of protest were most overt in the left-wing dances in the inter-war years in London and the USA, taking on Marxist binaries of class struggle. Similar aims are apparent on both sides of the Atlantic – raising consciousness of class through dance – however, crucial differences emerge in representations of workers and their agency, their relationship to the means of production and thematic presentations of the 'proletariat' in the USA and the 'people' in Britain. Part of the disparity can be attributed to larger ideological shifts with the emergence of the Popular Front in 1935. In both countries, distinctive class identities had been manifest in cultural and employment situations, with 'proletariat' inextricably linked to a Marxist ideology predicated on class conflict and often modelled on the factory labourer. In Britain representations of the 'people' tended to invoke a nostalgic vision of rural, pre-industrial peasantry rather than a factory worker in the workers dance that evolved in New York. The longing for the past resonates with Raymond Williams' analyses of the new social order that emerged with the 19th-century Industrial Revolution in England, linked to advances in mechanical production that altered social and cultural values.[3] Although the Popular Front impacted the range of representations in American modern dance and the gradual disappearance of the proletariat as worker, the rural ideal remained an iconic identity in Britain and was even central to the narrative of the 2012 Olympic Games Opening Ceremony. Other parallels are strong, however, seen in left-wing theatre connections, in an all-encompassing leftist culture with pageants and summer camps and their ideological drivers – the Communist Party USA and unions in New

2 Susan Manning (2007) '*Ausdruckstanz across the Atlantic*', in Franco and Nordera eds, op.cit.

3 Raymond Williams (1958/1983) *Culture and Society, 1780-1950*; and (1961) *The Long Revolution*.

York and the Co-operative Society in Britain. The international connections have some similarities, leaders of workers activities (Segal and Bush) in both countries spent time in Berlin and travelled to the USSR while singer-activist-actor Paul Robeson moved in and out of both worlds.

Questions remain regarding interrelationships between the leftist dancers in England due in part to policies of anonymity which precluded listing performers, and which also reinforced ideals of equality among participants despite their competencies. A few individuals were traced through their teaching and performing activities, such as Margaret Leona, revealing continued involvement in the left-wing theatre movement through mass declamations which were unison chants accompanied by stylised movement. Others, such as Kate Eisenstaedt, proved untraceable beyond 1939. Some creations emphasised a national imaginary through sharp portrayals of class divisions: Margaret Barr placed the action in a pub on a Saturday night, portraying fishermen, miners and ladies hunting. A London *Times* critic proclaimed that her work was 'essentially original and essentially English'.[4] Choreography for the 1938 *Towards To-morrow Co-operative Pageant*, however, centred on the universal themes of war and loss alongside the historical development of socialist ideals.

Whilst dancers were not always named in cast lists in the American performances, there was adequate documentation from other sources to reveal crossovers between the revolutionary dance and what was to become the mainstream modern dance community, providing a sense of the identities of the dancers. Affiliations with trade unions were fundamental to the movement, offering audiences, dancers and ideological support to articulate socially conscious choreographic messages. Workers joined recreational and performance union dance groups while many left-wing dancer-activists came from the working class and Jewish communities of the New York area. Although they may not have spent their days in repetitive labour, many of their parents did, thus offering insight to a worker's daily life. A specific political agenda underpinned the Communist Party events at Madison Square Garden, staged over a decade when the Soviet Union was heralded as a model society. Topical concerns were manifest, such as the communist struggles in Europe and the anti-fascist fight, however, a basic celebratory approach continued to perpetuate a mythical USSR, its past, present and future. Identification of a national identity – of the work as specifically American – is absent in accounts of the early left-wing dance. National themes emerged in Federal Theatre Project productions but they retained a subversive edge while recreational activities led by Segal reinforced secular Jewish culture and social justice themes.

Protest themes dominate the 1920s and 1930s choreography in both

4 Anon. (1935) 'The Arts Theatre, Dance-Drama Group', *The Times*, 12 February, p. 12.

countries, where anti-war, anti-poverty and social injustice themes inspired diverse creations, either as stand-alone dances or affiliated to left-wing theatre and pageants. For example, Segal's choreography took to heart binaries and gave voice to the marginalised. Black and white racial tensions were conveyed as being part of a broader struggle of the oppressed as the proletariat, standing up to the oppressor as the bourgeoisie. The dancers reflected on workers' lives, collective identities were prioritised above the personal. The dance practices in the San Francisco Bay Area reversed this balance later in the century – the practitioners engage with the collective through the individual as discussed below. In other creations, a counter-hegemonic inspiration arises from social inequities – such as topical incidents of oppression, discrimination, environmental destruction and anti-war sentiment. South Asian dance practitioners in Britain have also created dances inspired by social issues, such as Sundaram's *Awaz/Voice* and Jeyasingh's *Faultline* and *Bruiseblood*, but the majority of the dances in the public arenas of Trafalgar Square and other sites sit comfortably in relation to the multicultural mainstream ideals of harmony. The dominant representations reveal a spectacular and exotic heritage, a lineage to the classical dance forms, and the hegemony of the popular in Bollywood and bhangra styles. This is not a critique in itself, and the South Asian dance community has been innovative in using these productions to advance the aesthetics of the form and help professionalise the field.

Dance, ethnicities and the personal

Personal narratives abound in interdisciplinary creations in San Francisco area creations – queer identities, individual loss or disempowered migrants – which symbolise wider collectives. There is also an engagement with social space in contemporary practices, such as the site specific and aerial choreography by Joanna Haigood with Zaccho Dance Company and Jo Kreiter's Flyaway Productions, where the social histories inspire artistic reflection that brings contemporary injustices to light. Multiple ethnic and racial identities feature across these pages, representing acts of oppression and hope in narratives arising from the legacy of slavery in the USA. Stories of empowered free blacks in San Francisco contrasted to those of the hunted, still in chains, as well as emancipated African Americans still searching for equality at the turn of the twentieth century. South Asian dance in Britain, on the other hand, is a diasporic form presented as the exotic 'other' in many manifestations, underpinned by cultural symbols whose meaning can be gleaned on many levels – a knowledgeable audience responding differently to the uninitiated. Themes of resistance emerge in performances in the relatively new alternative venues, such as the Rich Mix performance space in the trendy Shoreditch area of East London. A generation of young choreographers are creating works that speak from individual experience and break from the canons of the classical forms, utilising physical theatre, text and diverse dance vocabularies. Similarities in inspirational sources rather than movement styles are seen in the reflective work of San Francisco Bay Area dancers such as Joe Goode and on the more alternative end of the spectrum, Contraband and Sara Shelton Mann, Keith Hennessy, Jess Curtis, Kim Epifano, Kathleen Hermsdorf, Stephanie Maher and Jules Beckman. Krissy Keefer and Dance Brigade place women's experience at the heart of much of their choreography, the female characters are survivors as well as leaders, healers and visionaries. Many of the new generation of South Asian choreographers are integrating western choreographic approaches, seen in dances about their diasporic experience in Britain (such as Divya Kasturi's *NowHere*, 2009). The personal as political with broader resonance is also evident in productions that derive from outreach projects – Sonia Sabri Company's *JUNGI* draws on women's stories of oppression, abuse and hope while *Fleeting Moments* arose out of Dance and Dementia workshops with Bisakha Sarker and Anusha Subramanyam in Liverpool. In both the Bay Area and Britain, the outreach and youth activities are integral to the social engagement of the dance communities.

Dance and Power

One of the resounding threads running through the performances and activities explored here is the sense of empowerment, derived from the act of dancing as well as the messages. Different relations of power were explored – the dance collective, the individual, and institution – be it government, dance school, union or lobbying group. The dancers are part of larger creative networks whose survival in difficult financial times rests on a strong commitment to artistry that pushes boundaries. San Francisco Bay Area performers have continued to shape an alternative culture which has blended into or influenced the mainstream over the years. The collective spirit that infuses productions extends to the structure of their dance organisations – from 848 Community Space to CounterPULSE and Dancers Group. Dance buildings are more than edifices for performance and training but sites for the community – ODC Commons, Alonzo King's Lines Dance Center and CounterPULSE. Their continuity rests on hard work and innovative funding searches, rather than on consistent arts funding from federal or state governments. Contrasts can be seen in the South Asian dance community's institution-building activities over the decades – Akademi, Kadam, Sampad, Milapfest, for example – who benefit from government arts funding in England and nationally. The relations of power run deeper than monetary support, however, as they help shape the delivery and understanding of the diasporic art form on a larger scale. Building networks and, significantly, sites for coverage of the field, exists in the specialist publication, *Pulse* which is helping educate the reader as well as circulate news and reviews, in symposia and other events sponsored by Akademi and CICD in Leiceister, and in the public arena through the spectacular site performances. Academic interaction has led to a wealth of scholarly research while the inclusion of South Asian dance as case studies within in the national curriculum and in various qualifications in education and training systems, has helped move it beyond its diasporic foundations.

California's dancers are increasingly shaping a wider discourse of inter-disciplinary, avant-garde performance rooted in collective processes. In addition to the flow back and forth between Europe, New York and the Bay Area, affiliations to universities are guiding upcoming generations of dancer/scholars/activists to reflect about their own creations as well as documenting the immediate history of their environment. Intellectual engagement has been a constant feature of their creative approaches, whilst the internet is helping to spread writing and viewing of the productions and choreographers discussed here (seen in Wikipedia pages on Contraband, Keith Hennessy and other seminal dance and performance activists). Only a snapshot is provided here, more recent activities are gleaned from correspondence and from the rich vein of published professional criticism – Rita Felciano and Ann Murphy among the long-standing commentators.

Institutional support for the American revolutionary dance in the 1920s-1930s came from being part of a larger radical arts movement. Segal's connections to John Reed Clubs, Artef and later the Federal Theatre Project were underpinned by her Communist Party affiliation although she maintained artistic independence throughout her career. The radical dancers joined together in the Workers Dance League (later New Dance League) which contributed to the codification and spread of American modern dance. In 1930s Britain, the leftist dancers' threads to the dance establishment were thin – Barr remained outside the mainstream and with the outbreak of war, the Central European strand of modern dance generally fell out of favour. The absence of written accounts reinforced the extent to which it was an outsider activity, with rare coverage in the specialist dance journal *The Dancing Times* and from professional critics. What is also missing from accounts of radical dance in Britain is evidence of activities involving young people and children. The Woodcraft Folk affiliated to the Co-operative Society fulfilled roles undertaken by the youth groups and summer camps in the USA. In contrast, San Francisco Bay Area companies such as Zaccho and Dance Brigade offer dance projects for children and young people who are economically disadvantaged. British students also have the potential to access South Asian dance and other styles through state education, dance examinations and outreach programmes, some of which have social inclusion objectives affiliated to dance companies and sponsored by organisations such as Akademi.

In setting out to explore the relationships between embodied politics in dance, protest and identities, novel historical accounts are offered to enhance dominant dance narratives. The first case study reveals new perspectives of left-wing dance activities in the USA, focusing on participatory activities in Segal's work which distinguishes it from the extensive scholarship cited in Chapter 2. The archival detail examines the specifics of the symbolism in her choreography and situates Segal within an international radical arts movement arising out of the intellectual and cultural hub of New York's Lower East Side. She contributed to the transformation of Progressive Era performance events such as pageants and recreational dance activities. The dancing workers brought together notions of collective resistance that parallel Mark Franko's analysis of theatrical dance and labour in the 1930s and Ramsay Burt's interrogation of diverse identity constructions and modernity in early American modern dance performance.[5] Segal's activism had a broad scope, continuing to awaken young people's social consciousness over the years.

The leftist modern dance in Britain had a fleeting existence, which is explored in relation to artistic practices informed by socialist and communist ideologies. The power of the dance institutions in formation at the time, the hegemony of ballet, the standardisation of examination systems, and the absence of an infrastructure to support alternative creative approaches was combined with the lack of a critical mass of participants, all formidable obstacles to overcome. The significance of the account lies in establishing connections to the wider leftist arts field, however, further research is required to determine whether the dance activities influenced political theatre practices. Seeds of resistance and avant-garde dance experimentation resurface after the war, but developed without a legacy from the 1930s dance activists.

Ever the innovators, the San Francisco Bay Area community has rich strands of practice responding to contemporary situations, some of which were briefly mentioned here – ethnic, gender, nation and sexual orientation issues as well as evolving class tensions and ecological concerns. Starting as powerful alternative performance collectives, a counter-hegemonic shift has occurred over the years, with dancer-activists shaping not just their communities but having a profound impact upon the wider cultural and social life of the Bay Area. This has occurred through their dances of resistance, of protest and politics embodied through performance and action, taking

5 Mark Franko (2002) *The Work of Dance: Labor, Movement and Identity in the 1930s*; Ramsay Burt (1998) *Alien Bodies: Representations of modernity, 'race' and nation in early modern dance*; and Tomko, op.cit.

dance into non-performance sites, and revealing marginalised histories. The entrance to the mainstream was as outsiders, as mavericks and iconoclasts, establishing studios, teaching and mentoring new generations in the local environment as well as in international arts centres such as Berlin and New York.

In contrast, the analysis of South Asian dance reveals a different trajectory of engagement with institutions and affecting change from within. Starting as the exotic 'other', the artists and their advocates have worked at grassroots and community levels to educate and enhance understandings of classical dance forms. Strategic decisions to move outside their communities resulted in opening up South Asian dance, working to create opportunities for performance, education and training in styles such as bharatanatyam and kathak. This study reveals the significance of broadening accessibility on multiple levels – for viewers, western dancers and members of the diasporic communities – they have succeeded in influencing the wider dance ecology. Hierarchies of style and notions of hybridity have become part of wider discourses about funding, arts policies and minority representation, all of which are engrained in dance scholarship and the development of critical voices from within, essentially constructing a Bourdieusian field of practice along the lines of the American modern dance. In addition to articulating concepts of heritage through classical dance foundations, some South Asian dance practitioners are absorbing creative practices from western performance that can enhance rather than replace expressive conventions in the diasporic styles. Significantly, the extent to which South Asian dance is placed within state education and training systems reinforces a political resonance.

In compiling this diverse range of research, I set out to challenge the sentiment that opens the book and proclaims the disappearance of dance as a weapon. The case studies examine diverse ways that dance is not merely reflective of the socio-political contexts of its existence but effects change. In each chapter, the significance of community and collective action is reinforced, the power of institutions, hegemony and how transformation can occur, whether arising from within or through dancers as activists who engage with existing mainstream organisations. Both Marxist informed ideas of praxis which celebrate a collective solidarity, and the personal as political which inspires individual agency, have shaped dance practices that impact upon the wider cultural ecologies linked to Britain and the USA.

Bibliography

Adair, Christy (2007) *Dancing the Black Question*, Alton: Dance Books

Anderson, Benedict (1991) *Imagined Communities*, 2d ed., London: Verso

Andrews, Irene Osgood & Margaret A. Hobbs (2008) *Economic Effects of the War upon Women and Children in Great Britain*, Charleston: BiblioBazzar

Anon. (1984) *Glory of the Garden: The development of the arts in England: a strategy for a decade*, London: Arts Council of Great Britain

Arnold, Aronson (2000) *American Avant-theatre: A History*, London: Routledge

Bell-Kanner, Karen (1998) *Frontiers: The Life and Times of Bonnie Bird: American Modern Dancer and Dance Educator*, Amsterdam: Harwood Academic Publishing

Benn, Tansin (2004) '"Race" and Physical Education, Sport and Dance', Physical Education: Essential Issues, Green, Ken and Kenneth Hardman, eds., London: Sage, 197-219

Birchall, Johnston (1994) *Co-op: The People's Business*, Manchester: Manchester University Press

Blanke, David (2002) *The Nineteen Tens: American Popular Culture through History*, Westport, CT: Greenwood Publishing

Blood, Melanie (2007) 'Cooper Heiresses take the Stage' in *Angels in the American Theater: Patrons, Patronage and Philanthropy*, introduction by Robert A. Schanke, Carbondale, IL: Southern Illinois University

Boggs, Carl (1976) *Gramsci's Marxism*, London: Pluto Press

Bonham-Carter, Victor (1958), *Dartington Hall: The History of an Experiment*, London: Phoenix House, Ltd.

Bordo, Susan (1993) *Unbearable Weight: Feminism, Western Culture and the Body*, Berkeley: University of California Press

Bourdieu, Pierre (1977) *Outline of a Theory of Practice*, Cambridge, MA: Cambridge University Press

Bourdieu, Pierre (1984) *Distinction: A Social Critique of the Judgement of Taste*, London: Routledge

Brah, Avtar (1996) *Cartographies of Diaspora*, London: Routledge

Bridgwood, Ann, Clare Fenn, Karen Dust, Lucy Hutton, Adrienne Skelton and Megan Skinner (2003) *Focus on Cultural Diversity: the arts in England*, ACE Research Report 34, London: Arts Council England

Brinson, Peter (1991) *Dance as Education: Towards a National Dance Culture*, Basingstone: Hants: The Falmer Press

Brown, Elena J. (2002) '"If I can't Dance I Don't Want to Be Part of Your Revolution': Edith Segal and the Revolutionary Dance Movement of the 1930s', *Society of Dance History Scholars Conference Proceedings*, Temple

University, 1-8

Buhle, Paul (1987) *Marxism in the USA: A History of the American Left*, London: Verso

Burns, Susanne and Sue Harrison (2009) *Dance Mapping Report*, London: Arts Council England

Burt, Ramsay (1998) *Alien Bodies: Representations of modernity, 'race' and nation in early modern dance*, London: Routledge

Burt, Ramsay (2013) 'The Biopolitics of Modernist Dance and Suffragette Protest', in Gerald Siegmund and Stefan Hölscher, eds., *Dance, Politics and Co-immunity*, Zurich, Berlin: diaphenes, 247-258

Bush, Alan (1980) *In My Eighth Decade & other Essays*, Chicago: Kahn & Averill

Bush, Nancy (2000) *Alan Bush, Music, Politics and Life*, London: Thames Publishing

Carlsson, Chris and Nancy Peters, eds. (1998) *Reclaiming San Francisco: History, Politics, Culture*, San Francisco: City Lights Books

Carter, Alexandra (2011) 'Constructing and Contesting the Natural in British Theatre Dance', in in Carter, Alexandra and Rachel Fensham, eds., *Dancing Naturally: Nature, Neo-Classicism and Modernity in Early Twentieth-Century Dance*, London: Palgrave Macmillan, 16-30

Chakravorty, Pallabi (1998) 'Hegemony, Dance and Nation: The Construction of the Classical Dance in India', *South Asia*, XXI:2, 107-120

Chakravorty, Pallabi (2008) *Bells of Change: Kathak dance, women and modernity in India*, Calcutta: Seagull

Chambers, Colin (1989) *The Story of Unity Theatre*, London: Lawrence & Wishart

Chambers, Colin (2006) *Here we Stand: Politics, Performers and Performance*, London: Nick Hern Books

Clark, Jon, Margot Heinemann, David Margolies and Carole Snee, eds., *Culture and Crisis in Britain in the Thirties*, London: Lawrence & Wishart

Clive Gray (2000) *The Politics of the Arts in Britain*, London: Macmillan Press

Cohen-Stratyner, Barbara Naomi (1982) 'John Bovingdon', *Biographical Dictionary of Dance*, New York: G Schirmer Books, 116

Coorlawala, Uttara Asha (2002) 'Response to Dr Andrée Grau's "Dance, Culture and Identity"', Animated, Autumn, 30-33

Croft, Andy (1998) 'Introduction', in Andy Croft, ed., *A Weapon in the Struggle: The Cultural History of the Communist Party in Britain*, London: Pluto Press

Crow, Susie, *Invisible Women*, Ballet Magazine, March 2002, http://www.ballet.co.uk/magazines/yr_02/mar02/sc_invisible_women.htm, accessed August 28, 2013

Culleton, Claire A. (2000) *Working-Class Culture, Women, and Britain 1914-*

1921, London: Macmillan

Daly, Ann (2003) *Done into Dance: Isadora Duncan in America*, Middletown, CT: Wesleyan University Press

David Gere, 'Contraband premieres elegant 'Mira' excerpts,' *The Oakland Tribune*, April 2, 1990

David, Ann R. (2003) 'Where have all the courses gone...?' *Pulse*, Issue 4, Winter, 6-8

David, Ann R. (2005) *Performing Faith: Dance, Identity and Religion in Hindu Communities in Leicester and London*, unpublished PhD thesis, DeMontfort University

David, Ann R. (2010) 'Negotiating Identity: Dance and Religion in British Hindu Communities' in Pallabi Chakravorty and Nilanjana Gupta, *Dance Matters. Peforming India*, ed. London & New Delhi: Routledge, 89-107

David, Ann R. (2012) 'Sacralising the City: Sound, Space and Performance in Hindu Ritual Practices in London'. *Culture and Religion*, 13:4, 449-467

DeFrantz, Thomas (1996) 'Simmering Passivity: The Black Male Body in Concert Dance', in Morris, Gay, ed., *Moving Words: Re-writing Dance*, London: Routledge, 95-106

Denning, Michael (1997) *The Cultural Front: the Laboring of American Culture in the Twentieth Century*, New York: Verso

Devlin, Graham (1989) *Stepping Forward: Some suggestions for the development of dance in England in the 1990s*, February 1989, London: Arts Council of Great Britain

Diner, Hasia R. (2000) *Lower East Side Memories: A Jewish Place in America*, Princeton & London: Princeton University Press

Duberman, Martin Bauml (1989) *Paul Robeson*, London: The Bodley Head

Eade, John (2000) *Placing London: From Imperial Capital to Global City*, Oxford & New York: Berghahn

Elton, Helen (1998) 'Vienna Revisited in Memory', in Bettina Vernon-Warren and Charles Warren, eds., *Gertrud Bodenwieser and Vienna's Contribution to Ausdruckstanz*, Amsterdam: Harwood Academic, 85-96

Epifano, Kim, 'A Red Thread: Creating Dance Across Cultures and Politics', *In Dance*, September 2008, http://www.dancersgroup.org/content/programs/articles/2008/2008September_125.html, accessed July 24, 2013

Felciano, Rita (2004) 'Best Wishes – and curses,' *SF Bay Guardian*, October 20-26, www.sfbg.com, accessed January 13, 2006

Felciano, Rita (2005) 'The Home Inside,' *Dance View Times*, June 17, http://www.danceviewtimes.com, accessed January 16, 2007

Felciano, Rita (2011) 'Top flight: Year in Dance 2011', *SF Bay Guardian*, December 20, http://www.sfbg.com/2011/12/20/top-flight, accessed July 28, 2013

Felciano, Rita (2011) 'Zaccho Dance Theatre Review', *Dance Magazine*, April 2011, http://www.dancemagazine.com/issues/April-2011/Zaccho-Dance-Theatre, accessed online, September 4, 2013

Felciano, Rita (2012) 'Fly, on the wall: Niagara Falling' takes to the air to take on the recession', *SF Guardian,* September 26, in http://www.sfbg.com/2012/09/26/fly-wall, accessed July 28, 2013

Fensham, Rachel (2011) 'Nature, Force and Variation', in Carter, Alexandra and Rachel Fensham, eds., *Dancing Naturally: Nature, Neo-Classicism and Modernity in Early Twentieth-Century Dance*, London: Palgrave Macmillan, 1-16

Foley, Barbara (1993) *Radical Representations: Politics and Form in U.S. Proletarian Fiction, 1929-1941*, Durham: Duke University Press

Foner, Eric (1998) *The Story of American Freedom*, New York & London: W.W. Norton

Foner, Eric (2010) *Give Me Liberty: An American History*, v. 2, 3d ed., London: W.W. Norton

Foster, Susan Leigh (2003) 'Choreographies of Protest', *Theatre Journal*, 55, 295-412

Foucault, Michel (1979) *Discipline & Punish: The Birth of the Prison*, trans. by Alan Sheridan, New York: Vintage Books

Foucault, Michel (1980) in Gordon, Colin, ed., *Power/Knowledge: Selected Interviews & Other Writings, 1972-1977*, New York: Pantheon Books

Franko, Mark (1995) *Dancing Modernism/Performing Politics*, Hoboken, NJ: John Wiley & Sons

Franko, Mark (2002) *The Work of Dance, Labor, Movement, and Identity in the 1930s*, Middletown, CT: Wesleyan University Press

Franko, Mark (2007) 'Dance and the Political' in Franco Susanne, and Marina Nordera, eds., *Dance Discourses: Keywords in Dance Research*, London: Routledge

Garafola, Lynn (2005) 'Writing on the Left: The Remarkable Career of Edna Ocko', *Legacies of Twentieth-Century Dance*, Middletown, CT: Wesleyan University Press, 293-304

Geduld, Victoria Phillips (2008) 'Performing Communism in the American Dance: Culture, Politics and the New Dance Group', *American Communist History*, 7:1, 39-65

Genné, Beth (2000) 'Creating a Canon, Creating the 'Classics' in Twentieth Century British Ballet', *Dance Research*, 18:2, Winter, 132-162

Gere, David (1994) 'Center for the Arts at Yerba Buena Inaugural Fall Season,' *Dance Magazine*, March, 88

Gere, David (2001) '*29 Effeminate Gestures*: Choreographer Joe Goode and the Heroism of Effeminacy,' in Jane Desmond, ed., *Dancing Desires*, Middletown: Wesleyan University Press, 349-391

Gere, David (2004) *How to Make Dances in an Epidemic: Tracking Choreography in the age of AIDS*, Madison: University of Wisconsin Press.

Gilroy, Paul (1993) *The Black Atlantic: Modernity and Double Consciousness*, London: Verso

Gilroy, Paul (2002) *There Ain't No Black in the Union Jack*, London: Routledge (2nd ed.)

Gladstone, Emma (2007) *Dance, Film and the Curriculum*, London: Arts Council of England.

Glassberg, David (1990) *American Historical Pageantry*, Chapel Hill, NC: University of North Carolina Press

Gomery, Douglas (1979) 'The Movies Become Big Business: Publix Theatres and the Chain Store Strategy', *Cinema Journal*, 18:2, 26-40

Gordon, Mel (1975) 'Foregger and the Dance of the Machines', *TDR*, T65, 68-73

Graff, Ellen (1997) *Stepping Left: Dance and Politics in New York City, 1928-1942*, Durham & London: Duke University Press

Graff, Ellen (2003) 'The Dance is a Weapon', in Dils, Ann and Ann Cooper Albright, *Moving Histories/Dancing Cultures*, Middletown, CT: Wesleyan University Press, 315-322

Gramsci, Antonio (1971) in Quentin Smith & Geoffrey Nowell, eds., *Selections from The Prison Notebooks*, London: ElecBooks

Grau, Andrée (1992) 'Intercultural Research in the Performing Arts', *Dance Research*, 10:2, 3-29

Grau, Andrée (1997) 'Dance, South Asian Dance, and Higher Education', in Iyer, Alessandra, ed. (1997) *'South Asian Dance: The British Experience'*, *Choreography and Dance*, Amsterdam: Harwood Academic Publishing, 55-62

Grau, Andrée (2001) 'Dance and Cultural Identity', *Animated*, Autumn, 23-26

Grau, Andrée (2002) *South Asian Dance in Britain*, London: Leverhulme Trust, with research by Alessandra Lopez y Royo and Magdeline Gorringe

Grau, Andrée (2008) 'Dance and the Shifting Sands of Multiculturalism', in Urmimala Sarkar Munsi, ed., *Dance: Transcending Borders*, New Delhi, Tulika Books, 232-252

Gray, Clive (2000) *The Politics of the Arts in Britain*, London: Macmillan Press

Gregory, Katie (2008) 'West End Girl, interview with Arlene Phillips', *Dancing Times*, 98:1176, August, 22-23

Hall, Duncan (2001) *'A pleasant change from politics': Music and the British labour movement between the wars*, Cheltenham: New Clarion Press

Hall, Fernau (1938) 'Modern Dancing at King's Cross: The Dance-Drama Group', *The Dancing Times*, no. 328, January, 526-528

Hall, Fernau (1950) *Modern English Ballet: An interpretation*, London:

Melrose

Hall, Stuart (1991) 'Old and new Identities, Old and New Ethnicities' in King, Anthony D., ed., *Culture, Globalization and the World-System*, London: Macmillan, 41-68

Halprin, Anna (1995) *Moving Toward Life: Five Decades of Transformational Dance*, Rachel Kaplan, ed., Middletown: Wesleyan University Press

Hanlon, Richard and Mike Waite (1998) 'Communism and British Classical Music' in Andy Croft (ed.) *A Weapon in the Struggle: The Cultural History of the Communist Party in Britain*, London: Pluto Press

Harrington, John (2007) *The Life of the Neighborhood Playhouse on Grand Street*, Syracuse: Syracuse University Press

Harris, Joanna Gewertz (2009) *Beyond Isadora: Bay Area Dancing, 1915-65*, Berkeley, CA: Regent Press

Hay, Marie (2010) *Changing Positions: Dance and the FE-HE transition in the UK*, Report for SCHODE and Palatine, http://78.158.56.101/archive/palatine/files/Changing_positions.pdf accessed March 7, 2013

Hazzard, Wayne, Michelle Lynch, Laurie MacDougall and Kegan Marling (2013) *Dance Activity in the San Francisco Bay Area: A Report on Key Benchmarks*, San Francisco: Dancers' Group

Hennessy, Keith (1995) 'Hype or Revolution or What?', Hennessy, Keith and Rachel Kaplan, eds. *More Out Than In: Notes on Sex, Art and Community*, Abundant Fuck Productions: San Francisco

Hewison, Robert (1995) *Culture and Consensus: England, Art and Politics since 1940*, London: Methuen

Hinton, James (1983) *Labour & Socialism: A History of the British Labour Movement, 1867-1974*, Brighton, Sussex: Wheatsheaf Books

Hobsbawm, Eric (1983) 'Mass Producing Traditions, Europe, 1870-1914', in Hobsbawm, Eric and Terence Ranger, eds., *The Invention of Tradition*, Cambridge: Cambridge University Press, 263-308

Hobsbawm, Eric (1984) *Worlds of Labour: Further Studies in the History of Labour*, London: Weidenfeld & Nicolson

Hobsbawm, Eric (1995) *Age of Extremes: 1914-1991*, London: Abacus

hooks, bell (2000) *Where We Stand*: Class Matters, London: Routledge

Houston, Sara (2002) *Quiet Revolutions? Philosophical and other concepts of community dance during the New Labour Years, 1997-2001*, unpublished PhD, University of Surrey, Roehampton

Houston, Sara (2005) 'Participation in Community Dance: the Road to Empowerment and Transformation?', *New Theatre Quarterly*, XXI: 2,166-177

Howard, Rachel (2005) 'Joe Goode finds a safe place to end trio in *Hometown*,' *San Francisco Chronicle*, June 13, http://www.sfgate.com. accessed January 13, 2006

Howard, Rachel (2008) 'Zaccho Dancers Slip Through Time in Yerba Buena Show', *San Francisco Chronicle*, http://www.sfgate.com/default/article/ Zaccho-dancers-slip-through-time-in-Yerba-Buena-3199332.php, accessed July 28, 2013

Howe, Irving (1976) *World of our Fathers, The Journey of the Eastern European Jews to American and the Life they Found and Made*, New York: Harcourt, Brace and Jovanovich

Hutera, Donald (2012) 'London 2012 Olympic Games: Keeping the Dance Flame Alive', *Pulse*, Issue 117, Summer, 6-9

Iyer, Alessandra, ed. (1997) *'South Asian Dance: The British Experience'*, *Choreography and Dance*, Amsterdam: Harwood Academic Publishing

Jackson, Anthony (2007) *Theatre, Education and the Making of Meanings: Art or Instrument?* Manchester: Manchester University Press

Jackson, Naomi (2002) *Converging Movements: Modern Dance and Jewish Culture at the 92ⁿᵈ Street Y*, Middletown, CT: Wesleyan University Press

Jeyasingh, Shobana (1998) 'Imaginary Homelands: Creating a New Dance Language', in Carter, Alexandra, ed., *Routledge Dance Studies Reader*, London: Routledge

Jones, Steve (2006) *Antonio Gramsci*, London: Routledge

Kepley, Vance Jr. (1983) 'The Workers' International Relief and the Cinema of the Left, 1921-1935, *Cinema Journal*, 23:1, Autumn, 7-23

Khan, Naseem (1976) *The Arts That Britain Ignores: the arts of the ethnic minorities in Britain*, London: The Arts Council of Great Britain

Khan, Naseem (1997) 'South Asian Dance in Britain', in Iyer, Alessandra, ed., *'South Asian Dance: The British Experience'*, *Choreography and Dance*, Amsterdam: Harwood Academic Publishing, 25-30

Khan, Naseem (2008) 'Dance Heritage: Stone or Water?', *Pulse*, Issue 101, Summer, 6-8

Khan, Naseem, Chitra Sundaram, Ginnie Wollaston and Piali Ray (2001) 'Moving Margins: South Asian Dance in the UK', http://www.narthaki. com/info/articles/article13.html, accessed November 17, 2008

Kirtin, Gil (2006) *The Making of Women Trade Unionists*, London: Ashgate Publishing

Klehr, Harvey (1984) *The Heyday of American Communism: The Depression Decade*, New York: Basic Books

Kloetzel, Melanie and Carolyn Pavlik, eds. (2009) *Site Dance: Choreographers and the Lure of Alternative Spaces*, Gainsville: University of Florida Press

Klugmann, James (1979) 'Introduction', in Clark, Jon, Margot Heinemann, David Margolies and Carole Snee, eds., *Culture and Crisis in Britain in the Thirties*, London: Lawrence & Wishart, 13-36

Kolb, Alexandra (2011) 'Cross-Currents of Dance and Politics: An Introduction' in Alexandra Kolb, ed. *Dance and Politics, Dance and Politics,*

Oxford: Peter Lang, 1-36

Krasner, David (2001), '"The Pageant is the Thing": Black Nationalism and the Star of Ethiopia', in Jeffrey D Mason & J. Ellen Gainor, eds., *Performing America: Cultural Nationalism in American Theater*, Chicago: University of Michigan Press, 106-122

Kucheria, Ambika (2006) 'In your site; in your mind', *Pulse*, Issue 14, 14-15

Lansman, Jon, 'A Big Thank you to Ken for the multicultural olympics', *Left Futures*, August 2012, http://www.leftfutures.org/2012/08/a-big-thank-you-to-ken-for-the-multicultural-olympics/, accessed June 4, 2013

Lester, Gary (1997) 'Margaret Barr: Epic Individual and Fringe Dweller', *Proceedings: Society of Dance History Scholars*, Riverside, California: Society of Dance History Scholars, 9-19

Levy, Susan Carbonneau (1990) Unpublished PhD, *The Russians are coming: Russian dancers in the United States, 1910-1933*, New York University

Lieberman, Robbie (1990) *My Song is my Weapon: People's Songs, American Communism and Culture, 1930-1950*, Chicago, IL: University of Illinois Press

Lifson, David S. (1965) *The Yiddish Theatre in America*, New York: Thomas Yoseloff

Lloyd, Margaret (1987) *The Borzoi Book of Modern Dance*, Princeton: Dance Horizons Republication [orig. pub. 1949]

Lopez y Royo, Alessandra (2003) 'Classicism, Post-classicism in Ranjabati Sricar's work: Re-defining the terms of Indian contemporary dance discourse', *South Asia Research*, 23:2, 152-169

Madood, Tariq and Stephen May (2001) 'Multiculturalism and Education in Britain: An internally contested debate', *International Journal of Education Research*, 35, 305-317

Manning, Susan (2004) *Modern Dance, Negro Dance: Race in Motion*, Minneapolis and London: University of Minnesota Press

Manning, Susan (2007) '*Ausdruckstandz* across the Atlantic', in Franco Susanne, and Marina Nordera, eds., *Dance Discourses: Keywords in Dance Research*, London: Routledge, 46-60

Marr, Andrew (2007) *A History of Modern Britain*, London, Macmillan

Marx, Karl (1963) *Selected Writings in Sociology and Social Philosophy*, T.B. Tottomore & Maximiliaen Rube, eds., Harmondsworth: Penguin Books

Massey, Doreen (2000) 'Space-time and the politics of location', in Read, Alan, ed., *Architecturally Speaking: Practices of Art, Architecture and the Everyday*, London: Routledge, 49-61

Massey, Doreen (2005) *For Space*, London: Sage

Massey, Doreen (2011) 'For Space: Reflections on an Engagement with Dance', *Proceedings of the 10th International NOFOD Conference*, Odense:

University of Southern Denmark, 35-44

Meduri Avanthi,(2004) 'Bharatanatyam as a Global Dance: Some Issues in Teaching, Practice and Research', *Dance Research Journal*, 36:2, Spring, 11-29

Meduri, Avanthi (2008) 'Labels, Histories, Politics: South Asian Dance on the Global Stage', *Dance Research*, 26: 2, 223-244

Meduri, Avanthi (2008) 'The Transfiguration of Indian/Asian Dance in the UK: Bharatanatyam in Global Contexts," *Asian Theatre Journal*, 25:2, 298-329

Mendelsohn, Epstein (2007) *At the Edge of a Dream: The Story of Jewish Immigrants on New York's Lower East Side, 1880-1920*, New York, John Wiley & Sons

Mendelsohn, Joyce (2009) *The Lower East Side: Remembered and Revisited (updated and revised), A history and Guide to a Legendary New York Neighborhood*, NY: Columbia University Press

Miles, Andrew and Alice Sullivan (2010), 'Understanding the relationship between taste and value in culture and sport', DCMS report

Miller, James (1987, 1994) *Democracy is in the Streets: From Port Huron to the Siege of Chicago*, Cambridge: Harvard University Press

Mishler, Paul C. (1999) *Raising Reds: The Young Pioneers, Radical Summer Camps, and Communist Political Culture in the United States*, New York: Columbia University Press

Mitra, Royona (2011) *Akram Khan, Performing the Third Space*, unpublished PhD, Royal Holloway University of London

Mitra, Royona (2012) 'Performing Cultural heritage in *Weaving Paths* by the Sonia Sabri Dance Company', in Jackson, A. and Kidd, J. eds. *Performing Heritage: Research, Practice and Innovation in Museum Theatre and Live Interpretation*. Manchester: University of Manchester Press, 144-157

Morris, Gay (2006) *A Game for Dancers: Performing Modernism in the Postwar Years, 1945-1960*, Middletown, CT: Wesleyan University Press

Morris, Geraldine (2012) Frederick Ashton's Ballets: Style, Performance, Choreography, London: Dance Books

Murphy, Ann (2002) 'Wise Bird,' *SF Weekly*, January 16, http://www.sfweekly.com, accessed May 19, 2006

Murphy, Ann, 'Parades and Changes over the past 43 Years, an Interview with Anna Halprin', *Writing Dance*, February 14, 2013, http://www.writingdance.blogspot.co.uk/, accessed July 19, 2013

Nicholas, Larraine (2007) *Dancing in Utopia: Dartington Hall and its Dancers*, Alton: Dance Books

Nicholas, Larraine (2010) 'Leslie Burrowes: A Young Dancer in Dresden and London, 1930-34', *Dance Research*, 28:2, 153-178

Nicolas Whybrow (2011) *Art and the City*, London, New York: I.B. Tauris

Novack, Cynthia (1990) *Sharing the Dance: Contact Improvisation and American Culture*, Madison: University of Wisconsin Press

O'Higgins, Rachel, 'Rhapsody in Red' summary of BBC Radio 4 programme, July 2002, www.alanbushtrust.org.uk, accessed March 3, 2009

O'Shea, Janet (2003) 'At Home in the World? The Bharatanatyam dancer as Transnational Interpreter', *TDR*, 47:1, 176-186

Osumare, Halifu (2007) *The Africanist Aesthetic in Global Hip-hop: Power Moves*, London: Palgrave

Palmer, Michael (no date) 'Crossroads/Collaboration Part 2,' *The Poetry Society Journal*, http://www.poetrysociety.org/journal/articles/collaborations/index.html, accessed January 7, 2007

Perlman, Joshua (2008 *Choreographing Identity: Modern Dance and American Jewish Life, 1924-1954*) unpublished PhD thesis, New York University.

Power, Richenda (1996) 'Healthy Motion, Images of "Natural" and "Cultured" Movement in Early Twentieth-Century Britain', *Women's Studies International Froum*, 19:5, 551-565

Prevots, Naima (1990) *American Pageantry: A Movement for Art and Democracy*, Ann Arbor, MI: UMI Research Press

Prickett (2007) '*Guru* or Teacher? *Shishya* or Student?: Pedagogic Shifts In South Asian Dance Training in India and Britain', *South Asia Research*, 27:1, 25-41

Prickett, Stacey (1989) 'From Workers' Dance to New Dance?', *Dance Research*, 7:1, 47-64

Prickett, Stacey (1990) 'Dance and the Workers' Struggle', *Dance Research*, 8:1, 47-61

Prickett, Stacey (1994) 'The People: Issues of Identity Within the Revolutionary Dance', in Garafola, Lynn, ed., *Of, By and For the People: Dancing on the Left in the 1930s*, Studies in Dance History, V:1, Spring, pp. 14-22

Prickett, Stacey (2003), Degrees of Change, *Pulse*, Issue 4, 9-11

Prickett, Stacey (2004) 'Techniques and Institutions', *Dance Research*, 22.1, 1-21

Prickett, Stacey (2007) 'San Francisco Innovators and Iconoclasts: Dance and Politics in the Left Coast City', *Dance Chronicle*, 30, 237-290

Prickett, Stacey (2011) 'Dancing the American Dream during World War II', in Kolb, Alexandra, ed., *Dance and Politics*, Oxford: Peter Lang, 167-192

Prickett, Stacey (2012) Defying Britain's Tick-Box Culture: Kathak in Dialogue with Hip-Hop', *Dance Research*, 30:2, 169-185

Purkayastha, Prarthana (2008) *Bodies Beyond Borders: Modern dance in Colonial and Postcolonial India*, unpublished PhD, Roehampton University

Purkayastha, Prarthana (2010) 'Performing Identity Politics: South Asian

Dance in Britain'. In Moura, A. & Coquet, E. eds., (coords) *Diálogos coma Arte II*. Braga: CESC - Universidade do Minho: 71-84

Rampersad, Arnold (2001) *The Life of Langston Hughes, Volume I, 1902-1941, I too Sing America'*, London: Oxford University Press.

Rosenwaike, Ira (1972) *Population History of New York City*, Syracuse University Press

Ross, Janice (1980) 'Bay Ways: A Climate for Free Spirits,' *Dance Magazine*, January, 78-85

Ross, Janice (2004) 'Anna Haprin's Urban Rituals',*TDR*, 48:2, 49-67

Ross, Janice (2007) *Anna Halprin: Experience as Dance*, Berkeley: University of California Press

Rossen, Rebecca Leigh (2006) *Dancing Jewish: Jewish Identity in American Modern Dance and Postmodern Dance*, unpublished PhD thesis, Northwestern University

Rowell, Bonnie (2000) 'An Expanding Map', in Grau, Andrée and Stephanie Jordan, eds. *Europe Dancing*, London: Routledge, 188-212

Samuel, Raphael (1985) 'Introduction: Theatre and Politics' and 'Theatre and Socialism in Britain (1880-1935), in Samuel, Raphael, Ewan MacColl and Stuart Cosgrove, eds., *Theatres of the Left, 1980-1935: Workers' Theatre Movements in Britain and America*, London: Routledge & Kegan Paul, 3-73

Sanchez, Erin N., Imogen J. Aujla and Sanna Nordin-Bates (2012) 'Cultural background variables in dance talent development, findings from the UK centres for advanced training', *Research in Dance Education*, http://www.tandfonline.com/doi/abs/10.1080/14647893.2012.712510#.Um0FZ-dFBtQ

Sanders, Lorna (2006*) Dance education renewed: A re-conceptualisation of the subject of dance in England and Wales with particular reference to GCSE and GCE A Level*, unpublished PhD thesis, University of Surrey

Sanders, Lorna (2008) 'Power in Operation: a case study focussing on how subject-based knowledge is constrained by the methods of assessment in GCE A Level Dance', *Research in Dance Education*, 9:3, 221-240.

Saner, Emine (2009) 'Let's Dance: We will if Arlene Phillips has her way', *The Guardian*, August 15, http://www.theguardian.com/society/2009/aug/15/arlene-phillips-dance-tsar, accessed August 16, 2013.

Schwartz, Peggy & Murray (2011) *The Dance Claimed Me: A Biography of Pearl Primus*, New Haven & London: Yale University Press

Shay, Anthony (2002) *Choreographic Politics: State Folk Dance Companies, Representation and Power*, Middletown, CT: Wesleyan University Press

Siddall, Jeanette (2001) *21st Century Dance: Present position, future vision*, London: Arts Council England

Siddall, Jeanette (2013) 'Youth Dance Contexts (Part 2): Health and Youth

Justice', in Sanders, Lorna, ed., *Dance Teaching and Learning: Shaping Practice*, 2d edition, London: Youth Dance England

Siegel, Marcia B. (1987) 'Modern Dance Before Bennington: Sorting it all out', *Dance Research Journal*, 19:1, 3-9

Smith, Clyde (1999) 'Mandala and the Men's Movement(s),' http://www.culturalresearch.org/mandala, accessed October 9, 2005

Sporn, Paul (1985) 'Working-Class Theatre on the Auto Picket Line', in McConachie, Bruce and Daniel Friedman, eds., *Theatre for Working Class Audiences in the United States*, Westport, CT: Greenwood Press, 155-170

Sporn, Paul (1985) *Against Itself: The Federal Theatre Project and Writers' Projects in the Midwest*, Detroit: Wayne State University

Stourac, Richard and Kathleen McCreery, eds. (1986) *Theatre as a Weapon: Workers' Theatre in the Soviet Union, Germany and Britain, 1917-1934*, London: Routledge & Kegan Paul

Stratyner, Barbara (1994) '"Significant Historical Events...Thrilling Dance Sequences": Communist Party Pageants in New York, 1937', in Garafola, Lynn, ed., *Of, By and For the People: Dancing on the Left in the 1930s*, Studies in Dance History, V:1, 31-37

Susman, Warren I (2003) *Culture as History: The Transformation of American Society in the Twentieth Century*, Washington & London: Smithsonian Institute Press [orig.pub. 1973]

Thomas, Helen (2003) *The Body, Dance & Cultural Theory*, Baskingstoke: Palgrave Macmillan

Thompson, E.P. (1980) *The Making of the English Working Class* [orig. pub. 1963]

Toepfer, Karl (1997) *Empire of Ecstasy: Nudity and Movement in German Body Culture, 1910-1935*, Berkeley: University of California Press

Tomko, Linda J. (1999) *Dancing Class, Gender, Ethnicity and Social Class in American Dance 1890-1920*, Bloomington, ID: Indiana University Press

Ulrich, Allan (2003) 'Dissent and the Dance Brigade', *Dance Magazine*, 77:6, June, 32

Van Geyseghem, André (1979) 'British Theatre in the Thirties: an autobiographical record' in Clark, Jon, Margot Heinemann, David Margolies and Carole Snee, eds., *Culture and Crisis in Britain in the Thirties*, London: Lawrence and Wishart, 209-218

Von Sturmer, Caryll (1993) *Margaret Barr: Epic Individual*, Syndey: Wild & Woolley

Wallis, Mick (1988) 'Heirs to the Pageant: Mass Spectacle and the Popular Front', in *A Weapon in the Struggle: the Cultural History of the Communist Party in Britain*, edited by Andy Croft, Pluto Press, 48-67

Wallis, Mick (1994) 'Pageantry and the Popular Front: Ideological Production in the 'Thirties', *New Theatre Quarterly*, 10:38, 132-156

Wallis, Mick (1995) 'The Popular Front Pageant: Its Emergence and Decline', *New Theatre Quarterly*, XI:41, 17-32

Walthall, Caroline, Dancing the Dialectics of Change: American Site-Specific Dance as Public History in the Twentieth Century, 2011, http://hdl.handle.net/10022/AC:P:10430, unpublished senior thesis, Columbia University

Weigand, Kate (2001) *Red Feminism: American Communism and the Making of Women's Liberation*, Baltimore & London: The John Hopkins University Press

Wiener, Martin J. (1981) *English Culture and the Decline of the Industrial Spirit, 1850-1980*, Cambridge: Cambridge University Press

Williams, Raymond (1961) *The Long Revolution*, London: Chatto and Windus

Williams, Raymond (1983) *Culture and Society, 1780-1950*. New York: Columbia University Press [orig. pub. 1958]

Wilson, Amrit (2006) *Dreams, Questions, Struggles: South Asian Women in Britain*, London: Pluto Press

Worley, Matthew (2002) *Class against Class: The Communist Party Between the Wars*, London: I.B. Tauris Publishers

Zinn, Howard (2003) *The Twentieth Century*, New York: Harper Perennial

Audio-Visual sources

Artists in Exile: A Story of Modern Dance in San Francisco, directed by Austin Forbord and Shelly Trott, 2000, Rapt Productions

Towards To-Morrow: Pageant of Co-operation, produced by Frank H.W. Cox for the CWS National Film Service, 1938, available from the National Co-operative Archive

Index

UNIVERSITY OF WINCHESTER
LIBRARY